LONG TIME COMING

LONG TIME COMING

An insider's story of the Birmingham church bombing that rocked the world.

Elizabeth H. Cobbs / Petric J. Smith

State's witness against Birmingham church bomber Robert Chambliss

Published by

CRANE HILL
PUBLISHERS

2923 Crescent Avenue
Birmingham, Alabama 35209

Printed in the United States of America
Published by Crane Hill Publishers
First edition, First printing September 1994

Front cover photo: The "Wales Window" of Sixteenth Street Baptist Church, donated by the
people of Wales to replace the original window destroyed by a bomb blast in 1963.
Photographed by permission of Sixteenth Street Baptist Church.
Photo by Keith Boyer.
Book design by Bob Weathers.

Library of Congress Cataloging-in-Publication Data

Smith, Petric J., 1940-
    Long Time Coming: an insider's story of the Birmingham church bombing that rocked the
world / Elizabeth H. Cobbs/Petric J. Smith
— 1st ed.
        p. cm.
    Includes bibliographical references (p.).
    ISBN 1-881548-10-4 : $19.95
        1. Bombings—Alabama—Birmingham—History—20th century.
2. Birmingham (Ala.)—Race relations. I. Title.
F334.B657S65 1994
976.1'781063—dc20   94-28721
                                                                               CIP

10   9   8   7   6   5   4   3   2

Crane Hill Publishers
2923 Crescent Avenue
Birmingham, Alabama 35209

Dedicated to the memory of my grandmothers,
Katie Jane Howard Manning Whitaker and
Lula Belle Leslie Hollifield, who each in her own way
taught me the meaning of unconditional love;

and to the memory of Judy Cole White,
who made me believe that this book was possible
though she did not live to see it completed.

TABLE OF CONTENTS

CHRONOLOGY

1940-55 Elizabeth grows up a member of the extended Chambliss family residing in the northeast section of Birmingham, Alabama.

1949 At age nine, she attends a major Klan rally.

1954 U.S. Supreme Court orders school desegregation.

1955 Elizabeth elopes and six months later returns home pregnant.

1956 Elizabeth's son, Robin, is born.

Racially motivated bombings and other terrorist activities in Birmingham are on the increase.

Robert Chambliss and three other Klansmen are arrested in Tuscaloosa for disorderly conduct in demonstrations against the entry of black student Autherine Lucy to the University of Alabama.

On Christmas, the parsonage of Bethel Baptist Church in Birmingham is bombed. No arrests are made.

1958 Bethel Baptist Church bombed again. (J. B. Stoner was tried and convicted of this crime in 1980.)

1959 Elizabeth's marriage breaks up; she divorces, and she and Robin move in with her maternal grandmother, "Mama Katie" Whitaker.

Elizabeth's beloved step-grandfather, Roger Whitaker, dies.

Elizabeth gets a job in the window-display department of New Ideal department store in downtown Birmingham.

1961-62 Robert Chambliss takes Elizabeth and other family members on tours of his Klan "secret places."

Aunt "Tee" Chambliss and Elizabeth visit a "bomb factory."

Detective "Stevens" warns Elizabeth about the danger of her position as the niece of Robert Chambliss.

1962 Birmingham voters reject the three-man commission form of government in favor of a mayor-council government.

1963 Albert Boutwell is elected mayor of Birmingham.

KKK terrorism increases.

Civil rights demonstrations heat up under the leadership of Dr. Martin Luther King, Jr., and the Sixteenth Street Baptist Church becomes headquarters for civil rights activism.

On September 4, Robert Chambliss purchases a case of dynamite from Leon Negron, and Arthur Shores's home is bombed.

On September 15, a bomb explodes at the Sixteenth Street Baptist Church. Four young black girls die in the explosion.

The FBI moves in to investigate.

Author Shores's home is bombed again.

Robert Chambliss, Charles Cagle, and John Wesley Hall are arrested for possession of dynamite.

1963-68 Elizabeth and Dale Tarrant cooperate as informants in the FBI investigation of the church bombing.

1965 During the Selma-to-Montgomery march for voting rights, demonstrators on Selma's Edmund Pettus Bridge are clubbed and gassed by state troopers and county deputies.

Civil rights worker Viola Liuzzo is shot and killed by four Klansmen in a car, one of whom is FBI infiltrator Gary Thomas Rowe.

Two female FBI informants die mysteriously.

Based on information allegedly provided to him by Dale Tarrant, FBI agent Mel Alexander files a report stating that Dale and Elizabeth witnessed the planting of the Sixteenth Street church bomb on the night of September 14-15, 1963.

Elizabeth and Robin move out of Mama Katie's house and into their own apartment.

CHRONOLOGY

1967-68   J. Edgar Hoover pulls out of the bombing investigation not long before the federal statute runs out on civil rights violations.

1970   Elizabeth remarries and starts selling real estate.

1975   Elizabeth begins to study for the ministry in the United Methodist Church.

1976   Elizabeth is appointed to her first pastorate, Acmar United Methodist Church.

Alabama Attorney General Bill Baxley reactivates the investigation of the Sixteenth Street Baptist Church bombing.

1977   Elizabeth is appointed pastor of Denman Memorial United Methodist Church in Birmingham. She is the first female Methodist minister in Alabama to receive an urban pastorate.

State investigator Bob Eddy persuades her to secretly participate once again in the church bombing case. Dale Tarrant also cooperates but declines to testify.

On November 15, state's witness Elizabeth Cobbs testifies in court against her uncle, accused murderer Robert Chambliss.

On November 18, the jury convicts Chambliss. He receives a life sentence; he died in jail in 1985.

1978   Bob Eddy is sent by Alabama Governor George Wallace to Huntsville to serve out the term of that county's deposed sheriff.

Elizabeth divorces for the second time.

Baxley loses his bid for governor.

Charles Graddick is elected attorney general of Alabama. No further arrests are made in the bombing case. The case remains inactive.

1979   Elizabeth Cobbs continues to receive death threats and harassing phone calls. She leaves Birmingham under an assumed identity.

ACKNOWLEDGMENTS

This story spans half a century. There are hundreds of people who have influenced me and steered me toward choices I have made, thus contributing to the story. Only a few can be acknowledged here.

I need to mention my teachers: the amateurs—my grandmothers, to whom the book is dedicated, and my step-grandfather, Roger Whitaker; and the professional ones—from Roberta Stanley and Gladys Secord in grade school to professors Earl Gossett, Roy Wells, Barbara Lester, Sam Stayer, and Nancy Campbell at Birmingham-Southern College. All of them are part of the story.

For their help in the preparation of this book, my heartfelt thanks go first to Joni, my partner and friend whose help with research and photography made it all possible; to the staff of the archives department of the Birmingham Public Library, Dr. Marvin Y. Whiting, Don Veasey, and James Baggett; to *Birmingham Post-Herald* reporter Kathy Kemp for her encouragement and critique; to the Reverend Christopher Hamlin, pastor of the Sixteenth Street Baptist Church, whose kindness and helpfulness have been both enabling and inspirational; and to photographer Keith Boyer.

I feel a debt of thanks to my son, James Robin Hood, who though not a chip off the old block is a hero in his own right.

Also, deep bows and kudos to the staff at Crane Hill Publishers: new mother Catherine O'Hare; the gentle, smiling, and always helpful Kim Cox; computer wizard Bob Weathers; graphics whiz Robin McLendon; reader and critic Norma McKittrick; and last (but no means least) publisher/editor/newfound friend Ellen Sullivan.

There are others, of course, who are not named here for one reason or another, but none are forgotten. Thank you all.

INTRODUCTION
AND CALL TO ACTION
by Reverend Fred L. Shuttlesworth

Long Time Coming by Elizabeth H. Cobbs took a long time indeed to congeal, but I hope it won't be a long time before this book opens the eyes and enlightens the minds of Birmingham, the South, and the nation.

The dark deeds of the Ku Klux Klan, which for many years were aided and abetted by law enforcement and the highest political officials, are here at long last presented in human terms, in a book worthy of reading by all Americans who truly believe in justice. Together with the recollections of the civil rights struggles by Southern Negroes, this should be, and must be, compelling educational reading for all Americans—but especially our American youth, who must finally outgrow the past and put an end to the effects of segregation and racism in America.

God's word tells mankind over and over to "fear not," to love mercy, and to do that which is kind, true, just, and compassionate. Sometimes, because we are human, we feel that in order to appreciate God's law, we must suffer too much from that which is evil.

Long Time Coming chronicles at long last the fear, violence, intimidation, beatings, bombings, castrations, and murders of the civil rights era. It is a powerful story because it is a painful personal view of both the causes and effects of these atrocities, which were planned with the KKK by law enforcement officials high and low; these were the tools, the agenda, and the operating tactics of the Klan.

Reared in Robert Chambliss's turbulent family, Elizabeth Cobbs learned under a mantle of fear of many out-of-the-way places where dynamite was stored, many unmarked graves of Klan victims, and the power of the Klan to ruin the lives of the living. And she learned of the businesses of respected officials who were the buddy-buddy boys of the KKK.

She correctly states that the "atmosphere in Birmingham and the South as I grew up was not one to give honest people faith in law enforcement while crooks and conspirators consorted openly with their neighborhood cop."

As pastor of Bethel Baptist Church in North Birmingham and organizer and leader of the Alabama Christian Movement for Human Rights, I can say that very few people have suffered more physical Klan brutality than I have. At one point, I honestly felt as if I would not live to reach age 40.

In 1956, a Christmas night bombing destroyed my parsonage home as I lay in bed. No one was ever arrested or prosecuted for that bombing. For a second bombing in 1958, J. B. Stoner was given a 10-year sentence, but 22 years later. That trial's testimony for the prosecution revealed that Stoner and law enforcement officials were observed in a prominent white Baptist church as they planned the second bombing attack that should have run me out of town, or later they would attack and leave me dead.

The list goes on, with mobs and beatings, bombings, jailings, and water hosings in 1963, not to mention countless atrocities to so many others in Birmingham and all over the South. To this day, I truly believe that only the Books of Heaven can fully record the crimes of the KKK and the consenting officials who facilitated them, from governors down to the lowest backwoods constable.

This book rightly takes the FBI to task for its continuing indulgence of and participation in these crimes, and it underscores the dubious mentality of J. Edgar Hoover, who arbitrarily closed the Sixteenth Street Church bombing case because "a conviction could not be obtained at that time in the South."

And it was still merely politics that caused Alabama Attorney General Bill Baxley to reopen the case 14 years later and obtain, with only a portion of Hoover's evidence, Chambliss's life sentence for murder. It is also clear that charges against several co-conspirators were dropped by Baxley's successor, Charles Graddick, in pursuit of his single-minded desire for an election win—not for a continuing and full justice in the matter.

Mrs. Cobbs correctly states that "there's more to life than walking in victimization."

Her own studies, her preaching, her reorganization of her life were all done in a continuing crucible of morbid fear, which she struggled constantly and valiantly to survive. And indeed she has both survived and escaped, compelled by truth, but not without some basic changes in her personality, as she describes in this book.

INTRODUCTION

While she and many others may have turned to human and clinical remedies to reach peace of soul, mind, and body, it is my firm conviction that no new lifestyle can better the one that made and sent us forth from the Creator's Hands as men and women.

Since Elizabeth Cobbs's compulsion for truth has caused her at last to step forward, I know she hopes—and I truly hope—the value of this book will be measured by its desire to end violence, and official condolence of violence, by the Klan and anyone else in America. I especially pray that this book will make a difference to the youth of America today, over whom a pall of violence has fallen. Our young people desperately need to read this story, to hear this voice, and to know what the legacy of violence begets. Dr. King was so right and true in saying that we must put an end to violence, or violence will put an end to us. Oh, if we had just heard and heeded his voice!

If America is ever to become a brotherhood, we must have people of all races, colors, and creeds contributing and sharing together. Brutes and brutality must not be allowed a place in the governance of our people.

Having lived on the edge of darkest night but also on the cutting edge of change in the Deep South for most of my youth and adult years, I feel Elizabeth Cobbs's book brings to life the essential tragedy of the ruling whites of the South: They were shackled by the fear and terror they allowed to be created, and allowed to remain; they made themselves prisoners as they sought to repress others.

Tragic indeed is the way the Klansmen ran their own families, in fear, violence, treachery, and the elimination of anyone designated as a threat to Klan ways.

But more tragic is the fact that blacks and whites in those days couldn't openly and honestly work together for change in the Deep South. For the most part, freedom then didn't mean the same for black and white; although we have evolved somewhat, it does not fully mean the same thing today.

One could easily imagine what a vast and different change might have been obtained without bombings and beatings, violence and mass jailings, if Elizabeth Cobbs, David Vann, Fred Shuttlesworth, Martin Luther King, Edward Gardner, Abraham Woods, Colonel Stone Johnson, James Armstrong, Lola Hendricks, Georgia Price, Julia Rainge, Anne and Carl Braden, James Dombrowski, and so very many others who sincerely desired, worked, and suffered for change might have been allowed to openly meet, discuss, plan, and work for that Birmingham which might have been. That Birmingham would have locked horns with and challenged Atlanta for the richest growth and diversity in the South—a future that fell to Atlanta because of racial strife and lack of vision by those who led Birmingham and the South far too long, and allowed the Klan to share their reign.

To me, finally, this book urgently calls by its pages of unanswered questions for a coalition of freedom and justice lovers to unrelentingly demand by petition and legal efforts the opening, under the Freedom of Information Act, of all files in possession of the FBI, Justice Department, and local law enforcement agencies; and for the full revelation of all the sordid acts and decisions made by the FBI and local authorities, especially as they relate to involvement—or lack thereof—in the Deep South during the Civil Rights Era.

I will gladly volunteer my name as leader of such a coalition, and I challenge all who read this to join me in this long overdue quest for Truth and Justice.

In this way, the bombing of the Sixteenth Street Baptist Church may yet hasten meaningful and true justice, and the deaths of the four young girls there, and so many unnamed others in the Deep South, will not have been in vain.

Cincinnati, Ohio 1994

Reverend Fred L. Shuttlesworth founded the Alabama Christian Movement for Human Rights in Birmingham in June 1956. He was the leader of the Birmingham civil rights movement and served as friend and aide to Dr. Martin Luther King, Jr.; a member of the board of the Southern Christian Leadership Conference; member of the board of the Southern Conference Fund; and later president of the latter group. He is the recipient of many awards and honors for his efforts in the civil rights struggle, including the SCLC Founder's Award and Rosa Parks Award, the Martin Luther King Civil Rights Award, and the PUSH Award for Excellence. He is currently co-chair with Anne Braden of the Southern Organizing Committee, a South-wide grassroots organization for environmental justice, as well as organizer and, for the last 28 years, pastor of the Greater New Light Baptist Church in Cincinnati, Ohio.

PROLOGUE

Journalists and scholars have written much about the times we have come to call the Civil Rights Era. Most of these civil rights chroniclers, however, were not directly involved and have little intimate personal knowledge of the events or principals who catalyzed the movement. Most civil rights books and articles draw upon formal interviews, newspaper reports, police reports, and FBI investigative reports, which is proper but incomplete.

There have been few direct accounts told by those of us who watched and waited and wailed over the events in Birmingham in those dark days. We who watched in horror and fear, waited with dread, and wailed because we were powerless to stop the madness.

This account will try to explain how I came to the day in November 1977 when I was led into a packed courtroom, through a cordon of sheriff's deputies, to testify against my aunt's husband, Robert Chambliss—the man accused of murder in the bombing of the Sixteenth Street Baptist Church.

How I came to be the surprise witness the defense did not anticipate and had not prepared for.

How I came to tell Chambliss's own words against him; for they were his words and his actions that convicted him. They were words against us all, whether black or white, Southern or Yankee. They were, indeed, words against all humanity.

I cannot tell his story and fail to tell my own story or the stories of others. Stories of people who loved and people who hated. Stories of people who struggled as life died in their hearts, breaking them. It was with broken hearts that many of us watched, helpless, as our world exploded.

As I write in 1994, it has been 17 years since one man was convicted for one crime that day in court. On November 18, 1977, Robert Chambliss was convicted for the murder of 11-year-old Denise McNair in the bombing that also killed three other young girls.

This is an account of what I know about that man and the way he affected the lives of so many, not only the victims of the most publicized racist bombing of the Civil Rights Era, but also those of us who grew up and lived under the shadow of his hatred and cruelty.

Yet we must not lose sight of the fact that Robert Chambliss was not a singular enigma. He was not a freak of society. He represented a breed of men and women whose lives were driven by prideful defense of what they believed to be right.

Born near the turn of the twentieth century, Chambliss was typical of his generation and social status. Lacking position and power of either education or birth, he clung fiercely and pridefully to the values of white Southern manhood. He saw his role as a protector of those things he held to be holy. He did not see his actions as crimes of conscience, only as crimes of law—a law that had unfairly changed on him.

Chambliss was a vigilante, and for many years he was applauded by those in power who could have, but did not, stop him. Then he went too far—he fought too long. Of the many criminals responsible for the murders that resulted from the September 15, 1963, bombing of the Sixteenth Street Baptist Church in Birmingham, only one, Robert Chambliss, was tried for that crime. And of Chambliss's many crimes, he was tried for only one felony.

For many years I've said that someday I would write this book. People who were close to the situation have pleadingly responded, "Please wait until I'm dead."

I've said that someday I would need to tell the story for my own sake, and public officials have pointedly said, "Use the records, don't get personal about people who will never be tried."

I've said that someday the story had to be told even if there were people embarrassed or angered. Now, I've come to the point in my life when that day can't be put off any longer.

My hope is that someday truth will be more important than politics, and justice will be more important than pride. That day has been a long time coming. Although there are many people who do not want this account to be published—now or ever—for me, that day is now.

Alabama 1994

LONG TIME COMING

1

THE KISS OF DEATH

November 15, 1977

I waited at home Tuesday morning November 15, 1977, for the call to come from Bob Eddy, an investigator with the State of Alabama attorney general's office.

Home, in November 1977, was the parsonage of Denman Memorial United Methodist Church located on Fourth Avenue West in Birmingham, Alabama. I was pastor of this small church, which sat on the corner half a block away. Assistant Attorney General Jon Yung had called the night before to tell me that this would be the day. At our last meeting he had asked me if I planned to wear my clerical collar to the courtroom when I came to testify. I had told him that I would not.

"What about the cross?" he had asked. He was concerned, it seemed, that I make a good appearance.

"I always wear the cross," I had told him. "But I don't think it's appropriate to wear the collar when I'm not performing ministerial duties."

I had, however, dressed carefully: a black crewneck sleeveless blouse under a pantsuit—tan blazer and dark-brown slacks, with a subtle check in the fabric—and the low-heeled sensible black shoes that I always wore except to school.

I thought little about it as I put the cross around my neck. Wearing it was almost as routine as combing my hair.

After I dressed, I sat at my kitchen table for another cup of coffee and another cigarette and waited for the telephone to ring with instructions.

I was theirs now. As if "Property of the State of Alabama" had been stamped across my forehead, my choices had been made. I had seen every event in my life seemingly flow into a funnel and compress into this day. And when this day was over, nothing in my life would be the same.

When the phone rang, I answered it immediately. Bob Eddy said that I should drive my car downtown. He would meet me on the street beside the 2121 Building, which housed the Birmingham offices of the Federal Bureau of Investigation. I left the parsonage within minutes and drove first north past Legion Field, where local football games were played, to Eighth Avenue North; there I took a right and drove east about two miles.

Bob was waiting when I parked at the curb on Twenty-second Street. He fed coins into the parking meter, and we got into a state-owned car, he in the front passenger seat and I in the back. He sat sideways watching behind and around the car as the driver took us to the Jefferson County Courthouse.

We entered the courthouse through a doorway hidden from the street under the massive front steps. In moments I found myself alone again—waiting.

Bob left me in an out-of-the-way room with instructions to stay until he came for me. I wandered into an empty adjacent courtroom. It was small; its gallery would perhaps seat 50 people. The wood was polished and new-looking. I touched the railing and the tables set up for defense and prosecution. I looked at the judge's high bench and the witness stand.

I was trying to acclimate myself to the formality, the unfamiliar feel of a courtroom. I had never been arrested nor charged with any crime. I had been in a courtroom with a friend once, and I had appeared in traffic court against another driver who had hit my car—but that time the officer testified and I just listened. My lack of familiarity made the scene awesome and intimidating.

For weeks fear had been a constant, just as it had been a part of my everyday life for many years earlier; and the morning of Tuesday, November 15, 1977, I was grave, grim, and determined. I had almost functioned on autopilot since I had made the decision to testify, but in the stark stillness of that empty courtroom, my fear rose to the level of panic, and I felt like the bottom of my stomach had dropped out. What was I doing? I was about to risk my life, the lives of my family, everything I knew and cared about to testify against Robert Chambliss, "Dynamite Bob," the accused Birmingham church bomber. I was the surprise prosecution witness, the one person on whose testimony Alabama Attorney General Bill Baxley, Assistant Attorney General Jon Yung, and Investigator Bob Eddy were pinning their hopes for justice.

THE KISS OF DEATH

Chambliss was my uncle, married to my mother's sister. Like the rest of my family, I had lived all my life in the shadow of this man and his personal code, a law of life that he and his fellow Klansmen spoke of as "the kiss of death." It meant that those who did not interfere and kept silent were allowed to live unmolested. Those who opened their mouths, who dared to question or speak of Klan atrocities ... well, things happened. Sometimes we never knew exactly what. Or how.

My stomach twisted and churned. My body shivered as waves of anxiety swept over me. With the whole world watching, I was about to shatter the Klan-imposed silence into a thousand irretrievable pieces. Baxley, Yung, and Eddy had done their best to reassure me, but there was no telling what the outcome of this trial would be. Still, I had made my decision. There was no going back now.

In a few minutes Bob Eddy returned and escorted me to the third-floor courtroom where Robert Chambliss was being tried for first-degree murder in the death of Denise McNair, caused by an explosion at the Sixteenth Street Baptist Church on September 15, 1963. Four girls had died in that explosion. And now, 14 years later, one man was being tried for causing the death of one of them.

Bob Eddy's firm grip on my arm was reassuring as we approached Courtroom 306. Uniformed officers from the sheriff's department lined the hallway, and a walk-through metal detector guarded the courtroom door. Reporters and television crews crowded around, craning to get a glimpse and asking each other who I was and what was going on.

We were abruptly stopped at the courtroom door—the room had been sealed in anticipation of the next witness, and the deputy guarding the door would not let us enter until, after an embarrassing moment, he verified with someone inside who was expected. "Is that Elizabeth Cobbs?" he asked Bob Eddy.

Bob told him that it was. Although the crowd wasn't physically close enough to touch me, I felt crushed. I felt exposed. Vulnerable. My cooperation with law enforcement officers and agencies was no longer a secret. There had only been potential danger before; now there was certain danger.

Once inside the courtroom, it seemed to take forever for me to walk down that aisle, one step behind Bob Eddy. He escorted me to the witness stand and then stood aside while the bailiff swore me in. Every eye in the courtroom had watched as I entered, and I shrank inside, under the stares of all those people.

I had seen Robert Chambliss and one of his attorneys, Art Hanes, Jr., who were seated at the defense table, turn toward the door as we came in. Robert had started shaking his head from side to side, the way he would at a child who was both naughty and simpleminded. His lips were pulled back in scorn.

Once seated, I tried to avoid looking at him, but my eyes were drawn unwillingly. He was glaring at me as though his disapproval would halt my actions, silence me. His pale-blue eyes were hard and cold.

I was afraid of this man. I had always been afraid of him. Through the years I had occasionally seen his eyes show sorrow and I had even more rarely seen his eyes show laughter—but mostly I had seen his eyes show anger and hate, as they did now.

Finally I was able to shift in the big chair so that the corner of the judge's bench was between me and Robert, blocking my view of his eyes. I knew that from that point on, it was a life and death struggle. Either he got life imprisonment, or I got death.

2
FAMILY MATTERS

The first time I remember Robert Chambliss speaking directly to me was in 1944, when I was four years old.

"Whose little boy are you?" Robert had asked, looking down at me as I sat on the sidewalk in front of our house playing. It was the sort of remark calculated to confuse and perhaps ridicule a girl child.

"You know me, Robert. I belong to John and Libby," I reminded him. Robert Chambliss was married to my mother's oldest sister, Flora, whom my cousin and I called Tee; I was defensive, and puzzled about him not recognizing me. He laughed and stepped around me, heading for the front porch. I watched him go inside, and then I returned to playing with my toy cowboys on the sidewalk.

At times I wondered why he came alone to my house. It was different when he and Tee came together. Then it was a "visit," and it was pleasant because it was always pleasant to be around Aunt Tee.

Tee was warm and soft, and, except when she was nervous, she was funny. Sometimes she was so nervous she was funny anyway, but sometimes she was so nervous she only watched Robert and clenched her jaw and pulled down her eyebrows and wrung her hands.

Robert mostly wore khaki work clothes or a white shirt and dress pants as if he was going somewhere, but when he went somewhere in particular he wore a suit and tie. Sometimes, usually at night, he would bring Aunt Tee to our house and leave her while he went to "take care of something." Those times I saw him coming and going in his long white robe. I didn't know at the time what this signified, only that it was important and mysterious.

He talked angry-talk most of the time, so it seemed best for him not to talk to you at all. It seemed best if he didn't see you either. But if he did see you, you had to be brave and not let it show that he made you afraid.

It was also pretty clear that everybody watched what they said around Robert. The grownups would whisper or be angry or laugh about him when he wasn't there, but they would always act like he was okay when he came around.

I usually found it much more comfortable to stay outside when he came to my house. Or I'd hope that the men would play dominoes or pinochle so he would stay in one place and I could avoid him easily.

When they played games in the kitchen—of whichever house the family was gathered—Robert made everybody uncomfortable. He whistled when he wanted Tee to bring him something, a long loud three-note whistle like you would use to call a New York cab. He expected Tee to wait on him and the other men. He implied that they were not quite "real" men because they didn't yell and cuss and whistle for their wives like he did. He would laugh at them, and his laugh was a "hee, hee, hee" under his breath. He always laughed at people, never with them.

I thought that it might be a joke that day he pretended not to know who I was, because he didn't sound mad and he would have run off any child he really didn't know, even though this wasn't his house. If it was a joke, though, it didn't feel funny—it felt scary.

In fact, when Uncle Robert was around, what I mostly felt was fear. It was frightening when you didn't know what was expected. Or when you thought you knew what was expected and then found out that you really didn't. Every situation was suspect, and you never really relaxed.

You learned to be still and quiet and act like you knew what was going on. Then when you really didn't, it wasn't embarrassing and you wouldn't have to cry or swallow the tears until your throat hurt.

These were war years, but Robert didn't go to war. He was too old. He was always old, it seemed to me. Thinking back, it seems impossible that he was only 36 when I was born. He had married Tee, his second wife, several years before I was born, so he was already family when I was born.

He was tall and thin and strong and beige. His thin straight hair was always cut the same way: short on the sides and back, longer on top so that it parted and combed over and back. He never had a mustache or beard; he was always clean and pressed. He usually ate oatmeal for breakfast and used Eagle Brand canned milk in his coffee, which was usually A&P brand or Luzianne.

I remember him from very early on, but not distinct things about him—just his face, his laugh, his hands, his house, and the fear. I was afraid of him, afraid in his house, but not afraid of his wife, my Aunt Tee—though she did not make me feel safe.

Tee would babysit for me and my cousin a lot. One time when she was babysitting, she was very sick and had a fever. In later years I was told that her tonsils had "rotted out" with infection, but at the time, I only knew she was sick and there wasn't anyone to help except us two children.

Tee lay on the couch, moaning and muttering. Having seen cold cloths used to soothe and bring down fever, I searched for something and found a white sock. I couldn't reach the sink, so I wet the sock in the toilet and bathed Tee's forehead.

I was afraid she was going to die that day. I was afraid that I couldn't keep her from dying. I was afraid Robert would come home. I knew he could either be mad or friendly, and Aunt Tee wouldn't be there to keep him from noticing us. But to my relief, our mamas came home first and took over caring for Tee.

Everyone tried to take care of Tee, even though her role in life seemed to be caretaker of others. She was "poor little Flora" to her mother, and to her sisters and brothers she was "poor little Sister," although she was the oldest of the seven. When my cousin and I tried to say "Sister," it came out "Tee Tee," and soon became just "Tee," a nickname she would be known by years later in newspaper articles, investigative reports, and books. But Robert always called her "Mommy."

From the beginning, Tee was both a victim of and a partner in Robert's life and passions. She witnessed unimaginable terror through the years. Because of her fear, because of her Victorian sense of loyalty, and perhaps because she shared his views about segregation, she lived with Robert Chambliss, cared for him, covered for him, and participated in his political activities for nearly 45 years.

Although Tee recovered from her bout with tonsillitis, apparently none the worse for the toilet-soaked sock, she was sick for a long time. In later years, she would suffer illness, abuse, hypertension, and strokes. She would die less than three years after Robert Chambliss went to prison in 1977 for the murder of Denise McNair.

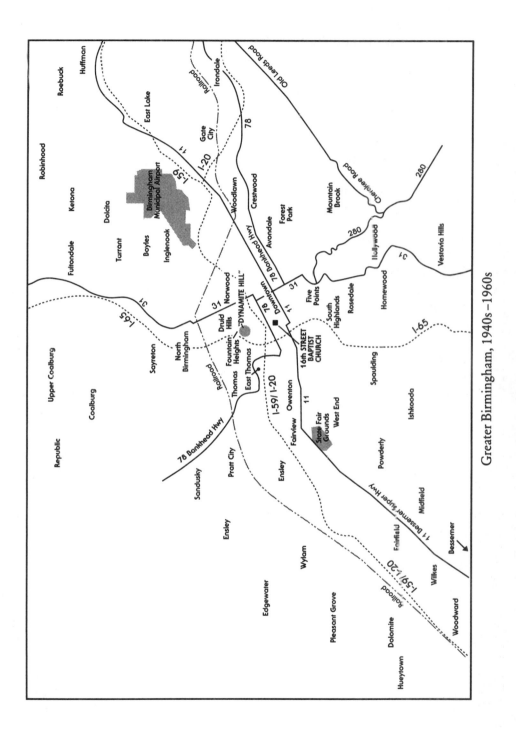

Greater Birmingham, 1940s–1960s

Detail of Birmingham
City Area

1. Robert Chambliss home
2. Bethel Baptist Church /
   Shuttlesworth home –
   bombed twice
3. Author's childhood home
4. McArthur School
5. "Dynamite Hill" – site of
   multiple bombings in the
   1950s
6. Arthur Shores home –
   bombed three times
7. Birmingham City Hall
8. Jefferson County Courthouse
9. Sixteenth Street Baptist
   Church – bombed 9/15/63
10. A.G. Gaston Motel – bombed
    once
11. Holiday Inn – site of "decoy
    bomb threat" 9/14 - 9/15/63
12. Parsonage, Denman Memorial
    Church
13. Denman Memorial United
    Methodist Church

*Taken from Shell Street Guide and
Metropolitan Map of Birmingham.
Chicago, IL: The H.M. Gousha
Company, 1963. Rucker Agee Map
Collection Birmingham Public Library*

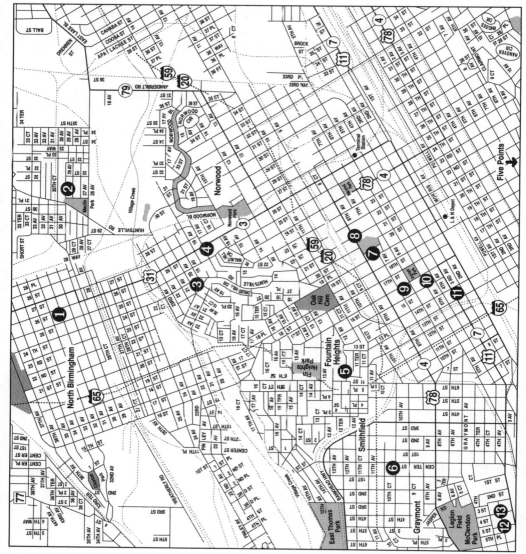

3

WAR YEARS

Like most large cities, Birmingham is a collection of neighborhoods. The city sits in a rolling valley stretching between two mountain ridges. Small towns and mining camps grew together as the Magic City reached out to them with city services. Just north of downtown, for instance, are Fountain Heights, Druid Hills, and Norwood. Immediately west are West End, and Ensley. To the east are Woodlawn, Avondale, East Lake, Inglenook, Roebuck, and Huffman. To the southeast are Forest Park and Crestwood. All of these neighborhoods and others fall within the city limits of Birmingham.

Before transportation became easy after World War II, the separate areas were more like small towns than they are today. My family mostly lived on the north and east side of town. My maternal grandmother, Mama Katie, divorced her husband more than a year before I was born, and from then on she would rent a house and several of her children would live with her, pooling whatever income they had for rent, electricity, coal, and food. As a child I thought in terms of "our room" rather than "our house"; and until I was 15, my parents and I lived, in one place or another, with Mama Katie.

I remember the day in 1944 when all of us moved into the house at 2004 Twenty-fourth Street North. Daddy had left for navy boot camp that April, so the residents of the new house would be me and Mama, Mama Katie and her second husband, my mother's younger sister Mary and her daughter, and mother's older sister Viola. Like my daddy, Mary's husband had been called to war. My new step-grandfather, Roger Whitaker, had bought the house, and we all moved in. Roger didn't actually sleep there for the first several months; he married Mama Katie that fall and then moved in. It seemed I had always known him, and I liked him.

Between the time I was four and six, the only men in my life regularly were Robert Chambliss and Roger Whitaker, the only two family men who were not in military service. Roger was patient, quiet, and altogether pleasant. I'll never forget the time he came home wearing an overcoat and a felt hat. Standing in the living room, he opened his coat and started emptying pockets. He had milk, cigarettes, Hershey bars, and fruit stuffed in the pockets of his coat and suit. It was like a party. All of those things were scarce and rationed, and even with ration books, there were short supplies and very little money to buy anything. Of course, at that age I didn't understand the economics, but I did understand the excitement.

Roger would sit in a chair on the front porch with my cousin on one knee and me on the other, allowing us to play with his double chin and ears and shirt collar until we went to sleep. Often we would wake from the nap without his having moved. He smelled of Old Spice aftershave and friendly sweat, and he had a steamer trunk that held his life and his history. Roger would go into that trunk for important papers or some item he needed, and I would "help" as he sorted out his things. He had military identification from all five branches of the armed forces, and he had an ID card from the Treasury Department. He kept his trunk locked, and it seems that no one but me ever saw some of those papers.

Roger was on a disability pension from the army and carried in his back several large pieces of shrapnel that could not be removed. He lived in constant pain and wore a custom back brace, but he was the kindest, most gentle man I have ever known. I have been thankful that during my formative years, I had Roger's pleasantness to balance Robert's gruff, fearsome arrogance.

Our house on Twenty-fourth Street had originally been built as a four-room cottage with a wide hallway down the middle. Onto the back of the house had been added a kitchen with wooden walls painted green, a screened porch, and a bathroom. The bathroom and the kitchen opened to either side off the back porch. Another doorway led into the kitchen from the middle room, but the only entrance to the bathroom was from the screened porch. In winter this was often difficult or impossible to manage, so we treated it as if the bathroom were outside and used chamber pots at night. The hallway became a common living room, and the other four rooms were used as bedrooms. Daddy and Aunt Mary's husband, William, came back from the military in 1946. Uncle William built two rooms onto the back of the house, making a separate apartment for himself, Aunt Mary, and my cousin.

My cousin and I started school when we were six at Seventeenth Avenue School, a two-story building with six classrooms. The first few weeks were rough, as they are on any first grader, but my cousin and I had such a close and dependent relationship that we clung together yet behaved as sibling rivals in the new environment. Our teacher talked to our parents about separating us so we would become part of the class rather than two kids in a tough situation together.

My cousin was transferred to North Birmingham School, and after a few more months she and her parents moved out of the house to live closer to the school she attended. It was awful at first, but soon the sheer joy of learning took over. I had been taught nursery rhymes and poems and songs at home, but I had not yet learned to read. Learning to read, for me, was nothing short of spectacular. I loved words. And numbers. And colors. And I loved to sing.

I grew up hearing my mother and her sisters and brothers sing in three- and four-part harmony, so I was ignorant of the fact that many people don't hear music in their heads. I had simply always sung with my family, and I loved the way the harmony resonated. My teacher got excited when I tried out for the school Christmas show, and she put me on the program; she also arranged to take me to every class in the school to perform. I was in heaven. The only spotlight I had previously known was criticism. I was scolded at home anytime I did anything to stand out—I was taught not to do anything to call attention to myself. In school, for the first time, I was experiencing what it felt like to shine just a bit.

Even though I wasn't a healthy child and suffered frequent bouts of respiratory problems and eye trouble, those first few years of school were an exuberant time.

When I was in fourth grade, the city built a new addition to my school, and the name was changed to F.D. McArthur Elementary School. The construction was exciting to watch, and the new school was exciting to occupy. So at nine years old, my world expanded into a much larger building and a larger, more diverse group of kids.

All of my schoolmates, of course, were white. The only black persons at my school were the janitor and a couple of women who worked in the lunchroom. I don't recall that I even wondered where the black children who lived three blocks from me, across Village Creek, went to school. Nor did I wonder whether any of the children I went to school with were taken to a Ku Klux Klan rally, as I was later that year.

Tee and Robert lived in Lewisburg, north of Birmingham, until the mid-1940s. In 1946, Robert built a house on Thirty-second Avenue in North Birmingham. This house would be their home until Tee died in 1980. I remember being taken there while the house was being built. Robert used red brick tiles—not bricks, not concrete blocks. The tiles were cheaper than bricks and nicer than the blocks. I recall that he ran into a problem with an inspection because he had not left air space between the outer walls and inner walls for insulation.

For many years Robert kept an old gray-green panel truck that did not run in the backyard. The back of that truck served as storage for many things, and it was not to be touched or bothered in any way. The backyard was chain-link fenced, and they always had a junkyard dog guarding the place. There were several in succession named Sport. Each was a German shepherd Robert had trained to be mean. He beat and abused his dogs so they instantly obeyed him. Every dog he had would cower before him, and it would attempt to eat anyone he pointed to and said, "Sic 'em." It wouldn't let anyone it didn't know into the backyard. Even the people it knew were not allowed onto the porch without orders from Tee or Robert.

One day Mama and I had walked to their house and entered the yard through the alley gate. The dog waited until we got onto the porch before it lunged and pinned my mother against the wall. Front paws on her shoulders, snarling into her face, he did not let her go until Tee pulled him off.

We went to visit Tee and Robert a lot during those years. But since we lived with Mama Katie, who tended to stay home and let her children come to her, Tee and Robert were often at our house too. The domino and card games the men played migrated between our kitchen and their kitchen. Shortly after mother's younger brother Howard married Mary Ida, they moved in with Tee and Robert and lived there through the birth and early childhood of their four children. The Chambliss house seemed to get smaller and smaller.

In 1950 either Robert or Howard bought a television set. It was the first one in the family, providing an even better reason to go visit Tee and Robert. I believe that our visits would have diminished otherwise, because I recall that my parents were not often enthusiastic about going there. One or the other, or both, would insist on not staying late. The television changed some of that. But still, while we were there watching TV with Tee and Robert, we got to hear Robert's version of the news broadcasts, and we heard him curse and rail whenever a black face appeared on the screen. He especially hated Sammy Davis, Jr., and the white performers who appeared with Davis.

Tee was a born comic and could turn almost any situation into a comedy routine. Whichever dog they happened to have was usually made to be part of the show. She fed and petted the animals, and her nature was such that they were invariably loyal to and indulgent of her. She taught each in turn to speak and sing, which of course were forms of howling, yet she would ad lib dialogue with the dog so that it seemed as though it were actually responding appropriately.

When she would be particularly aggravated with Robert and had no defense against him, she would dress the dog in Robert's clothes, and as the dog walked on its hind legs, she would dance with it and carry on conversations, calling it insulting things in a very sweet tone of voice and smiling all the while.

We children and her sisters were usually her only audience, with perhaps one or the other of her brothers or an in-law present. The routine would progress from funny to hilarious, and Tee would find it funnier than even we, who delighted in her antics. Eyes streaming with tears of laughter, she would usually end by laughing so hard she would have to race to the bathroom, thighs clenched holding her bladder. We often said that Tee would rather make someone laugh than eat when she was hungry. Her sense of humor served her well much of the time, but it failed as time passed and the pressures of the life she was forced to live bore down upon her, lining her face, stooping her shoulders, and driving her blood pressure to dangerous heights.

Robert would not allow her to wear slacks nor to smoke. Old-fashioned and straight-laced, he was a Bible-believing man though only an occasional churchgoer. There were certain protocols of "faith" and doing "right" that simply constituted the-way-things-were with him. These protocols he expected everyone around him to observe. For example, at every meal Robert said the blessing. He called it "returning thanks." I can hear him now, every word, every inflection, every pause:

Kiiind heavenly Faaather,
We thaaank thee
For theeese table blesssings
We nooow booow to receive.
Huumbly baag.
For Chriiist's sake.
Aaamen.

Always precisely the same. Humble and plaintive. Never a variance. Then he would raise his head and resume the sentence he had been in when interrupted to pray. As often as not the first words he uttered after saying grace were "Goddamn sumbitch … ."

One time when we were sharing a meal with them, Robert's grown son, and his wife and son, were visiting from out of town. Robert's son was asked to return thanks, and when everyone had bowed heads he recited his father's blessing word for word. However, he said it rather more rapidly, in a normal tone of voice, and at a normal pace rather than in the plaintive drawl that characterized his father's delivery.

Robert drew back his fist and threatened to knock his son away from the table if he didn't say it right, and he was dead serious. It was not that Robert felt himself mocked, it was that the son had not been properly humble and pious. The son said it "right," and the meal progressed.

4
THE FIFTIES WEREN'T LIKE TV

When I was about nine years old I was taken with Tee, Robert, Mama Katie, and Roger to a barbecue staged by the Ku Klux Klan. (Not being very familiar with streets and highways outside my neighborhood at that age, I don't know the exact location, but I think it was near Bessemer.) The event was well-attended, with Klan members swarming over a large park or farm. The place was decked out with both United States and Confederate flags, so it may have been the Fourth of July or Labor Day.

The scene was impressive, meant to be patriotic and religious. I had heard about the Klan all of my life, but I had never seen anything like this. I had seen Robert in his robe. I knew he went out to meetings and did secret things. I had heard him talking to other adults, so I knew that the Klan would take people out of their homes and "teach them lessons." I understood physical discipline. I had not, however, been to a large-scale rally before. There were hundreds of people gathered on this vast piece of land.

Robert was very proud this day and had assumed his public persona, which was jovial and strutting. I think his intent was to impress my step-grandfather, Roger, into joining the Klan—for this was a special occasion that lasted all afternoon and evening, providing the perfect setting for recruiting new members. To heighten the effect, there was a large platform some three or four feet high and probably twenty feet across. Behind it were three crosses made from what looked like telephone poles, the center one taller than the other two. Throughout the evening, Mama Katie stayed fairly close to the car and kept me with her so I didn't mix and mingle very much. But both Tee and Robert would go off into the crowd and come back, bringing someone with them to introduce to the adults. Some of the women, including Tee, had on white robes without hoods, and some had on hoods with the face mask tucked up inside. Many of the men were in robes and hoods, though many were not.

Off and on there was music: Christian hymns and patriotic tunes. I heard the same songs that I heard in church: "The Old Rugged Cross" and "Onward Christian Soldiers." And, of course, there were "Dixie" and "America." Then came the speakers. Angry men. And passionate men. There were two that most stick in my mind. One was a man in a red and purple embroidered satin robe and pointed cap, and the other man wore green satin, also elaborately embroidered.

Although I don't remember much of what was said, I recall that I felt uneasy and out of place. The men in satin robes drew great applause and were treated like celebrities—held in awe, it seemed. I asked at one point and was told, "That's the Grand Dragon and the Wizard." I didn't really understand what was going on, but young as I was, I did know that I wasn't intended to—only insiders were supposed to be fully informed. There were secrets and things said that meant nothing to me. And I knew it was supposed to be that way.

During the last speech, someone lit the larger of the crosses, and it burned high—reaching flames into the night sky. The satin robes of the men on stage glowed in the firelight, and the crowd became very loud. We left after that—Mama Katie insisted. Robert was testy about leaving. Tee was nervous. I was frightened. My step-grandfather had little to say except for something in a joking undertone to Mama Katie about so many "people out in public in their bathrobes."

As frightening as that burning cross and those strange men were, I would have been even more frightened if I had known then that the fear I felt would underscore the rest of my life. I had already learned to hide my feelings and to behave in public as expected. But that night I did not understand that this was not the way life should be.

Although most occasions were not this extraordinary, I did spend a great deal of time with Tee and Robert, as a child. There were several reasons why. My mother was often sick, and when that happened, Mama Katie was my primary source of parenting. When she went with Tee and Robert somewhere, I often was taken along. And when my mother was up and around, we would go to Tee's to visit and, of course, Robert would be there. Sometimes Mama and I would walk from our house on Twenty-fourth Street to North Birmingham or ride the bus to shop, and after shopping, we'd go by the Chamblisses' to visit or rest before heading home.

It was only 13 blocks from our house to theirs. We would walk past Salamone's store and the Armour meat-packing plant, which we called the "packing house." Next came Village Creek, a wide, open ditch that traversed the city from east to west for the transport of sewage. We would walk across the bridge and railroad tracks into the "nigger quarter," then through more light industry, and eventually emerge at the edge of the white neighborhood surrounding the already declining commercial district of North Birmingham.

I knew the way, but I did not know the people. Our contact with black people was limited despite the proximity in housing. Mama used to hire a black woman to help with ironing, and when no one was around to interfere, that woman's little girl and I would talk and try to play. But there was an element of the unknown and a gap in communication which made play difficult.

I came to understand that it was hard to play because we weren't "supposed" to. So why start something that would stop abruptly if an adult came in? It only took my mother briskly removing me once or twice to another room, or the ironing lady's stern look to know that something was wrong. (Twenty years later I hired that little girl to do day-work for me in my modest home, and we did talk. We still didn't quite reach friendship, but we did learn about each other.)

My folks were afraid of black people. There was fear everywhere. Some of the fears were nameless fears, but many had names. The greatest fear was of black men. For years I had no idea just why they were supposed to be so scary, especially since most of the ones I actually saw were very old, like the elderly man who delivered ice in a mule-drawn wagon through the alley. He would bring the ten-, twenty-five-, or fifty-cent block of ice to the back door with tongs, and Mama would take it and struggle it into the wooden icebox because the iceman was not allowed to come into the house.

There were other black men who came to our back door in those early years, too. They would ask for work to earn food, and my grandmother would usually find something they could do for a half hour or an hour and then give them food through the back door. They would eat on the steps and knock on the screen door to hand back the plate and jelly glass with a polite, "Thank you, Ma'am. God bless you Ma'am."

Salamone's grocery store, about two blocks north of our house, served white customers from our neighborhood, but they also welcomed business from the black neighborhood on the other side of Village Creek. The general attitude in my family was that Italians and Jews were somewhere between white folks and black folks, and when they chose to be with black folks, they became not acceptable as white anymore. So our dealings with Salamone's store were limited to times when the smaller store closer to home didn't carry what we needed.

I was forbidden to socialize with either Italians or Jews or to make friends with them beyond school hours, although one of the

Salamones' daughters was in my class at school. The prejudices were not all racial. Catholics were also rejected with the attendant stories about "their" hatred for "us" and the sinister power priests held over parishioners. There was another Catholic girl in my class whose uncle worked with Daddy at Southern Line Material Company; his wife worked at New Ideal department store in downtown Birmingham, and she later helped me get my first job. Daddy and Mama and my friend's uncle and aunt sat together at company parties, but they did not socialize otherwise.

We lived on the cusp of Norwood, which at that time was a moderately affluent community of large and beautiful homes, most of which are now either divided into apartments or have gone through deterioration and emerged into restoration. The area was totally white in the forties and fifties and is now predominantly black, as is the case with North Birmingham. Even then, our street was barely respectable—lower to lower-middle class—home to industrial workers, a bus driver, an insurance salesman, and retirees.

When everybody had moved out of Mama Katie and Roger's house except my family, which now included my only brother, Johnny, the hallway of the house was divided in half with a plasterboard partition, and the front half became my bedroom. Prior to that I had slept in the room with Mama and Daddy, but their room was awfully crowded with their double bed, my single bed, and the baby bed. So at age 12, I got a room of my own. The back half of the hallway was converted into a kitchen for my grandmother. The front door was changed into a window in my room, and two new front doors were put into the front rooms on either side. The house then had two living rooms, three bedrooms, and two kitchens, but we all still shared the bath. The year I got my own room, we also got our first television, a sewing machine, and a vacuum cleaner.

Many afternoons and Saturdays were spent washing diapers in the ringer washer and hanging them on the line in the backyard to dry while we cleaned the house. From the time I was eight I had taken on more and more of the household chores, kneeling or standing on a kitchen chair at the sink or ironing board. After the chores were done, on Saturday evenings and Sunday afternoons, the family would gather either at our house or at Tee and Robert's house. The men would play dominoes or pinochle, and the women would sit on the porch or in the living room and talk or sing.

Mama would send me to the kitchen to get a lighted cigarette from Daddy for her since he kept the package with him. During the summer I was six, I started sneaking a draw or two from the sweet-smelling Lucky Strike as I carried it carefully back to the porch to give to her. Before I finished elementary school, I was holding back lunch money to buy my own cigarettes and hiding to smoke.

It wasn't until May 1955, when I was fifteen and my brother was three, that my parents bought a new house in Tarrant City. During this time I had entertained thoughts of college after I graduated high school, although no one in my family had ever been to college. My friends were making decisions in tenth grade to take either the college-prep courses or the commercial courses. They were talking about Chapel Hill and Sewanee, and some from more affluent families spoke of Bryn Mawr and Smith, and the really bright ones were talking about scholarships. Those who knew they couldn't afford to go out of state talked about the University of Alabama, Auburn University, and Birmingham-Southern College. I was truly excited and brought these conversations home. I had been double-promoted once, loved school, and the promise of higher education thrilled me.

I was told to forget it. I was told that my plan would be to finish high school and help my mother until I found a husband; then I would marry and raise a family. "You don't need to think about college," my parents said. "We're not going to waste money like that. And you can't go away like that by yourself."

High school that fall was insufferable. With no hope of college, I had to sign up for commercial courses, so there were no algebra, chemistry, or physics classes—studies I had looked forward to with great anticipation. To make matters worse, the misery of home was now unbearable. If all I could look forward to was more of the same, why bother. With that reasoning, I eloped to Mississippi with my teenaged boyfriend in October. We returned to Birmingham, but within a few weeks I quit school.

Six months after eloping, I was six weeks pregnant and in excruciating pain. The week of my sixteenth birthday, my mother went with me to see a doctor in Tarrant City. "If you want this baby, go home and go to bed," he told me. "And stay there. Don't get up except to go to the bathroom. Then you have a fifty-fifty chance of carrying." He leaned against the door of the examining room and tilted his head to one side and said, "If you don't want the baby, walk around the block and come back. I'll take care of the damage." Mama took me home with her in a cab and put me to bed. My young husband moved our things in, and we stayed in the bedroom that had been mine before I eloped.

One day that summer, Tee called my mother to say that Robert and his fellow Klan members were planning to have new robes made and were going to pay to have the sewing done, and she wanted to know if we would help her do it. I had noticed that after the demonstrations against school desegregation at the University of Alabama during the past February that the Klan seemed to grow and take on a more public image. Members of the press sometimes showed up at rallies, and they had started running pictures in the newspapers, so apparently the Klan leaders felt a need to put on a better public appearance. My mother agreed to do the sewing, partly because extra money was hard to pass up back then, but mostly because Robert and his fellow Klansmen would think we were unpatriotic if we didn't help out.

So Tee, my mother, their sister Viola, and I spent much of the summer of 1956 making Klan robes and hoods, cutting the pieces from bolts of white fabric. We followed a basic pattern and cut out several robes at a time. I worked on the handmade emblems that were sewn onto the left breast of each robe. The emblem was a circle containing a white cross, upon which was sewn a diamond. In the center of the diamond was a single red drop representing blood. Each component was a separate piece of cloth, and the components were stacked and then hand-stitched.

For the life of me, I can't recall how much I was paid for each robe I sewed, nor do I remember actually receiving the promised money. I was enormously pregnant at the time and money was pretty tight, yet I saw the whole episode as an intrusion. It made me angry the way Robert preened and straw-bossed through it all. I didn't like that my mother's involvement with the sewing project that summer had turned my parents' house into a temporary Klan robe factory. But participation was much easier than escape. So I sat on the sofa, stitched Klan badges atop my huge pregnant stomach, and resented every minute of it.

While this feverish activity to spruce up the Klan's image was taking place in private homes like mine, the political push for states' rights continued to evolve. Hill Furguson, Chairman of the Board of Trustees of the University of Alabama, and Governor "Big Jim" Folsom postured and plotted ways to block desegregation of the university, while the Klan continued to gain a strength and visibility it had not known for several decades.

In November 1956, my son, Robin, was born, and the next month Mama Katie and Roger moved into a house on Thirty-fifth Avenue in North Birmingham. My husband and I continued to live with my parents for about three months after Robin was born, and then we moved to an apartment.

Unfortunately the young man I had married was as immature as I was, and he expressed his frustration by beating me. During the year we had lived with my parents his behavior was moderate, but when we moved into our own place, his actions became more violent as he progressed from instability to serious mental illness. After two years the abuse grew so extreme that I felt our son was also in danger.

In April 1959, the month I turned nineteen, I left with my toddler on one hip, a cardboard suitcase on the other, and the diaper bag slung over a shoulder, taking refuge with Mama Katie and Roger. Roger told me, "You'll always have a home as long as I'm alive." But in September of that year, my beloved Roger died.

The afternoon of the day he died, Roger, Robert, and my daddy had played dominoes while Tee and my mother visited with Mama Katie and me. My Uncle Howard and his family had stopped by for a visit, too—their oldest son had a birthday that weekend. And my Aunt Viola with her children had come. After everyone else had gone home, Roger, Mama Katie, Robin, and I sat down in the living room to watch Sunday night TV. Before long Roger told us he felt sick. He turned pale and started holding his chest. He told Mama Katie to call Uncle Howard, rather than an ambulance, to take him to the hospital.

When Howard arrived about a half hour later, he took Roger and Mama Katie to the Veterans Hospital on Birmingham's south side. Not long after they left, Tee and Robert came to the house and sat with me while we waited for word from the hospital. Robert sat at the kitchen table and played solitaire and smoked, while Tee and I talked and puttered around the house. Robin napped, but he would not go to sleep soundly.

As we spread the word through the family, another uncle went to the hospital to join the vigil there. His wife called a little after one o'clock in the morning and asked if we had heard from the hospital. There had been so many calls that I thought she was asking for news, but when I told her that I had not heard anything in close to an hour, she told me her husband had called and told her that Roger had died just a few minutes earlier. Melodramatic as it may seem, the first thing I did was to pass out. Although the news was not unkindly delivered, it was abrupt and unexpected; and the hours of tense waiting had worn badly on nerves still frayed from my abusive marriage and emotional divorce.

When I came to, Robin was sitting on the floor near me, crying softly, the wall telephone was hanging clear, and my aunt on the phone was calling my name over and over. Tee was running—around and around through the kitchen into the middle bedroom, into the hall, back toward the rear of the house, through the small back hall and into the kitchen to start the circuit again. She was also screaming—keening really. And Robert was chasing her, trying to catch up and stop her. They made several circuits like that after I regained consciousness—I don't know how long I had been out. When Tee saw me faint, she didn't ask for information. She knew, of course, and lost her fragile grip on self-control.

I took up the telephone again and concluded the conversation with my aunt. Meanwhile Robert caught Tee and held her until she calmed down. A short while later Mama Katie came home supported by her two sons, other family members arrived, and the days and weeks of mourning began. I felt I had lost the person in my life who had been kindest to me, who had always shown that he really cared about me. And I didn't ever have to earn his love—he gave it freely.

Later during that difficult fall, I started my first job, working at New Ideal department store. I was hired before the holiday season and kept on afterward, a part-time job that paid 75 cents per hour. I worked hard and got a few nickel and dime raises until I was making a dollar an hour. When the first minimum wage law became effective in 1962, everybody, even the black maids and porters, were also making a dollar an hour. It says something about social conditioning that I complained; it says something about the climate in Birmingham that I was given a ten-cent raise to maintain the differential.

5
FEUDING

Robert seemed to have a strong desire to involve family members in his Klan activities. He would talk about the Klan and extend invitations to rallies, and he would brag about his nighttime adventures. Although we women and some men were rarely told specifics, I think Robert wanted all of us to be impressed, and to a certain degree, we were held hostage by the information and events he shared with us.

Only men were allowed to join the Klan; their wives joined the women's auxiliary. To my knowledge the only person in our family whom Robert was able to cajole or coerce into actually joining the Klan was Jim Hillhouse, who had married my Aunt Viola in 1947. However, Viola did not join the Klan along with Jim, and even his membership was short-lived. Jim went to meetings with Robert, but he was not extremely active. After a while as a rank-and-file member, he was taken along on some of the group's more clandestine activities. On one of the first night rides, Jim became so appalled at the mistreatment of a Negro man the group had kidnapped that he refused to participate further, and he left the group of Klansmen and their victim near an abandoned coal mine.

Neither Jim nor Robert would discuss the details when they were asked about that night, but because of that incident Jim decided to leave the Klan. The next day Jim had Viola take his Klan robe to Robert's house and turn it in, to emphasize his disassociation from both Robert and the Klan. Robert, enraged, retaliated by taking a Klan robe with blood on it to the police, accusing Jim of the murder the group had committed the night before. Jim was questioned by the authorities, but no charges were brought against him—or anyone else. Apparently it could not be demonstrated that a killing had actually taken place. In the early fifties there was little incentive for law enforcement officers to search the many abandoned mines around Birmingham hoping to find a missing black man.

Robert somehow ensured Jim's silence about the incident. I don't know exactly how, but I do know for sure that there was a long-term threat, with Robert holding something over Jim's head. Perhaps it was the gun that was used in the incident, because the Klansmen had used a gun that night—a gun that Jim had handled. That circumstantial evidence coupled with the bloodied robe might have been enough to convict Jim, especially if he had gone into court without Klan backing. As I've mentioned, no charges were ever filed in the case, but Robert's hold on Jim's silence was secure.

The two men called a tacit truce in September 1959 during the wake and funeral service for my step-grandfather, Roger Whitaker, who was father-in-law to them both. They agreed to keep peace at least that once so that their wives and mother-in-law would not be further burdened. But the atmosphere between them was still volatile, especially when Robert walked over to Jim and, smiling, started a seemingly casual conversation. Jim met Robert's overtures with quiet, clenched-teeth responses, but Robert kept at him, goading and prodding, until one of the other men at the funeral intervened and peacefully broke up the encounter.

A few months later, Jim went to Robert's house and "called him out." For years Robert had harassed Jim, and he had recently made public remarks again, bragging that Jim was afraid of him. Jim stood on the sidewalk in front of the Chambliss home and demanded that Robert come out and settle things once and for all. Robert went out to the front porch, and he, at least, had a gun. According to Aunt Viola, Jim had probably also taken his gun from home when he left to confront his brother-in-law. Intervention by the women prevented one of them from being killed then and there. Their wives being sisters was the only thing that kept Jim from being taken out and "taught a lesson" the same way the black man had been taught a lesson that night years earlier in a coal mine.

It was much to Jim's chagrin when, several years later, Viola borrowed three thousand dollars from Robert to go into business. She established a beauty shop on the main street in North Birmingham, and she was still operating the beauty shop with her daughter, Kathy, in 1972, when a small store known as Hamer's Sundries was put up for sale. Hamer's, as we all called the store, had done business on a nearby corner for more than 25 years and had an established clientele in the neighborhood. So Viola borrowed from Robert again and purchased Hamer's, which had a soda fountain and also sold groceries and patent medicines. To assist in the business, Jim quit his job as an automobile mechanic at a local filling station, where he had worked most of his adult life. With Jim's help at the store, they appeared to be on their way to a second successful family venture.

Ten days after they opened the store, I scared everyone at my house at seven o'clock one morning when I woke up from a nightmare screaming, "Every time he starts to get ahead, he gets shot out of the saddle." I couldn't recall what I had been dreaming about, but we learned a few hours later that I had awakened at the very moment a lone robber, a black man, had entered Hamer's, taken cash and groceries, and shot Jim and two of his customers in the head, leaving them for dead. Jim survived the shooting, but he didn't fare well in surgery. He had suffered from heart disease for a decade, and during the operation he went into coronary arrest of sufficient duration to cause brain damage, which disabled him for the few remaining years of his life.

It wasn't surprising that Viola's newly opened business suffered in the wake of the robbery and shooting. Today customers will come into a robbed convenience store as soon as the police okay it, but in the early seventies, fear was a hallmark of everyday life in Birmingham, and for the folks in the neighborhood, the atmosphere of the place was tainted by the incident. Viola, however, refused to give up, and believing that Hamer's might still be the more promising of her two businesses, she and Kathy closed the beauty shop and stored the equipment. After a few months of diminishing returns, though, Viola closed the store and worked elsewhere until she went to work with Kathy in a second beauty shop. Despite Viola's business acumen and spitfire nature, Robert used the loan he had made to her as an excuse to justify an attitude of authority over her for several years, saying such things as, "If she don't make it, I'll have to sell her hair dryers and sinks to try to get my money back."

Jim lived until July 1977, the year the Alabama attorney general's office presented evidence against Robert to a grand jury and gained an indictment charging him in connection with the 1963 bombing of the Sixteenth Street Baptist Church. On the day of Jim's death, I was at my grandmother's home helping Aunt Viola and her children make the funeral arrangements when Robert called the house offering to serve as a pallbearer. I had answered the phone, and I winced at the sound of his voice. When I had heard his offer, I put my hand over the mouthpiece and told Viola. Jim's son and namesake overheard what I said and became livid, shouting that Robert had not been "fit to associate with my daddy while he was alive, and I won't let him touch my daddy's coffin."

As a way of minimizing prolonged contact with Robert at Jim's funeral, we decided not to have a chapel service, which also eliminated the need for the formality of pallbearers. It was just another instance of my family adjusting plans to avoid confronting Robert and risking his ire, knowing that he would not hesitate to disrupt any occasion if he were angered.

Robert was at the cemetery for the funeral, though, and as the simple service progressed in the humid Alabama July heat, Robert smoked and flicked ashes, moving about restlessly. When the service ended and mourners began milling about in small groups, Robert stood close by the coffin and purposely flicked his cigarette ashes toward the bier, as casually as if he were standing on a street corner. By the time of Jim's funeral, Robert had had many years to relax with the assurance that he and his fellow Klan members would never be called to account for the night's work he had held over Jim's head. Standing by Jim's coffin, Robert surely felt that he had won—at least he was the survivor of the long years of enmity between the two men.

By then, it had been almost 14 years since he had participated in the bombing of the Sixteenth Street Baptist Church and almost a decade since he and his cronies had been assured the FBI had aborted their investigation of the bombing. On the day of Jim's funeral, Robert thought that he had accomplished a degree of security, even though there had been noises about the state attorney general reactivating the case. Even so, most of the people who might have been "weak" enough to break the Klan code of silence and betray Robert were dead. As he stood at the graveside, he must have felt smug.

As I watched Robert that day, my mind went back over past events, scanning other days when I had seen that same smug look, when his half-grin had caused fear or dread, when his cold, half-closed, pale-blue eyes would cut with anger and hatred. By that summer of 1977, my primary interest in Robert was to avoid being around him as much as possible and to avoid conflict. I had moved to a point in my life when I thought I was far beyond the strife and violence of the fifties and sixties. I was relieved that period was over, even though I resented that Robert had never been brought to justice for the part I was certain he had played in the racial bombings in Birmingham. I was resigned to the belief that there would be no justice.

Although I disliked Robert intensely, I feared the fact that he was a liar and without scruples more than I feared personal physical injury. I had simply distanced myself from association with him, except on family occasions such as funerals and weddings. I would, periodically, run into him when I visited my grandmother, but thankfully those were rare encounters, and there were very few occasions during the mid-seventies that I visited in the Chambliss home.

I had worked hard to get on with my life. In their own way, all of the members of my family had moved through that horrifying period and into saner days ... or so we thought.

6
FUN AND GAMES

It seemed to me during the fifties that Robert thoroughly enjoyed himself most of the time. He was a politically oriented person and the advent of court-ordered school desegregation in 1954 gave him a cause célèbre along with the usual night riding and Klan work.

In later years, I became fascinated with the history of the Klan, and I began to research this organization that drove, and was driven by, men like Robert Chambliss. I learned that the Ku Klux Klan had been born in 1866 near Pulaski, Tennessee. It had been formed, some say, as a prank, by half a dozen reputable, well-educated young men who felt themselves oppressed and bored during the Reconstruction era following the Civil War. After an evening of talk and drink in a local judge's office, these men put sheets over themselves and went riding through the streets; they were amused at the fear this raised in superstitious Negroes, who reputedly thought the night riders were ghosts of the Confederate dead. Their hooded night riding soon took the nature of protecting newly disenfranchised southern whites, particularly southern white women. The night riders denied, however, any involvement with violence or attacks on innocent or unarmed Negroes.

Ku Klux Klan spokesmen held that their power was in their anonymity, but that very "invisibility" allowed others, who might be less honorable, to perform acts of violence under the guise of being Klansmen. Violent activities such as floggings, lynchings, and tar-and-featherings prompted passage of laws attempting to curtail vigilante night riding.

After being officially disbanded by its Imperial Wizard, former Confederate General Nathan Bedford Forrest, in 1871, the KKK did not function again as an organizational entity until 1915, when "Colonel" William Joseph Simmons revived it. Alongside a newspaper advertisement for the D. W. Griffith classic film *Birth of a Nation* in Atlanta, Simmons advertised the newborn Klan as "The World's Greatest Secret, Social, Patriotic, Fraternal Beneficiary Order." He also renamed the brotherhood the "Knights of the Ku Klux Klan." Simmons was a professional fraternalist and a skilled organizer who, with the aid of a public relations team, built the reborn Klan into an empire. At its peak in the 1920s, Klan membership was estimated at between four and five million, with, surprisingly enough, more members in the North than in the South.

In 1922, amidst a rigorous power struggle, leadership of the Klan passed to Dr. Hiram Evans, a dentist from Texas. Under Evans's hand the Klan grew to phenomenal levels, which made election of Klansmen to high office and appointment of Klansmen to important posts a rich complement to its numerical and financial strength. Supreme Court Justice Hugo Black, Alabama Governor Bibb Graves, and President Harry Truman top the long list of sheriffs, policemen, mayors, state and U.S. senators and representatives, attorneys general, governors, cabinet members, judges, and justices who stood shoulder to shoulder with farmers, truck drivers, small businessmen, laborers, and just ordinary folks in the hooded Empire.

It was during this flurry of growth that 20-year-old Robert Chambliss joined the organization in 1924. I don't know much about Robert's joining or his early Klan activities, but it wouldn't surprise me to learn that he joined after viewing *Birth of a Nation;* that film became the epic of self-definition for Klansmen, and Robert and other members of the Birmingham klaverns were using it at meetings into the sixties and seventies. I do know that by the 1940s, when I first became aware of Robert's activities, the Klan had lost much of its glitter and influence. By the time the Internal Revenue Service filed a lien against the Klan for $685,000 in back taxes in 1944, fewer prominent people were members and the national organization had splintered into a number of independent groups.

I believe, as I've mentioned earlier, that a large part of what attracted Robert and men like him was the fraternalist status of the Klan. Although Klan influence was waning by the forties, Robert and his cohorts still enjoyed rank equal to, and perhaps more awesome than, the Masons, the Elks, and the Woodmen of the World. A Klansman knew that his "brothers" would see that he was buried decently and would look after his widow and children, and he expected their backing if he got into trouble. The Klan also gave white men a sense of place and power in a world that often afforded them neither; white men were often competing for low-paying jobs with black men and living as we did, in neighborhoods separated only by railroad tracks or a stand of trees.

I knew that the Klan traditionally supported public education, family, the Protestant fundamentalist churches, the southern version of the Democratic party, individual freedoms as guaranteed by the Bill of Rights, states' rights, and segregation of the races. They also generally supported a right-to-work, anti-union position, declaring labor unions to be Communist.

When the Klan was reborn under Dr. Samuel Green in Atlanta in 1946, it again started to grow as thousands of working-class men returned from Europe and Japan expecting the spoils of victory as returning heroes. What they found was an economy geared to war, trying to retool itself to peacetime production. Many of the jobs they had had before their military service were no longer available, although the women who had held down the fort were going home to make room for the returning men. They found a shortage of housing and a scarcity of consumer goods, even though rationing had been lifted. World War II had ended the Great Depression, but the boom days of the fifties had not yet arrived. The revived Klan attracted some of these returning young men, providing the esprit de corps that returning military men had grown to need.

Robert was one of the many old-heads who had kept the home fires of the Klan burning, unofficially, waiting for a fresh start. He had continued to hood up and ride with a few cronies in a loosely formed Alabama Klan during the war years, and the remnants of his original Birmingham Klan group, the Robert E. Lee Klavern, were far from dead.

During my childhood and early teen years, the Klan activities I was aware of were mostly clandestine night riding, involving small groups targeting a single person or a couple. I heard only few details about these occurrences, though—this was in the days before television, when radio mostly provided music and half-hour dramas like "The Shadow" and "Inner Sanctum." There were no lurid news reports or tabloid extravaganzas of Klan atrocities. Sometimes I heard talk of fires and dynamite, but this was usually styled as "punishment" for people who "got out of line." The Klansmen were vigilantes. Arrests in these incidents were rare, and convictions almost unheard of.

Many times, Robert would tell about a black man who had been picked up, taken to a remote area, and beaten, tortured, or sometimes merely "harassed" into promises of "behaving." If the presumed infraction was serious enough, however, the punishment was also severe—perhaps even fatal. At least one of those men that Robert told about was castrated by the Klan. Robert said he and his cronies had poured turpentine on the man's wounds because "we didn't want to kill him. We wanted him to live with what happens to a nigger who rapes a white woman." They then left the man alone to make his way to help or die in the effort. One Klansman was arrested in that incident, and Robert and his buddies raised money for his bail and defense.

Another black man, Robert said, was forced to dig a hole, and then he was buried to his neck; thus rendered helpless he was kicked, beaten, and taunted. Robert said that they left him alive, also. But did he survive, I wondered. Others similarly buried had gasoline or syrup poured on them. Still others, men and women, were said to be tied to trees and beaten. I often heard tales of beating, dismemberment, and potentially fatal injuries, with mine shafts, rivers, shallow graves, fields, and roadsides considered adequate disposal sites for the victims. I recall Robert laughing as he told about the night that he and a group of his buddies "scared a nigger so bad he jumped off a bridge to get away." According to Robert and his fellow Klansmen, the most serious offenses a black man could commit were paying too much attention to or showing a lack of respect for a white woman—rape of a white woman being the ultimate crime, requiring the ultimate penalty.

As I recall these stories, I also recall emotions. I felt revulsion, and I felt fear. My fear was rather primitive, stemming from my sense that the violence was actually indiscriminate; anyone might fall victim if the Klan were to judge them deserving. Even women, white women, were "punished," I knew. Robert had told us this was done to women who engaged in extramarital or interracial sexual activity, as well as to their partners. Often the beatings of women were carried out by members of the Klan's women's auxiliary, who would hood up and go along on a night ride especially for that grisly purpose.

So I grew up being warned about the importance of protecting one's reputation and having a good name. I was also warned that, if given an opportunity, Robert would tell lies accusing females (and males) of promiscuity or loose morals whether there were any truth to the story or not. It was paradoxical, because we all feared his wandering hands and eyes. "Don't ever be by yourself with him," Mama warned. At least two of my young cousins were victims of his inappropriate fondling, and a male cousin told me, "I think he has tried to molest every child in the family—boys and girls."

I have often questioned why Robert would feel secure enough to talk so openly about his Klan activities. I have also questioned how I avoided becoming completely jaded to tales of this violent life, especially when I look back and consider what a routine part of life it was at the time. But Robert had policemen and public officials among his associates, and by the time I became aware that he should be stopped, I was also aware that there was no one to tell.

I realize now that it was not as amazing that so few arrests were made as it was that any arrests were made at all.

7

THE CAHABA BOYS

By 1954, when the U.S. Supreme Court ordered desegregation of schools, the national Klan association had been reorganized yet again, this time under the leadership of Eldon Edwards, who held the post of Imperial Wizard until his death in 1960. Meanwhile, in Tuscaloosa, Alabama, a young Klansman named Robert Shelton was gaining a reputation and a following in eastern Alabama, while a disc jockey named Ace Carter, with patter that was increasingly political and unrestrainedly racist, was gathering an audience in the north-central part of the state, including Birmingham. In Selma, Alabama, a businessman named Sam Englehardt saw the need for open and organized political resistance to integration. His response was to form the first White Citizens' Council.

Englehardt's council sounded good to a lot of people. Among other groups to spring up in its mold was the North Alabama Citizens' Council formed by Ace Carter in Birmingham. Robert Chambliss claimed to be the first member of this group and openly said so in a letter he wrote threatening the president of the University of Alabama during the 1956 struggle to prevent Autherine Lucy from becoming the school's first black student.

I had heard Robert talk about the Klan "going soft" during the early fifties. He and a dozen or so others who shared sentiments on what the Klan should be had drawn apart into what he called simply his "buddies," a group that initially functioned as a violent-action arm of the old Robert E. Lee Klavern. There would be several official Klan klaverns formed in the Birmingham area, moving and changing every few years. Chambliss and his buddies were, whenever possible, attached to a group with a charter and recognition.

I haven't been able to document the exact date when Robert and these fellow Klansmen came to identify themselves separately, but their handiwork began to show up in newspaper reports of violent acts as the decade of the fifties progressed. Initially they apparently were loyal to Charles Pearson, a grocer in the Fountain Heights area, who is said to have paid the men with groceries for their night riding. In the late fifties, Pearson assumed the leadership for a short time of a Klan group known as the Cahaba Ridge Klavern, when its first leader, Troy Ingram, resigned. Troy was one of Robert Chambliss's "buddies." The two of them had organized the Cahaba Ridge Klavern, which met in downtown Birmingham and had eighty-five to ninety members. The group took its name from the nearby Cahaba River and surrounding valley.

Although its time as a chartered group was short, the "Cahaba" did not die. Its members aligned with other klaverns, while the group's inner circle, which included Robert, continued as a tight-knit, secret society. This small Klan group, known as the "Cahaba Boys," has been given a great deal of attention in books, articles, and television documentaries. It has also been variously called Klavern 13 and the Cahaba Group. Klavern 13 was actually the chartered group that met in Woodlawn during the late fifties and early sixties; it had its own klokan, or secret militant-action group, as did all the klaverns. The Cahaba Boys, however, was a separate entity, although it did share some cross-membership with Klavern 13.

In the early sixties the Cahaba Boys met at a place on the Cahaba River, near the river bridge on Highway 280; they carefully limited access and information and were not chartered by the Klan. This group was originally composed of the same men who had operated out of the Robert E. Lee Klavern and had given "Dynamite Hill" its name when they bombed and burned numerous homes, churches, and businesses in the Fountain Heights community to oppose integration of the area in the fifties. Their penchant for violence and overt as well as covert action caused them to operate outside the established klaverns, though, as I have mentioned, the established klaverns each had militant klokans or "action" squads. As far as the official Klan was concerned, the Cahaba Boys were outsiders and their activities were disclaimed, yet they were fully led and supported by Robert Shelton, whose rise to power coincided with turmoil over school desegregation.

Shelton's leadership in Alabama grew during the late fifties and, when Eldon Edwards died in 1960, the squabble over leadership of the various Klans saw Shelton emerge as Imperial Wizard. His particular Invisible Empire (United Klans of America, Inc.) would soon stretch across state lines and include groups from Louisiana, southern Mississippi, Tennessee, Florida, and parts of Georgia, as well as Alabama by the time his power peaked in the sixties. The reason for isolating the Cahaba Boys from the main body of the Klan was to ensure secrecy and security and insulate the Klan from responsibility. Entry into this circle was for those proven loyal—and not squeamish. As more men were drawn to these violent outsiders, the core group repeatedly isolated itself from the larger body.

Although the now well-known FBI informant Gary Thomas (Tommy) Rowe was a member of Klavern 13 and was present at Klan meetings and "actions" from 1960 to 1965, I do not believe, from remarks made by Robert Chambliss and others, that he ever penetrated the core of this particular group of elite troops. The group's membership shifted over the years, but the core group consisted of Robert, Troy Ingram, Thomas "Pop" Blanton (and later, his son Tommy, Jr.), latecomer Bobby Cherry, Herman and Jack Cash, Charles Cagle, John Wesley "Nigger" Hall, Ross Keith, and a handful of others whose roles varied from starting fires to securing and hauling dynamite; building and placing bombs; providing alibis, surveillance, and diversions; and just generally keeping track of each other. Meanwhile they moved in and out of other groups.

Through it all, there was the "routine" work of harassing, beating, and occasionally killing blacks who could be caught alone or dragged out of their homes with little resistance. And there was also the "disciplining" of whites whose conduct or morals or loose tongues justified the Klansmen's attention.

Gary Thomas Rowe was in the Klan in Birmingham and knew, or knew of, all the men involved in the Cahaba Boys. Rowe stayed busy earning his FBI informant's pay and creating situations to take part in, as well as participating in violence himself whenever possible. Rowe had his heyday in 1961 with his participation in attacks on the busloads of civil rights activists, known as Freedom Riders, who traveled the South to integrate interstate transportation. His undercover career would end when he testified against fellow Klansmen in the murder of civil rights activist Viola Liuzzo near Selma, Alabama, in 1965, just after the Selma-to-Montgomery march.

I know from Robert that among these Klansmen Rowe was not trusted enough to penetrate beyond Klavern 13 local planning meetings and overt actions of the group. He did, however, apparently follow the other men on a few occasions and then place calls to his FBI contacts to say he was on the scene of a bombing or riot. During his five years on the FBI payroll, Rowe never gave substantive information about any of the bombing cases. After passage of the Freedom of Information Act, I learned that Tommy Rowe also instigated violent acts on his own and at the direction of his FBI handlers.

Robert, of course, knew Rowe and called him "that old crazy Tommy." On the several occasions Robert spoke of Rowe in my presence, he said that he thought Rowe was an informer and couldn't be trusted or that Rowe had done something "crazy" again that was going to get the whole Klan in trouble.

When a large group was needed and the police were firmly in hand, such as the 1961 Mother's Day attack on Freedom Riders at Birmingham's Trailways Bus Terminal, almost anybody could come along. When the planning was serious and security tight, however, there was a core group of no more than a dozen men involved in planning and execution of the violence in Birmingham.

There were also other small groups and klokans from other klaverns at work in the Birmingham area, as well as disruptive and violent demonstrations by members of the National States Rights Party led by Atlanta attorney J. B. Stoner. These men, in turn, helped smaller groups in other locations and on occasion received help from them; a few of them were active in several small groups simultaneously.

The members of the Cahaba Boys group shared a relationship somewhat like that made familiar to the public by Mafia movies. They had a mutual trust based on the very real knowledge that betrayal meant death. I heard Robert say that the "kiss of death" was his reason for never giving any information about any other Klansman, and he said that the "kiss of death" was on his wife, as well.

If any of the Cahaba Boys came to Robert's house when family or friends were there, Robert would either take them into another room or banish family members into the kitchen. At times, he would take his buddies down to Gafford's Auto Parts on the corner, an establishment operated by Bob Gafford (who was elected to the Alabama House of Representatives in 1966), or Gafford would come to Robert's house to meet with whichever visitor had arrived.

Several times Imperial Wizard Robert Shelton came to the Chambliss house, and at least once he and Bob Gafford were there at the same time when I happened to be visiting. J. B. Stoner was also there on several occasions, and I recall the first time I was told who he was. I had heard his name and discussion about him as the attorney who defended Klansmen in court and who was also a popular speaker at Klan rallies. Stoner was a leader in the National States Rights Party, which he helped form in 1958, taking the insignia and philosophy of the defunct neo-Nazi Columbians, a fanatical right-wing group. The NSRP replaced the Anti-Jewish Party, which Stoner had formed in the forties.

I had expected an impressive and powerful person, but I found Stoner to be a creepy little wild-eyed man who appeared both nervous and leering. He would come to Birmingham quite often, and during the late fifties and early sixties, he was said to have expanded his work with Klansmen by holding classes on bomb building.

These classes were held at various places including Troy Ingram's house, Jack Cash's restaurant in West End, and a meeting place north of town. Often when Robert left home he would tell us that he was "going over to Troy's house," and it was an understood code for Klan work. Although Robert had been arrested once for beating a black man, his goings and comings still remained relatively low profile until 1954, when the school desegregation directive was handed down by the U.S. Supreme Court. That was the spark that seemed to ignite a new, more active, more public role for Robert and his cronies.

In 1954, at Phillips High School where I was a freshman, the desegregation directive was disturbing news. I remember my science teacher explaining, though, that we didn't need to worry because the directive would not affect us. "Nothing will happen for at least a decade," she assured the class.

The next year, 1955, Autherine Lucy and Pollie Myers applied for entrance to the University of Alabama in Tuscaloosa, which was then and is now homebase to the Alabama Klan; Robert Chambliss and other Klansmen avidly followed the progress of the various suits and motions through the courts. When Lucy finally started classes in February 1956, Robert was in Tuscaloosa taking part in demonstrations to stop desegregation of the university and have her removed from school. Of some three thousand demonstrators, there were four arrests for disorderly conduct, one of whom was Robert Chambliss.

When the NAACP brought suit against the university for conspiracy to violate the court-ordered attendance of Lucy, they named Robert Chambliss and the three others who had been arrested as codefendants, probably one of the greatest tactical errors the NAACP could have made. That was a very proud day for Robert. Previously he had had scrapes with the law and had already earned the nickname "Dynamite Bob" among his Klan buddies and in police reports. But now this man, whose education had stopped with the third grade, was sharing a spotlight with university administrators and some of the most prominent names in the state. And after Robert and the three others who were named in the suit countersued the NAACP for four million dollars, he joked about being rich when he got his "nigger money." These legal battles resulted in the NAACP being barred from operating in the area, and Chambliss took a great deal of credit for "running the N-double-A-C-P out of town." It would be several years before the

NAACP voice would be heard again, although the organization's attorney, Arthur Shores, maintained prominence and was a frequent target of Klan attack.

Chambliss and his cronies operated with the approval of and often at the direction of the political power base. Chambliss's job, working in vehicle maintenance for the City of Birmingham, was said to be a reward for his efforts to prevent integration of housing in Fountain Heights. When Chambliss was arrested for a house bombing in 1950, Police Commissioner Eugene "Bull" Connor would not allow Birmingham detectives or state investigators to question him. Chambliss was ordered released within a few hours, and his police record shows "material witness" for the incident.

Although his job with the city ended when Mayor Cooper Green finally refused to continue putting up with his embarrassing shenanigans, Chambliss continued to enjoy protection from prosecution and outright patronage from law enforcement. Even in 1963, after Bull Connor and Mayor Art Hanes, Sr., had been ousted from city hall, Robert Chambliss's career as a terrorist continued unabated.

Throughout all of this, I and the rest of my family lived on in fear and silence.

8

TIMES ARE CHANGING

As the Klan became more visible, its night-riding activities became increasingly more terrorist. Attacks on individuals seemed to be fewer, while members of the small, secret violent-action groups like Robert's were beginning to use dynamite and bottle bombs against political targets.

Fountain Heights, a neighborhood close to where we lived just north and west of downtown Birmingham, and Smithfield to its west, were wracked with violence during the fifties and early sixties as black families started to buy houses in these formerly all-white areas. The neighborhood was dubbed "Dynamite Hill" because it was so frequently targeted for fires, bombs, and dynamite blasts.

I read in newspaper accounts in May 1957 that the Negroes had sent a telegram to U.S. Attorney General Brownell asking for federal intervention. The Reverend Fred Shuttlesworth, leader of the Alabama Christian Movement for Human Rights, estimated that there had been "twenty-one racial unsolved bombings, burnings, and explosive events in this area alone" since 1948. On Christmas night 1956, the parsonage of Bethel Baptist Church and home to the Shuttlesworth family had been bombed and literally collapsed into a heap of rubble. Miraculously no one inside the house was killed. The violence was nothing new.

Meanwhile, "Dynamite Hill" became more and more a focal point of news reports as houses sold to Negroes and houses merely on the market were systematically burned and bombed—to the point that on May 6, 1958, a *Birmingham News* headline asked, "Are Reds Behind Bombings?" with a subhead stating that "J. Edgar Hoover Says Communists Are Exploiting Race Issues on National Scale." The next month the Bethel Baptist Church itself, which was pastored by Shuttlesworth and served as civil rights movement headquarters in those years, was bombed. On June 3, Police Commissioner Eugene

"Bull" Connor asked the Negro pastor to take a lie detector test in an attempt to place suspicion of the bombing on him.

The accusations against blacks, from Bull Connor and J. Edgar Hoover, would echo through statements from politicians and law enforcement long after Connor had lost his position and Hoover had died. But Klansmen like Robert were quick to repeat these accusations and print them in propaganda, claiming that blacks were bombing themselves, backed by a Jewish-Communist plot.

During this time, I recall that Robert and other Klansmen often rode with police officers on their patrols. One policeman's statement to the FBI said that Robert would excitedly ask to be taken along on calls and allowed to "whip niggers." Even after he was fired from his job at the city garage, Robert hung around with beat officers and showed up at crime scenes. He kept a police band radio turned on most nights and "helped" police in his local area, often arriving before officers. He "caught" one man under the Twenty-sixth Street overpass and pistol-whipped him before the police arrived. Robert told us that the officer who arrived at the scene wasn't as pleased as his police buddies usually were and told him to stop answering calls. But Robert laughed it off, saying the officer was "mad because I'm doing his job for him."

A few days later, I went by to visit Tee and found Robert telling an account of his adventures the night before. "I shot at that nigger six times. He was just a runnin', pickin' up his feet jumping over things—and I farred at him six times and missed ever' time. I couldn't understand that, 'cause I never missed a nigger in my life, but this 'un got away from me."

"What had he done, Robert?" I asked, incredulous at his remarks. "Why were you shooting at him?"

"He was running from the police," Robert answered, still grinning broadly and continuing his story. "But, anyway, I'd shot my gun at him six times and he's still arunning and I'uz gonna chase him, but I thought an' taken an' sighted down the barrel of my gun and it was bent! I'd bent my gun when I pistol-whipped that nigger the other night! That 'un really had a hard head!" I had never seen Robert so genuinely amused and animated as he was over this episode. His marksmanship was "vendicated" by the fact that he had damaged his weapon on another man's head.

Robert continued to make these "citizen's arrests" well into the late sixties. On another occasion several years later, Robert and Tee were in bed resting when Robert saw a black man's head as the man ran past the window. The county was working a road crew of prisoners several blocks away on Highway 31 North, and this man had bolted. He made the mistake of cutting between Robert's house and the house next door to get to the alley. Robert's physical agility in his sixties was demonstrated by his actions in the next few minutes—he got up, pulled on his trousers, got his gun, and ran out the front door of his house. He rounded the corner, went past three houses, and caught the escapee as he emerged from the alley. Robert held him by the scruff of his neck and fired at his feet making him "dance" until the corrections officers arrived to rescue the prisoner from Robert.

The times were changing, but Robert never would.

I recall another incident that for me underlines his intransigence. It was 1968, and Robert was hospitalized in Carraway Methodist Hospital after surgery for stomach ulcers. I went to visit him in the hospital—because it was expected and failure to do what was expected might cause suspicion—and found him very quiet and uncommunicative. I asked him how he was doing.

"Awright," he muttered.

"You're awfully quiet, Robert. Are you still hurting from the surgery?" I asked him.

"Naw, that's all-right, but my arm sure does hurt." He was laying on his back with the covers up to his chest, and both arms were covered. An IV tube ran under the cover to his left arm. He turned his head slightly looking at that left arm, and my first thought was perhaps he was having a heart attack.

I lifted the bedspread and gasped. His IV had gotten out of the vein or the vein had perforated because his forearm was swollen more than twice its normal size. "Have you called a nurse?" I asked him, alarmed by the appearance of his arm.

"No," was his simple response. I turned on the call button and told the nurse who answered that his IV needed to be checked. In a few minutes a nurse came in, checked his arm and said something like, "Oh, my God! Why didn't you tell us when that started hurting!" While several nurses started taking care of the situation, I left.

The next evening, I called Tee at home and was told that Robert had come home from the hospital and was in bed there. Carraway Methodist Hospital was racially integrated by 1968, and a black male patient had been brought into the semiprivate room with Robert. He became enraged and demanded that the man be moved. When the hospital staff refused, Robert got out of bed and made a scene in the hall, going into other patients' rooms, ranting. During this tirade he demanded that his family be called to come get him because he would not stay in the room with a "nigger." Witnesses reported that he said he had bombed the church and would bomb the hospital.

Two days later, Birmingham police officers went to the hospital to investigate the incident and concluded that:

It is felt by the investigating officers, Robert Chambliss on other occasions, in a fit of anger, would do a lot of talking, etc. We think that the first report was in error of what was heard. He did not say he had bombed the church and he did not say he was going to bomb the hospital.

But at home later Robert said he would "blow up the damn place" before he would "sleep with a nigger."

9
SEEING THE SIGHTS

During the late fifties and early sixties, there were many Saturday and Sunday afternoons when Robert would chauffeur family drives in the country. I enjoyed these excursions into Tennessee, to remote parts of Alabama, and once to the docks in Mobile to watch banana boats unload cargo at midnight. Between April and September 1959, my son and I went along with Tee and Robert, Mama Katie, and Roger on several trips. While Roger was alive, he organized our outings, providing gasoline on the condition that someone else drive. After Roger died, the outings continued, with trips to Mineral Springs, Cullman, Nauvoo, Warrior, and other cities and towns. But there are two of those jaunts that particularly stand out in my memory.

First was a ride to a plot of former farmland north of Birmingham toward Gardendale; this was probably the same property that Robert would later show to FBI agents in 1963 when he explained that he had purchased dynamite to remove stumps in preparation for construction. At the time he took us there, he and his buddies had just acquired the land, which had a small shed-type building on it. He told us about their plans to build on it, although as it turned out, it would remain not much more than a depository for dynamite, caps, equipment, etc.

Robert's purpose in taking us there was to show off the land and brag about their having a secret place to gather and store equipment away from anybody's home, to have a place that was "their own." He seemed quite explicit that the land would be the property of the Cahaba Boys rather than the Klan at large, and that only those who did things their way would be allowed access.

Robert seemed to envision a meeting hall, something of a paramilitary installation. Since at least part of the Cahaba Boys' explosives were allegedly secured by way of theft from military installations, it made sense of a sort. He spoke of building underground space that would be concealed and impossible to access by outsiders.

"We can put stuff away, and they'll never know it's here," he said. I would recall those words a few years later when Robert warned that he had "enough stuff put away to flatten half of Birmingham," and that the police and FBI couldn't find it unless he should "point it out to them."

The second Sunday drive I particularly remember was to another rural area. We drove circuitously for several hours, so I'm not sure of the exact location. Robert slowed the car and pulled off the two-lane paved road onto a dirt track. In about 75 to 100 yards we came to the remains of a rather large antebellum house. We all got out of the car and walked around.

It was a two-story structure atop an above-ground basement with a stone-and-concrete foundation. The house was in extremely poor condition and could not be easily entered because both the exterior steps up to the front veranda and the interior stairway were badly deteriorated. The roof was partially open, and we could look up through the doors and windows of what remained and imagine days of gentility and prosperity.

On the left side of the house the foundation walls had openings that appeared to have once been windows and a doorway. Inside this basement was an inner wall that was recessed several feet as if it enclosed an inner room. Along the visible wall inside were rings set into the concrete. They appeared to be for shackles, and, in fact, two or three had links of chain attached to them. Near these, lower on the wall, were several dark stains that appeared to be blood. There were possibly a dozen such stained places, and within several there were a number of holes in the concrete, a few of which had what appeared to be bullet slugs embedded in them.

Robert explained that this had been a plantation and that the wall was a place of punishment for "niggers." He elaborated that "niggers" had been shackled to the wall and "disciplined." He told us that the beatings and executions had left the bloodstains on the wall.

He took us farther back on the property, off the left rear of the house, to a long, narrow, single-story building that looked like a stable, or a bunkhouse. Robert told us it had been slave quarters before the war. We didn't go in to explore; it was dark, overgrown, and altogether inhospitable, portions of it having collapsed long before.

A short distance from this building was a rather tall, old-looking though squat tree, and a large area around it was not as overgrown as the rest of the property. The ground was soft here, and Robert pointed out some sunken places that he said were graves. He more or less outlined the perimeters of several, pointing with his finger.

Quite frankly, I chose to behave as though he were speaking of relics of slavery days some hundred years prior, even though I sensed that he was "sharing," as he often did, and there was an air of braggadocio about him as he led the tour. He did, in an aside to my son that was repeated to me, say that putting lime or lye on a corpse would make it impossible to identify, even by dental work, within six weeks, and that the stains on the wall were not 100 years old. (This took place either in late 1961 or early 1962. My son, Robin, and I had not discussed this place until I started writing this book, but when he asked if I remembered this incident and I told him that I did, we compared notes. At five years of age, he was so affected by the scene that his recall of the details was perhaps sharper than my own.)

Robert would, at times, deliberately discuss his activities with an attitude of pride, as though he expected praise. It seemed that, in his mind, this also served to involve us to the extent we could hardly betray him. Yet his accounts were also sketchy, carefully omitting names and specifics that might give enough detail to make betrayal easy.

I was led to believe that this land was owned by someone in their group or a group member's family, so that Klan activities that might take place would not be disturbed. He did say that he and his buddies came out there when they had "business to take care of" where "nobody'll bother us."

After we were back in the car and driving on the two-lane highway leaving the area, Robert pointed out several small houses of obvious great age and poor condition. He explained that they were tenant farmers' houses, and he sounded angry and agitated that "niggers own these plots of land that their damned granddaddy had worked as a slave." He pointed out the poor condition of the houses and remarked that their occupants were "shiftless and lazy and had been better off as slaves."

Robert only took us to that place once, and I haven't been able to locate the property to find out whether any of the structures still stand more than 30 years after that day. There is even a possibility that there has been construction on the property in the interim. The graves would hold only sparse remains by now, if any, and the secrets of that plantation may be buried forever.

Another incident I clearly remember was during the summer of 1963 when my Aunt Tee asked me to take her to look at an empty house in Fountain Heights. Tee had always had a fascination with empty houses, loving to look through them and collect dolls and other odd things people left behind. So this, seemingly, was just an innocent adventure as far as I could see. Unlike today, going into vacant houses wasn't considered trespassing in those days, and realtors would purposely leave them unlocked for potential tenant or buyer access and inspection.

This particular house was a two-story frame with the lot sloping down from front to back so that the basement was above ground in the back and on the sides of the house. It was on the north side of the street, two or three lots from a corner. Although it was obviously vacant, there was no sign posted indicating that it was either for sale or rent.

We went through it from room to room on the first floor and then went upstairs where we found one of the doors wouldn't open. We struggled with the door a bit until we could see there was a mattress pushed against the door from the inside of the room. When we had gotten the door open a few inches, we could see that there were other things in the room. It appeared that someone was using the nearly bare room, for there were signs of recent food and drink consumption and a telephone visible on the floor. There was a noise that frightened us so we retreated at a near run down the stairs and into the basement.

The mattress against the door seemed to indicate that someone was actually in the room at the time, and I thought we should just leave, but Tee insisted on looking around the basement first. There was a workbench against one wall, loaded with paraphernalia: single-strand electric wire by the roll, boxes with what Tee told me was dynamite, gallon and half-gallon glass jugs of what appeared to be gasoline and kerosene, and an assortment of other things like small parts and hand tools.

I was still very frightened but curious nonetheless. Tee reached into a small cardboard box about four inches square and held up several small metal objects. Eyes wide, she told me that they were blasting caps. Finally Tee took me by the arm and pulled me toward the door. We left through the side door in the basement, which opened into the yard, and hurried away to my car, parked in front of the vacant lot next door.

Tee seemed to be as frightened and agitated as I was, but she insisted we keep secret that we had been in the house or even in the neighborhood. "If anybody knew we'd been here, it could get us killed. You can't tell anybody, not even Robert," she told me.

I kept expecting to be chased and grabbed before we could get away. Although Tee was excited and apparently frightened, she explained to me once I had the car in motion that the basement was "a bomb factory" and that she had "wanted to see for sure." I believe Tee got me to take her "to see for sure" so that this information could be passed on to authorities; yet if the makeshift laboratory had been discovered, the implication could have been made that blacks were, indeed, using the house—considering its location.

The "theory" that blacks were doing the bombing was put forth repeatedly during those violent years. While J. Edgar Hoover blamed the Communists for exploiting the race issues, local voices were also calling it a conspiracy by blacks and the Kennedys to justify sending in federal troops to enforce desegregation.

Robert had been a city employee, enjoying the benefits of being a crony of Birmingham's Police Commissioner Eugene "Bull" Connor. Robert had been fired from work as a garbage collector for the city of Bessemer some years earlier, and he had been subsequently hired to work in the Birmingham city garage. Part of his job was to clean out police cars, and he had bureau drawers at home full of interesting things that he had brought from work, including brass knuckles, handcuffs, bullets, and blackjacks. A collection of found police hardware was a standard in the Chambliss home for a number of years, from my childhood through my young adult years, when my brother, my young cousins, and my son were entertained by being allowed to play with these things. They were probably the only kids in Birmingham given real .38s to play cowboys with when they were growing up.

I shudder when I think about how much "evidence" was "cleaned" out of the police cars in those days. Robert told tales of having to quickly clean out a patrol car and remove blood before the car could go back out. More than once, he told of patrolmen letting a "nigger bleed to death in the back seat before they dropped him off at Hillman [hospital]."

On many occasions, Robert told us about visiting Bull Connor's office to demand that particular issues be handled in particular ways. But finally, on one occasion, Robert apparently went too far by banging his fist on Connor's desk and threatening him in front of other city hall employees. This happened after an altercation at a Klan rally that drew a complaint from a newsman Robert had attacked. Within the same time frame, Robert had harassed a black couple, identifying himself as a city employee; he later explained that he felt it would carry more weight with them than saying he was a Klansman when he tried to force them to move from a previously all-white area. Normally Connor would have covered for Robert when Mayor Cooper Green tried to terminate him, but Robert's open threat had pushed Connor into an untenable position. So he did not throw his weight at the termination hearing, and Robert was fired.

After that, Robert worked at several jobs, including clerking at Bob Gafford's auto parts store. Then he started driving a truck for another parts company, making road trips to Florida, Mississippi, and south Alabama. I know there were several occasions when Robert would leave his house to go on one of those road trips, and within an hour a bomb blast would detonate somewhere in the city. Every time he would return from the trip claiming that he had been "on the road" and well out of town by the time the bomb went off. I also remember times that Robert brought the loaded truck home before a trip, and while it was parked in front of his house, some of his buddies would pull up and off-load a box or two into their own cars.

10

POLITICS AND DYNAMITE

The years 1958 to 1962 marked the movement of Robert's political posture from opinionated and verbal to violently militant. His rabble-rousing and subsequent arrest during the desegregation of the University of Alabama in the mid-fifties had marked the beginning of his more activist approach to politics.

Demonstrations like those that took place at the university brought growth to local Klan klaverns and increased the powerbase of the up-and-coming Klan leader Robert Shelton in Tuscaloosa. Meanwhile, in Atlanta, attorney J. B. Stoner and chiropractor Edward Fields had put together the ultra-conservative National States Rights Party. They moved the NSRP headquarters to Birmingham in 1960 and claimed about two hundred members as they started to stage protests.

Naturally Robert counted himself among them. He would insist that anyone who came into his house during those years should stuff envelopes, and he pressed us all to pass out literature and bumper stickers and lapel buttons. Usually I would put the literature in the trunk of my car, where it would stay until the next time I cleaned it out.

Robert was also a member of the United Americans for Conservative Government (UACG), a third party formed out of southern disenchantment with both Democrats and Republicans, and that presented a more legitimate political face than the hate-mongering NSRP.

Despite this upsurge in "independent" politics and Klan visibility, by the sixties it was becoming less acceptable to have the open support of the Ku Klux Klan in an election. Sooner or later, people lose tolerance for sustained destruction, if for no other reason than it's bad for business.

Between 1948 and 1960 the faces of both the Democratic and Republican parties had changed almost completely, largely because of civil rights issues. Americans who were economically conservative and socially traditional began to recognize themselves among Republicans, while those who supported the principles of equality in the voting booth and the marketplace saw themselves in the new version of the Democrats.

As the increasing violence of Klan-affiliated former Democrats like Robert—people who now labeled themselves NSRP, UACG, or even Republican—began to stain the political arena, powerful Democrats of long-standing began to draw back from the negative publicity. Anticipating his own re-election in Birmingham, Police Commissioner Bull Connor even found it necessary to be publicly distanced from the Klan violence and bombings. It is a matter of record, however, that Connor not only attended Klan rallies but also spoke at them, sometimes standing on the hood of a car to be seen. This is confirmed by police reports and newspaper accounts.

While on the surface the politicians in power began to separate themselves from Klan activity, their covert intertwining remained intact. In my mind it was understood, from years of listening to Robert, that Klan activities were financed, at least in part, by money that flowed from Washington, D.C., through both J. B. Stoner in Atlanta and the Alabama state capital, into the Alabama state police headed by Colonel Al Lingo. As Robert told it (and FBI files record investigations of these allegations), several couriers were kept busy and well-paid for traveling between Stoner, Shelton, and Al Lingo with packages and messages. From there, according to Robert, the funds were channeled into the hands of Klan leaders and to whichever individuals were to secure materials or pay participants' expenses.

Of course, there is no documentation of the funds—no canceled checks or ledger pages. Robert and his cronies simply discussed the situation as fact, usually in terms of Klan complaints that officials were siphoning off the top and cheating the rank and file who did the actual work.

I also knew from listening to Robert and others that local politics still ran with the approval of the Klan. It was still difficult for anyone to be elected who was not favored by the Invisible Empire, in spite of (or perhaps because of) Klan activities that included harassing and killing Negroes, beating white men who had abused their wives or failed to provide for their households, and making life unpleasant for anyone who happened to be Jewish, Catholic, or unionist.

Women were not exempt from Klan discipline. A woman who was not a "good" wife (or daughter) or was having an affair, especially a woman known to socialize with a black man, was a target for Klan punishment. Informants were treated with special severity. A Klansman who beat his own wife or kept a girlfriend, however, was not usually molested by fellow Klansmen. On more than a few occasions, Tee sported bruises and lumps, moving slowly and painfully after Robert "straightened her out." His physical abuse of Aunt Tee seemed to lessen during the years that my mother's brother Howard, his wife Mary Ida, and their children lived in the house with them, but it was not gone altogether.

Nor was the abuse totally physical. As is so often the case, Robert's was a sinister, calculating brutality that caused fear greater than the pain. It was a cruelty that Tee could not be protected from, neither could she leave Robert—there was an overt threat on the head of each person she loved should she cross him. And it was clearly understood that she would not live long, and certainly not peacefully, should she try to leave him. There was nothing any of us could do to save Tee from her husband, and fear for her safety is what kept us quiet about Robert and his activities.

At the time, I wasn't really aware that I was also in danger. I had started working downtown at the New Ideal department store in the fall of 1959 and soon formed a friendship with a woman coworker at the store. During 1961 and 1962 I frequently visited her hilltop Fountain Heights home, and she introduced me to a city detective, "Don Stevens," who had used an upper room in her house in connection with the late-fifties Dynamite Hill bombings. The elevation of her house allowed easy surveillance of parallel and adjacent streets while Stevens remained unseen using binoculars in a darkened room.

During the Christmas season Stevens had been suddenly and inexplicably pulled from these duties, put back in uniform, and assigned to traffic duty downtown, at one of the busiest intersections. Within a few days he was severely injured by a hit-and-run driver. After months of treatment Stevens returned to work at a desk job, able to walk only with the aid of crutches and in great pain for many years. In fact, he was crippled for life.

Stevens asked me to meet him one day in the fall of 1962 in a restaurant, a greasy little out-of-the-way place on the near northeast side of downtown. When I saw the place I almost didn't go in to meet him, but I liked him and he had seemed distressed when he called. Over coffee and pie, he told me about the night he was injured and the big white car that hit him; how he had seen it bearing down on him and how he had run; how it had "chased [me] all over that intersection until it finally got [me]."

He told me the story with a strong warning for me to be careful. He said that he knew who was responsible for his injuries, and yet he would never testify against this person—he would not be allowed to live to do so should he try to press a case. He also cautioned me against the police in Birmingham, saying that it was impossible to know who could be trusted. He told me that even officers who would prefer to be honorable were often afraid to act for fear of danger to themselves or their families.

I was not quite able to appreciate the significance of his confidences that day. I felt that he was deeply troubled, and yet I wasn't sure why he was so clearly exposing his vulnerability to me. He was ahead of me by more than a year, but I would reflect on his warnings many times as events unfolded.

During these years, former FBI agent Art Hanes, Sr., ran Birmingham as mayor and president of the city commission, while Bull Connor ran the police and fire departments as commissioner of public safety. "Jabo" Waggoner rounded out the three-seat city commission as commissioner of public works. Clarence M. Kelley (who would succeed J. Edgar Hoover as FBI director) was special agent in charge of the FBI office in Birmingham.

The number and frequency of demonstrations, rallies, and destructive night rides increased and the scope of the targets became more and more political. I knew from Robert's mutterings and from what I heard on the news that the businesses and homes of prominent black leaders, black churches, and houses sold to blacks were primary targets. With increasing frequency the targets were also Jewish temples and businesses as the influence of J. B. Stoner, Ed Fields, and their National States Rights Party grew and talk of a "Jewish-Communist plot" grew more strident.

The Reverend Martin Luther King, Jr., whose ministry in Montgomery had served as support and guidance for the Montgomery Bus Boycott after Rosa Parks refused to go to the back of the bus in 1955, also was experiencing the lash of the Klan as churches and homes were bombed in Montgomery. The Klans in Montgomery, Birmingham, Tuscaloosa, and Anniston kept Highway 31 (North–South) and Highways 78 and 11 (East–West) busy as members in the four major areas supported each other and assisted with "actions" in smaller towns, all under the watchful eye of Imperial Wizard Robert Shelton.

Attitudes had not changed much since February 1957, when a grand jury in Montgomery returned indictments against seven men in connection with bombings and bombing attempts in that city. They issued a statement saying that the indictments "served notice today that segregation must be preserved without bombs and bullets," and further, "we believe we are expressing the feelings of our citizens who believe in law and order, and that they are a great majority of our people."

The men indicted in the bombings of four churches, the homes of the Reverends Ralph Abernathy and Robert Graetz, and an unexploded bomb at the home of Dr. King, were Eugene Hall, Charlie Bodiford, Donald Dunlap, Henry Alexander, James D. York, Raymond C. Britt, Jr., and "Sonny" Kyle Livingston, Jr. The latter four were also charged, when Britt confessed in 1976, in the 1957 death of Willie Edwards (who may have been the black man Robert had laughed about scaring so badly that he jumped off a bridge into the Alabama River). Britt apparently made a mistake about the fourth man being Livingston, though, and when Livingston was able to prove he was not at the scene of the crime, the case fell apart. (Alexander made a deathbed confession in 1993, but to date no one has been prosecuted for Edwards's murder.)

As the decade of the sixties opened, the black community in Birmingham hesitantly gained the leadership of Dr. Martin Luther King, Jr., and the Southern Christian Leadership Conference. King's nonviolent strategy was much more visible than the earlier legal/ political style of the NAACP, which had been banned in Birmingham after the Autherine Lucy/University of Alabama suits and countersuits in which Robert participated. The new civil disobedience was different, and it disturbed many, both blacks and whites. Naturally it disturbed Robert Chambliss, who had been enjoying taking credit for running the NAACP out of town. He called the new black leader "Martin Lucifer King" or "Martin Luther Coon."

These were very nervous days for Birmingham. Most of us felt we were caught in a war zone that we would just as soon avoid. We could feel the battle bearing down upon us as downtown Birmingham had a few attempted sit-ins and scuffles and the civil rights rallies began at Kelly Ingram Park, Sixteenth Street Baptist Church across the street, and other churches across the city. There was no real thrust to these efforts, but that didn't make them any less disturbing.

There were headlines and news comments. President Kennedy and the U.S. attorney general made carefully worded statements. There were talks and negotiations between some wise men of both races in Birmingham, including the Reverend Fred Shuttlesworth, attorneys Arthur Shores and David Vann, and Methodist minister John Rutland.

The year 1962 was punctuated by bombings and frequent reports of night riding. St. Luke's AME Zion Church was bombed. So was Triumph the Church and Kingdom Hall of God in Christ. So were some apartments near New Bethel Baptist Church on Thirteenth Avenue. At these times Robert would often leave the house, with the bomb blast occurring a short while later.

POLITICS AND DYNAMITE

Birmingham's white businessmen and black leaders reached a first agreement toward desegregation of the commercial area, and in November 1962, moderates led by David Vann won the right to reorganize the city government to a mayor-council form, effectively deposing at midterm the three-man commission powerbase of Bull Connor, Art Hanes, and Jabo Waggoner. The three commissioners campaigned vigorously against the proposed change, but they were defeated in a citywide vote. Not one to give up easily, Bull entered the race for the mayor's office, while he and Hanes and Waggoner contested the legitimacy of the new elections, insisting they had a right to serve out their duly elected terms of office. In spite of their efforts, the mayoral election was slated for March 5, 1963.

On December 17, 1962, the City of Birmingham announced a $1,000 reward for information in the bombings, and on December 18, the reward was increased to $3,000. On December 16, *The Birmingham News* ran a front page editorial entitled "Birmingham Merry Christmas with Dynamite."

In typical fashion, Robert Shelton, Imperial Wizard of the United Klans of America, distanced himself and the main body of the Klan from the violence with a pledge of $1,000, announced on Christmas Day, for information in the bombings.

11
HOT TIME IN THE OLD TOWN

As 1962 became 1963, Birmingham was in turmoil, but I was busy with turmoil in my own life and at times missed the import of things going on around me. My son, Robin, had turned six in November 1962, and I always tried to spend as much of my free time with him as I could. We still lived with my grandmother, and she took care of him while I worked, but if I went out at night, Robin usually went with me. We would often visit my friend in Fountain Heights, until she accepted a job out of state and moved. Sometimes Robin and I would go bowling or to a movie or to the zoo. I didn't have much money to spend, but we found things to do.

One of my family's close friends was "Dale Tarrant," whose only child, a daughter a bit younger than I, had graduated college and moved out of state. Dale and Robin and I spent a lot of time together at her home or mine, bowling, eating out, or just riding around town singing in the car. She, too, had grown up in a family that sang, and we enjoyed the harmony, especially on old folk songs and spirituals.

I was driving an old 1953 Chevrolet that was held together by ignorance and hope. It blew so much oil out the exhaust pipe that I carried a five-gallon can of recycled oil, and a coffeepot to pour it from, in the trunk at all times. I also carried an old inner tube and a pair of scissors—I used strips of rubber to hold the gear selector in place. I got so good at repairing it that when it came off, usually at a traffic light, I could hop out, pop the hood, put on a new strip of rubber, and be back in the car before the light changed.

I was still working in downtown Birmingham as 1963 started warming up. There were increased incidents of black agitation for desegregation and voting rights, and there were more bombings and burnings, Klan motorcades, and political posturing. As I said, I didn't notice as much as I should have: I was worn out from three years on a physically demanding job, I couldn't always make ends meet taking home less than 40 dollars a week, I'd had several bouts with respiratory problems and a case of lead poisoning from printer's ink, I was being stalked by the husband of a coworker, and my best friend Shirley, from high school days, had been murdered in September 1962 by her estranged husband.

By late March 1963, I was something of a wreck, and with mounting pressure of home, work, and a confusing social life, I suffered a fall, resulting in a concussion and a hospital stay of several days during which doctors ran tests. I left the hospital promising to return in three weeks if the pain in my head and numbness in my left side were no better. Instead, I started trying to change things in my life. I applied for admission to the University of Alabama in Birmingham, bought a new old car, and started looking for a new job.

In spite of my problems, I had noticed when the March 5 mayoral election resulted in a runoff between Bull Connor and Albert Boutwell, a less rabid segregationist but a segregationist nonetheless. I also took note when on March 8, 1963, local radio station WIXI hosted an event at Municipal Auditorium across Eighth Avenue from city hall. The event drew an enormous crowd—a fact I couldn't miss because I was in the middle of it. This was one of those times when Robert Chambliss made such a big deal about us being expected to go that I complied, taking with me Mama Katie and Robin.

Operation Midnight Ride was the brainchild and political vehicle of Major General Edwin A. Walker and the Reverend Billy James Hargis. Walker had been in the news since he had commanded the paratroopers sent into Little Rock by Eisenhower to enforce federal desegregation orders. Walker renounced those actions and backed up Mississippi Governor Ross Burnett when Ole Miss stood in violation of the Supreme Court in its own desegregation crisis. The ensuing riots in Mississippi had caused the federal government to bring charges of "insurrection and seditious conspiracy" against Walker. He was also ordered into psychiatric evaluation.

"Brother" Hargis, on the other hand, had his own following through his daily radio program carried on WIXI, and his fundamentalist rhetoric was liberally sprinkled with fanatical racism. Together Hargis and Walker promoted Operation Midnight Ride as a tour for God and country, and they came to Birmingham to help Bull Connor defeat Albert Boutwell in the April runoff election. Imperial Wizard Robert Shelton and large numbers of his United Klans of America were in attendance, including the members of Eastview Klavern 13 and the Cahaba Boys, although the latter was not an acknowledged group. Also there were WIXI disc jockey Ace Carter, the Citizens' Council of North Alabama, Dr. Edward Fields, and members of the National States Rights

Party, as well as leaders and members of United Americans for Conservative Government.

Back in those days, behavior was looser in public buildings, and I remember Robert, in his blue suit, standing around the doorway of the auditorium smoking and passing out literature, acting as a self-appointed usher/host. The event itself was a cross between a revival camp meeting and a political pep rally. Robert and several other men stayed around the door, clapping and cheering loudly, helping to stir up the crowd.

On April 2, Albert Boutwell won the mayoral runoff, but Art Hanes and Bull Connor refused to give up their offices, so both camps were in city hall for some weeks while Connor filed a challenge of the election results.

While all of this was going on, there had been little progress in the struggle to end segregation. Dr. Martin Luther King, Jr., by then based in Georgia, declared Birmingham the world's "most segregated city" and named it as a target for the next round of his nonviolent protests for voting rights and desegregation of public facilities. Birmingham's centrally located Sixteenth Street Baptist Church became the new base of operations for civil rights activism. The church was large and conveniently situated only four blocks from city hall. Dr. King and his staff stayed at the A.G. Gaston Motel, about a block away, while he was in town. The day after the runoff election, the first group of demonstrators stepped out from the Sixteenth Street Baptist Church and attempted to get service at city lunch counters.

On April 11, *The Birmingham News* ran an editorial cartoon by Charles Brooks proclaiming "WANTED, For the Attempted Assassination of Birmingham, Alabama." The cartoon was centered by a large question mark and the word "bombers." It showed in bold figures the reward offered at $87,125 and assured that the "Identity of person supplying information will be kept secret."

On April 12, 63 black leaders published a statement explaining why they could wait no longer and had to "lay our case before the general public." On that same day, Dr. Martin Luther King, Jr., was arrested in Birmingham. During his incarceration he wrote his now-famous "Letter from the Birmingham Jail."

On May 2 and 3, the Children's Marches took place downtown. Children and teenagers stepped out from Sixteenth Street Baptist Church and were stopped and arrested by police as Dr. King looked on. They were followed closely by another group—and another. Even though Bull Connor had been voted out of office, he continued to exercise his abusive authority against racial demonstrations, and he called out the police dogs and the fire department hoses to attack the crowd. Criticism was leveled at Dr. King for using children and at Bull Connor for using dogs and hoses against children and for arresting them by the busload—2,000 youngsters were hauled away.

"Saturday night, May 11, more than 2,500 Ku Klux Klansmen, some of them armed, gathered in the flickering light of two 20-foot burning crosses near Bessemer" reported the *Birmingham Post-Herald* on Monday. It was further reported that deputy sheriff R. E. Belcher and three others from the sheriff's office attended that gathering.

Later that Saturday night, at 11:08 p.m., three people were hurt when two blasts destroyed the Ensley home of the Reverend A. D. W. King, a brother of Martin Luther King, Jr. Forty-five minutes later, another blast ripped into the A.G. Gaston Motel, where King's headquarters were located. Neither Dr. King nor any of his staff was in the motel at the time, but the room Klansmen believed King was in was destroyed. The streets filled with angry black citizens.

Alabama highway patrol chief Colonel Al Lingo had become almost a fixture in downtown Birmingham, but he had suddenly pulled his troopers out of town a few hours before the blasts. Police Chief Jamie Moore responded to the scene downtown with police dogs and city officers. By 2 a.m. Sunday, Moore had the situation under control, but Lingo and 250 troopers returned a half hour later after being "requested" by Mayor Art Hanes. Lingo took a look around and ordered his troops into the streets, with clubs swinging, to beat and arrest those few blacks still out.

It was reported that four white men with their faces smeared in camouflage had been seen near the motel, but they could not be identified. Mayor Hanes denounced Dr. Martin Luther King, Jr., for having "masterminded the recent demonstrations." He added that King had been "encouraged by the White House and the attorney general." In Alabama by the spring of 1963, support of the Kennedy brothers was considered by white segregationists to be as great an insult as a charge of Communism.

The following Tuesday, May 14, was the day of the Black Wall, when an estimated 2,000 black demonstrators went through downtown en masse, taking up the street and the sidewalks and making token efforts to enter stores as they passed. All of the stores were locked—there had been public warnings that the demonstration would take place, and the owners of New Ideal department store, where I worked at the time, along with other merchants, ordered their doors locked.

I was at the New Ideal during the demonstration, and I remember that the male employees, armed with weapons ranging from pistols to a claw hammer held by the display department director, took positions at the doors and display window entrances. The rest of us were herded upstairs—out of harm's way. I stood with a dozen or more employees and watched from the mezzanine as the long line of protesters passed the front of the store. There was genuine fear among whites downtown that day and not a little anger. Caught between two warring factions, we could not change the situation and had no avenue of response.

The family who owned the New Ideal had warned their black employees that participation in demonstrations would cost them their jobs. William, a young black man about my age, worked as a porter and helped me in the display department when our boss was out sick (which happened often). William was a very talented young man, and I taught him as much as I could about setting up display windows and running the sign-making machine. Since the passage of the federal minimum wage law, overtime pay was discontinued, yet the owners expected the department to be covered during all business hours; consequently I sometimes worked 60- and 70-hour weeks with only regular hours reported.

I remember one night I had gone past the allowed number of hours the company would pay for and I left William in charge of the department rather than work "off the clock"—I knew there would be hell to pay, but I was too tired to care, and I knew that William was perfectly capable of handling whatever work might come up. I did get a dressing down when I came into work the next morning, but fortunately for William I got to the department office before the owners and destroyed the doodles he had made about "black power" and "equality" while he sat alone at the display office desk the evening before.

William did not come to work the day of the Black Wall, and I knew that he had been part of that mass demonstration—he could not have done otherwise. But I tried to convince our boss to stick up for him, saying that William had really been sick and should be allowed to return to work. I also talked to one of the owners about the matter, but I couldn't change the situation. I haven't seen William since his last day at the store and I don't remember his last name, but William knows who he is, and if he ever reads this book he will know that I admired his spunk, feared for his safety, and tried to stick up for him.

During late May and early June 1963, attention diverted from Birmingham to Tuscaloosa as the University of Alabama played out its hand of legal cards and prepared to admit black students Vivian Malone and James Hood for the summer term. Governor George Wallace was preparing to stand in the schoolhouse door, and the Kennedy brothers in Washington were preparing to respond with whatever was necessary to desegregate the campus.

Wallace told members of the Klan, the Citizens' Councils, and the National States Rights Party to stay away and let him handle the situation. There is a report that one carload of Birmingham Klansmen, including and apparently incited by FBI informant Gary Thomas Rowe, was detained at the Tuscaloosa city limits Saturday night, June 8, and an "arsenal" was confiscated. Arrested along with Rowe were Birmingham Klansmen Herman Cash, William Ross Keith, Herbert Eugene Reeves, Charles Cagle, and Ellis Denesmore. Otherwise there was no interference—the city of Tuscaloosa and the university campus were secured, and all traffic was checked. Although Atlanta attorney J. B. Stoner, founder of the National States Rights Party, spoke at a massive rally south of Tuscaloosa that Saturday night and at another on Sunday, there was no violence that weekend.

Robert Shelton got the six Klansmen out of jail early Sunday morning, but they had no opportunity to breach the carefully planned peace. Nor was there violence on Tuesday, June 11, when Wallace made his stand as the two black students were admitted. A third black college student was admitted without incident at the university's campus in Huntsville.

That same night, however, in Jackson, Mississippi, Medgar Evers, NAACP field secretary, was gunned down in his driveway by a sniper with a rifle. Byron De la Beckwith stood trial for the murder twice in 1964, but all-white juries refused to convict him, despite overwhelming evidence. (In February 1994, he was tried a third time and this time was convicted.)

Beginning in August 1963, Klan night riding again accelerated with several fires and blasts, including three attacks on Birmingham Businessman A. G. Gaston's home and one on the home of NAACP attorney Arthur Shores. On Friday, August 16, a *Birmingham News* headline reported that "City Fathers Pledge Effort To Get Bomber." The accompanying article stated that "Angry city council and Mayor Albert Boutwell pledged to apprehend the sick rabid animal who tossed a gas bomb into Loveman's Thursday." A tear gas bomb had been put in a wastebasket in Loveman's department store just before lunch time. One of Birmingham's largest downtown retailers, Loveman's had recently desegregated its eating facilities. National States Rights Party members demonstrated and picketed the store, and several were arrested.

Even though things were heating up in Birmingham, my life seemed to be improving. I had taken the high school equivalency test and gotten my G.E.D. in 1961, and I had started college courses at the University Extension Center in Birmingham during the summer term 1963. Also I had started a new job right after the Fourth of July holiday.

The money wasn't any better, but the work wasn't as physically taxing as my job in the display department at New Ideal. And the hours were better, making it easier for me to attend night classes. My efforts to change life for the better seemed to be working.

My son was due to start first grade at North Birmingham Elementary School in the fall, and the first black students were scheduled to desegregate Birmingham high schools. During the lull in activity between Wallace's stand in the schoolhouse door and the start of school for the fall term in elementary and high schools, many of the city's ministers were pressing for peaceful solutions. The pastor of Thirty-fifth Avenue Baptist Church, up the street from where we lived, was one of those who urged peace.

Robert Chambliss was not an avid churchgoer, but he was a member of the Thirty-fifth Avenue Baptist Church, as were several others in the family; I was not a member but went occasionally. Robert was convinced that his segregationist actions and attitudes were biblically justified, and he became enraged during an evening worship service and rose from his seat shouting at the preacher and waving his fist. He did not go to the aisle to head for the pulpit in confrontation—instead he started climbing over the pews from seat to seat, shouting all the while. He was blocked by ushers and suddenly seemed to realize what he was doing. He turned and abruptly left, still hurling insults. His wife, my Aunt Tee, hurried out behind him.

I was trying to see Tee regularly during this period. Her health was not good, and repeated bouts of hypertension were taking a toll on her. Often on Saturday, Robin and I would go by for a visit. Sometimes Robert would already be gone when we arrived, but other times he would be at home.

Most of our visits took place around the kitchen table with coffee and conversation. If Robert was gone, Tee would smoke a cigarette with her coffee, nervously glancing out as though she feared he would come back unexpectedly. Robin and I still lived with my grandmother a few blocks away, and sometimes Tee would call and tell me Robert was gone and ask me to come over.

They had a parakeet whose cage sat under the windows in the kitchen on a table with an enameled top. Robert would play with the bird, letting it sit on his shoulder while he ate, drank coffee, read, or talked. He would angle his jaw toward the bird and tell it, "Give me sugar," and it would peck his cheek. If he had not shaved, the bird would catch a whisker in its beak and pull. Robert would yell, the bird would fly around his head fussing, and then settle back on his shoulder.

Robert had also taught it to say a few words and to whistle the way he did when he called Tee. And he had taught the parakeet to call the cat—a great amusement for Robert. He would tell the bird to call the cat, and the bird would whistle and say, "Here kitty, kitty." The cat would always come running and put on a show of frustration trying to get the caged bird who would still be calling. Robert would laugh at the cat's frustration and put it out the back door.

One day when he and Tee had been out of the house, they returned to find the cage upturned and the bird reduced to a few feathers. Apparently, the bird had baited the cat when there was no one to intervene.

The Klan in Birmingham was also approaching a time when there would be no one to intervene and protect it.

12
CUSSING AND FUSSING

On September 4, 1963, Robert Chambliss purchased from Leon Negron's General Store in Daisy City, Alabama, a case of dynamite, along with caps and a roll of fuse. He had this case of dynamite—opened—in the trunk of his car late that night when he and other Klansmen gathered at Jack Cash's Cafe on Third Avenue West. They laughed and talked about the bombing of attorney Arthur Shores's home at 1601 Center Street a little earlier that evening.

About midnight, Robert left the cafe and went home, leaving a message for two of his buddies. Later that night, Klansmen John Wesley "Nigger" Hall and Charles Cagle, two of the men in the Cahaba Boys, went to Robert's house. They moved the box of dynamite from the trunk of Robert's car and put it into Hall's car, just as Robert's message had instructed them to do. (An FBI surveillance photograph on file shows Tee standing on the porch watching Hall and Cagle move the box from one car to the other.) Hall and Cagle took the case of dynamite to a field in the Gardendale area and hid it under kudzu vines. Cagle then told Klansman Levi Yarbrough where it was so Yarbrough could retrieve it and deliver it to Troy Ingram's house in Cahaba Heights.

The blast at Arthur Shores's home had been a "toss and run" bomb. It did not have a timing device, and several Klansmen had been seen in cars in the area. That type of bombing carries risk of being seen and of being injured, making it more exciting, and the group enjoyed it, just as high school boys enjoy a prank.

For the next ten days, there were demonstrations at local schools as desegregation efforts were begun in earnest. Members of the United Klans of America, the National States Rights Party, the United Americans for Conservative Government, White Citizens' Councils, and assorted parents and students staged protests and disruptions at each of the city's high schools. Emotions were running high, sparking new racial confrontations.

I heard a sketchy radio news report Friday night, September 13, 1963, about a white high school girl being stabbed by a young black male, and I read a brief article about it in the Saturday morning newspaper. I stopped at Tee and Robert's about 7 o'clock on my way to work that morning. Tee had not been feeling well, and to give Tee a break from Robert's demanding attention, I asked him if he had heard about the incident. Robert hadn't, and he immediately left the house by the back door and walked down the alley to a supermarket half a block away to buy a newspaper. When he returned, he sat at the kitchen table and read the front-page article while Tee served his oatmeal and coffee.

Robert scolded her for not having fixed me a cup of coffee in spite of my objections that I did not want any—I hated coffee at their house; it was thick and strong, and the Eagle Brand canned milk he used was too sickeningly sweet for me. I accepted the coffee, though, to avoid the harangue going on any longer—when he was agitated and angry like this, anything could set him off. After reading the article, he ranted about the "poor little [white] girl" on a bus returning from a school football game who had been stabbed through the bus window by a young black male who was outside the bus. She was the daughter of a city detective, and I had been in a grade or two of school with her older sister.

(That article in the morning newspaper later became important to substantiating my memory of the breakfast conversation that took place between Robert and myself. In the fall of 1977 as part of the pretrial investigation of Robert Chambliss, Assistant Attorney General Jon Yung and Investigator Bob Eddy from the Alabama attorney general's office questioned me about that morning, and I recalled that the newspaper story had been on the front page below the fold—near the bottom of the page. During our next meeting, they handed me a tear sheet of the 1963 newspaper with the article circled in red; it was, indeed, just where I had remembered it).

"Bob Gafford is going to offer a hundred dollar reward," I had told Robert that Saturday morning.

"By God, if Bob can put up a hundred, I'll put up a thousand," Robert bristled, it seemed, as much at Gafford as at the knife-wielding young black man.

"That's a lot of money, Robert. Do you think it'll do any good?" I asked.

"Nothin's gonna do any good except puttin' the damn niggers in their place and keepin' them there! That poor little girl, just ridin' a bus, doin' nobody no harm. They'd been to a ball game.... "

"Where does she go to school?" I asked him.

"I don't know … that goddamn nigger reached through the bus window and cut her on the arm."

"What happened before that? How could he reach into a bus window from the street, Robert? Was she leaning out or something?" I reflected that the account didn't add up.

"The bus stopped and the niggers on the street started yelling things cause they was white kids on the bus … trying to start something. She was just minding her own business," he defended.

"She was a detective's daughter, do you know him?" I asked.

"Bieker. He's a good man."

"I knew one of his daughters in school."

"This girl's still in school. She's too young for you to know."

"I know that. Bonnie was in school when I was. This must be the one who was real little when I went over to their house after school a couple of times." I added.

"This wouldn't have ever happened if we had put the niggers in their place a long time ago. I've been fighting a one-man war since 1942. If the boys would have backed me up, we'd have put the niggers in their place by now." His face was tight and his jaw jutted forward defiantly.

"How have you been fighting a one-man war, Robert?" I asked, still trying to occupy his attention and give Tee a rest.

"George Wallace is a lily-livered coward. That little bastard has sold us out. He used to be a man, but he just won't do anything now. We got him elected, and he's not gonna do what's right."

"He's just doing what he can," I replied. "He knew in the beginning that he couldn't keep any promises about the schools. The federal government passes a law, and all Wallace can do is make noise. He did exactly what he said he would—no more and no less—he stood in the door," I told Robert, knowing that he would react.

"That's why we've got to fight for states' rights. If Wallace wasn't such a coward, he would have done more to keep segregation."

"Maybe so. But when the laws change, there seems to be no way to keep things from changing. Do you wonder why they would even want to integrate?" Somehow this seemed logical at the time. In my mind, I could easily understand blacks wanting better jobs, education, and housing, but I could not understand why a black person would have any desire to run the risks involved in widespread integration of facilities.

My thoughts were heavily influenced, of course, by knowing that Robert and men like him created the danger, and I could not envision that danger ever going away. The abyss between the cultures of southern whites and blacks at that time was such that even though I had had almost four years of easy relationships with blacks at work, it did not occur to me that they would be comfortable interacting with whites in general. My black coworkers and I would laugh and cut up when we were by ourselves, but when customers or another white employee was around, we would "behave."

At that moment, however, Robert got my full attention. "You just wait 'til after Sunday morning. They'll beg us to let them segregate!" His face was grim and defiant.

"What do you mean, Robert? What's so important about Sunday morning?" I thought there was a rally or something planned that I had not heard about, and I expected him to furnish details about some huge show of force—a motorcade ... or a downtown demonstration.

Instead, he set his jaw and glared as he looked me squarely in the face and said, "Just wait. You'll see. Everybody will."

During this exchange, Tee had served his breakfast, refilled his coffee cup, and put juice and some sort of medication before him on the table. She had not said a word. Robert had eaten, paying little attention to the food, and Tee hovered in the background puttering about, pale and stooped. I remember being worried about her.

As he ate, he continued, "I can stop all this foolishness."

"How on earth can you expect to make any difference, Robert?" I asked him. By this time I had become disturbed, as I usually did, by his mood and the things he was saying. I think I wanted to see him admit helplessness even if it meant more of his anger. He did not—he caught me off guard again.

"I've got enough stuff put away to flatten half of Birmingham. And they'll never find it. I could take them right to it, and they couldn't find it if I didn't point it out to them," he told me with pride, leaning his head slightly back as though looking down his nose, his eyes partially closed. He looked smug. Perhaps "conspiratorial" is a better word, as though his boast was also a confidence.

"Robert, don't do anything that's going to get you into trouble. People don't need to be hurt. Besides, what would Tee do if something happened to you." A lot better, I thought to myself.

"I ain't gonna get caught doing anything. I know what I'm doing. Mommy, get some more coffee. My buddies and me can do what we need to. When I do something, I'll be in something I can get away in." He had finished eating and took his false teeth out. I knew from past experience that he would proceed to lick them clean, so with my stomach beginning to lurch, I stood and explained that I had to go to work.

I hugged Tee, told Robert good-bye, and walked with Tee to the door. She whispered for me to ignore him and not to tell anybody how he had carried on. I slipped Tee a couple of cigarettes, which she put into the pocket of her duster-style housecoat. Later she would sneak a smoke—Robert would not allow her to smoke because it was unseemly for a woman, so we all slipped her a few each time we went by. We hugged at the door, and I left, heading for the south side of town to work.

As the day progressed, Robert would be busy. During the day other family members and friends stopped by to visit, which was normal procedure on weekends. Robert was in and out of the house all day.

About dark Robert invited one of the youngsters to go with him "out to the airport." At the airport, Robert met the Klan's Imperial Wizard, Robert Shelton, and the three of them rode back into town in Robert Chambliss's car. The two men discussed the plans to bomb the Sixteenth Street Baptist Church—with the youngster in the car. Robert dropped the youngster at the Chambliss home and left to "go to Troy's house."

One of the women visiting that evening said he came home about 10:30 p.m., and she left while he was still there. Reports from other people indicate that Robert was at home for only a few minutes, didn't return until morning, and then left several times again before 10 a.m., and several times more later in the day.

Dale Tarrant was also at the Chambliss house that Saturday evening, and soon after Robert dropped off the youngster and left for Troy's, she went to find a phone. She called Deputy Sheriff James Hancock and asked to meet with him, saying that it was urgent; he did not agree to meet her and hung up on her.

For many months, Dale had been in and out of the Chambliss home—helping Tee serve coffee at meetings, stuffing envelopes with political literature, visiting—and listening, and watching. Everything she had heard and seen, she had passed on to the deputy. She had even helped him place a bug in the house ... but he would not talk to her that night when she called him.

Later that night, they spoke again and met at their usual area (north of Tarrant City) about 6 o'clock Sunday morning. Hancock asked Dale many questions, teased her, and drove around town and the rural areas for several hours, even stopping for coffee. She was frustrated that he apparently did not believe her. During the many months she had been giving him information about Robert's Klan activities, nothing ever seemed to be "enough" for him to bring charges against Robert and his buddies.

Before 10 o'clock that Sunday morning, Hancock dropped Dale back at her car, telling her he would "check it out." He later reported that as he drove back toward town, the bomb at the church exploded. He had not called in any alarm or bomb threat in the four hours he had Dale's information, and what's more, he had effectively kept Dale isolated so that she could not give her information to anyone else until the expected time for the explosion had passed.

Years later, when Hancock was finally questioned about his failure to perform his duty as a law enforcement officer, he insinuated that the two of them had spent the time being intimate and that her information was not "specific," even though she told him where a bomb had been placed. Hancock effectively neutralized Dale's role as an informant, a pattern that was repeated with other law enforcement officers and their informants on Klan activity.

As far as Robert's alibi, there were five people who saw him at his house when the explosion occurred on Sunday, September 15, at 10:22 a.m., and during the following half hour: his wife, one of her sisters, one of his sisters, one of his nephews, and one of his next-door neighbors. My grandmother and I spoke to Tee on the telephone minutes after the blast, and I could hear Robert in the background. So I knew he was at home ... at least at the time of the explosion.

I did not learn until quite recently about the youngster's trip to the airport with Robert or the incriminating conversation that was overheard. In all the years of investigating the church bombing, no one ever questioned the children in the Chambliss family. Not the local police, nor the FBI agents, nor the state investigators. They missed altogether the fact that kids were in the Chambliss home that evening.

My Aunt Viola had also gone to the Chambliss home that Saturday evening before the bombing, taking her two children with her. So she, too, was in a position to perhaps know firsthand about the visitors that evening and to overhear enough to piece together that something big was in the works. Robert had talked a lot that night.

Bob Gafford and Robert saw each other on Saturday, but Bob Gafford had witnesses to his whereabouts late that Saturday night. He and his wife, along with Hubert Page (a Klan leader in Klavern 13) and his wife and son, had gone to the bowling alley at Eastwood Mall. They said they were there from before midnight until after 2 o'clock Sunday morning. Robert Chambliss's employer came into the bowling alley and seeing Bob Gafford, teased him about offering the small one hundred dollar reward and Robert's one-upmanship in offering a thousand for information in the stabbing of the detective's daughter.

Bob replied that Robert was going to cost him a hundred dollars because the reward was in the name of United Americans for Conservative Government and had only been offered for publicity. The one thousand dollar reward, however, was big enough to get someone to give information, which would force the UACG to pay their pledge also.

With this incident, Bob not only got UACG publicity, which did turn out to be free, but he also established his own alibi and Page's for the time frame during which a bomb was being placed under the steps of the Sixteenth Street Baptist Church miles away. Few alibis for those hours were quite as neat.

13
SUNDAY MORNING COMING DOWN

Sunday, September 15, 1963, started like a lot of Sundays. I lived with my son and my grandmother in her home at 2320 Thirty-fifth Avenue North, and none of us got up to go to church that morning. Mama Katie was only 69 years old, but she suffered greatly from arthritis. We had gotten up at a leisurely hour and had put together an informal breakfast. My Uncle Howard often dropped off his children at the Thirty-fifth Avenue Baptist Church and came by to visit until it was time to pick them up.

Our television set was black-and-white, and the boxy cabinet was on wheels. We had pushed it into Mama Katie's bedroom the evening before so that she could watch it from either her bed or rocking chair. She had watched one of the television preachers that morning and had been up for awhile before she came out to the kitchen to drink a cup of coffee. She had left the television on, and we could hear it in the background while we talked.

We abruptly stopped talking and exchanged looks of question and worry when we heard and felt the rumbling vibration of ... a bombing? Usually they happened at night. In the dark. This was Sunday. It was broad open daylight. My stomach tightened as we decided that perhaps it was at ACIPCO or U.S. Pipe, two huge foundries a mile or so distant—one to the east, the other to the west.

Minutes passed, and other than the distant whine of a siren we heard nothing. Then we heard a voice on the television saying there had been an explosion, and I think it said "apparently a bomb"—a special report would follow. We turned up the volume on the television and listened to the reports about and from the Sixteenth Street Baptist Church. At first the voice-over was matter-of-fact, but it took on a somber note as the scene unfolded. There on the screen was the church building, with crowds of onlookers, fire trucks and police cars, and police officers with shotguns. The camera eventually focused on a gaping hole in the side of the building; rubble and pieces of the building were strewn across the sidewalk and on automobiles battered by the blast.

Instantly I knew that Robert had been in some way involved. It was a gut-level knowing that can't be shaken, but can't be proven either. It came from how we had grown to know that he was usually "on the road" or "at a meeting" when something happened.

We spent the rest of the day watching the reports. The voice on the television said that several people had been injured by flying debris. The minister, the Reverend John Cross, had a bullhorn and called for calm, trying to keep his people from losing self-control. At one point he seemed to be weeping as were many others. Reverend Cross helped dig through the rubble, and we watched as a small body, wrapped in a white sheet, was brought out on a gurney.

We wept and groaned as the small bodies were removed, one by one, from the rubble, through that huge hole in the wall where windows and concrete steps had been—across the crater in the ground where dirt and the sidewalk had been blown away to a depth of two and one-half feet, and more than five feet wide. Firemen and ambulance attendants stumbled and struggled across that chasm bearing their burdens ... children. One. Two. Three. Four. Five. One, only one, was alive.

That morning a special service had been underway at the Sixteenth Street Baptist Church—the youth were taking responsibility usually reserved to adults, and five girls were in the ladies' lounge preparing to take their places in the worship service.

They were combing hair, primping; one was tying the sash of another's dress. They were excited. They were nervous. They were happy.

Then the wall caved in. Pieces of the 30-inch-thick stone and concrete wall, metal security grating, and the glass and wood of the window filled the room with the impact of the explosion. The opposite wall of the room disappeared as debris traveled through the superheated air forced out from the center of the detonated bomb.

Four of the children were found in one place, felled by the wall as it came in: Denise McNair, age 11; Addie Mae Collins, age 14; Carole Robertson, age 14; and Cynthia Wesley, age 14. A few feet away, they found 11-year-old Sarah Collins, Addie Mae's sister, buried under the stone and glass. She was alive ... barely.

Earlier that morning, at about the time these girls had been arriving at their church, my cousin, 11-year-old Kathy Hillhouse, had also gotten ready to go to Sunday school.

She was going to walk to Thirty-fifth Avenue Baptist Church a block away from her home. She was running late, and as she rushed out of the front door, a man came up the porch steps. He was not a stranger to her, but he was a man she did not know well, so at first glance she did not recognize him. He was wearing dress trousers, a white shirt, and tie, and he told her he wanted to talk to her mother and father. Kathy turned in the doorway and called out, "Mother! There's a man here wants to talk to you."

Her father, Jim Hillhouse, was at work at Reid's Service Station on Twenty-seventh Street. My Aunt Viola came to the door, and when she saw who was on the porch, she pulled Kathy back inside the house.

"Mother, I'm going to be late," Kathy complained, trying to pull away from her mother's grasp on her arm.

"You're not going anywhere, go back inside," Viola snapped. Pushing Kathy into the house, Viola went out onto the porch, and she and the man sat in the porch swing for several minutes talking. As they talked, Kathy realized that this man was at Robert Chambliss's house occasionally and lived only a few blocks up the hill toward Fairmont behind the Hillhouse home. She had seen his children at church, although they were older than she. She had not recognized him at first, because every other time she had seen him he had had on his distinctive Birmingham police department uniform—with badge, gunbelt, and billy stick.

He finally left, and Viola came back inside. She was upset and crying. After she had fretted for a short while she telephoned Dale Tarrant. Kathy listened as Viola told Dale about the man's visit and what had been said. Kathy heard her mother saying that he had told her that a bomb was at the church and that she was to "keep your damned mouth shut. If anybody asks, you don't know anything. Understand?" He had further threatened that if she told anything she knew "we will put it on Jim."

After the man left, he went to his own home—he had apparently been on his way home but felt it imperative that he stop off and warn Viola into silence on the way. He had worked 3 p.m. until 11 p.m. Saturday and had been out all night. At home he changed clothes and, according to his statement later to the FBI, fed his dogs. He told FBI agents that his children went to Sunday school, and he said his wife left for church at 10 a.m. He said that he was called at 10:30 a.m. by the police dispatcher and told to come to work because of the bombing; the church was in his regular patrol beat. He told the FBI that he went to the Thirty-fifth Avenue Baptist Church to tell his wife he was going to work and then went to see his uncle, Robert Chambliss.

Robert told the FBI that this man, his nephew Floyd Garrett, had on "work clothes" when he came by the Chambliss house shortly after

10:30 a.m. Both Chambliss and Garrett said he came to borrow a shotgun to use in riot control because his own had jammed. Chambliss did not have a shotgun, so Garrett left without one.

Garrett said he got into uniform at the station and Sergeant Jones unjammed his shotgun for him. By the time the FBI questioned Garrett several days later, they knew that the bomb had been on a crude timing device. They also had a description of a car with white men in it near the Sixteenth Street Baptist Church at 2 a.m. that Sunday morning.

Garrett's alibi for the time the bomb was placed was that he had picked up his girlfriend at midnight, had taken her to buy groceries (at a supermarket a few blocks from the Sixteenth Street Baptist Church), and had then spent time with her until he went home early that morning. He did not tell the FBI that he had gone by the Hillhouse home. His story would be somewhat different when he testified as a defense witness in 1977. Under oath, he said that he had gone home from work when he got off at 11 p.m. Saturday night, that he was still asleep when the dispatcher called—and that his wife woke him up.

Questions. So many questions. The first question was how? Robert was at home when the bomb had exploded. I was so naive that I did not understand timers and drip buckets … yet.

When Floyd Garrett was questioned by the FBI, no one seemed to think it strange that a police officer would need to "borrow a shotgun" to go "on duty" when the police department furnished arms. In fact, he told his superior officer, Captain Maurice House, that he had gone by to see if Chambliss was home because he was suspicious of Chambliss.

And apparently it was months later before anyone thought to ask Garrett about his uniform—a man who was so impressed with his uniform that in the ten years he had been on the force, he was seldom seen out of it. Yet that morning, he was "on his way to work" when he went to see Chambliss but didn't have on his uniform.

Could it have been that he had to go to Chambliss to get his uniform before he could go to work? There were reported sightings of "policemen" not in police cars the night before the bombing.

Tee and Mama Katie and I had spoken on the telephone a few minutes after we heard the explosion. I called Tee later in the afternoon, and Robert was gone, but she again affirmed he had been home when it happened. It had become almost routine to check and see if Robert was at home when a bomb exploded in Birmingham. Many times, though, he would leave the house, and within an hour there would be a blast.

Attorney David Vann, who would later become mayor of Birmingham, said he saw Robert at the scene of the bombing that afternoon in the crowd. The witness who had seen white men in a car at

2 a.m. also saw the same car circling the area several times that afternoon. Were Robert and the others admiring their work?

Mama Katie fretted so that by mid-afternoon she took to bed and stayed there for several days. Her arthritis was apparently irritated by the circumstances and, I think, a profound sadness bound up in fear.

There was a lot of talk on the telephone that day, but no one voiced any open accusations despite whispered speculations. I can only guess at events in and around the Chambliss home that afternoon because I stayed away. I stayed home, watching the television, taking care of Mama Katie and Robin, and worrying.

During the afternoon two more black children died in other incidents in Birmingham: James Ware was shot on his bicycle by two white youths on a motorcycle, and Johnny Robinson was shot in the back by a policeman for throwing rocks at a car loaded with catcalling white youths displaying Confederate flags.

The juveniles who killed Ware were identified from photos taken at an NSRP rally that afternoon. One pleaded guilty to manslaughter, the other was convicted at trial. They each received seven-month suspended sentences.

Officer Jack Parker said he was firing at the feet of Johnny Robinson and his companion ... with a shotgun ... at 100 feet, and he was surprised when the youngster "appeared to stumble and fall."

Early that evening, our doorbell rang. I stepped into the hallway and saw Robert was standing on the porch. We had opened the wooden inside door for air circulation, but we kept the glass-and-aluminum storm door locked, so I saw Robert without him seeing me in the darkened hallway. I turned and went back to my grandmother to ask what she wanted me to do. She told me not to let him in. We were actually afraid of him at that moment—afraid that we could not hide our certainty that he had set that bomb.

I went to the door and spoke to Robert through the screen, wondering how I was supposed to keep him from entering the house, knowing that he had always done what he wanted. He came and went as he pleased, and I had certainly never barred him. There was conscious fear that he would notice behavior that wasn't "normal" and that thinking we might "tell on him," he would do something to us. He said that Tee wanted to know how Mama Katie was doing, and he wanted to see if we needed any help. He took hold of the door handle to pull it open, expecting me to unlock it to him. I ignored his hand as I told him that she was in bed and had said that she didn't want any company because she was trying hard to go to sleep. I don't know who was most lame in that exchange. It was obvious that he had come by in person to gauge our reaction to the bombing rather than calling us on the phone to check on Mama Katie, and it was obvious that I was making excuses to send him away.

He hesitated, and I saw anger cross his face. After a moment, he ran a hand through his hair, ducked his head, and grinned saying, "If y'all need us, call."

He turned, went across the concrete porch he had worked so hard helping to pour several years earlier, and down the three steps to the sidewalk that split the front lawn. He looked back once as he got into his car parked at the curb.

During the days that followed, the tension was thick in both the city and among Chambliss family members. Conversations were guarded, and yet everyone attempted to behave as though everything were normal. The greatest fear was that Robert would become angry and lash out if he thought anyone might speak out against him. There was no one to tell of our suspicions, though, and no proof.

During the following week, the Sunday morning bombing was a regular item in news broadcasts, reward monies were increased, and the investigation continued. The FBI was brought in because of indications of possible police involvement, and even though local FBI agents had gone to the scene almost immediately, J. Edgar Hoover sent in additional men.

The next Saturday afternoon, September 21, I visited Tee again. I was in the Chambliss living room when the evening news came on the television and Robert came into the room, sitting down on the sofa to watch. I was sitting in a chair near the front door, and although there were other family members in the house, only the two of us were in the dimly lit front room at the time. I don't think Robert even realized that I was there.

He leaned forward toward the television across the room. The news anchorman was updating the story of the bombing and stated that murder charges were being considered rather than the lesser charge of bombing or even bombing of an occupied building. Robert spoke, apparently to the man on the screen, saying, "It wasn't meant to hurt anybody. It didn't go off when it was supposed to."

He looked and sounded upset as though pleading to be believed. It struck me that he may not have meant to have anyone, especially children, killed in the blast, yet wasn't there always that danger when they planted explosives? Was he speaking for himself or from a knowledge of the mind and motives of some others who were guilty? After that evening I never doubted that he had, in fact, been responsible for those deaths because he had known exactly when and where the bomb was supposed to explode. I felt certain that he had either put the dynamite in place and set the timer with his own hand, or he knew the hand that had. And he could have called a warning when the planned explosion time passed and there were people in the building. He seemed to want it understood that they had believed the bomb had failed to detonate or that it had been discovered, so they sat back and kept quiet.

In subsequent days, Robert's remarks were more guarded and angry, and they often came in the form of criticism of others. Where he had, in the past, laughed about arguing with Troy Ingram over which of them was the better bomb-maker and claiming that Troy was just a braggart, now he would snarl comments about Troy and renounce his stupidity. His anger seemed to be directed toward J. B. Storer, Ed Fields, and other National States Rights Party men as well as his "buddies" and Robert Thomas, Grand Dragon of Eastview Klavern 13 He spoke with Robert Shelton several times (or said he did) but later expressed anger that he couldn't reach Shelton when he wanted to. He expressed fear that Robert Thomas was going to "put me and Cash, Blanton, and Cherry in the electric chair."

Between September 15 and 29, when the state would make a move against them, the Klansmen were not sitting back quietly. They were still at work. The same day that Robert had talked to the television saying that the bomb didn't go off when it was supposed to, a fellow Klansman brought a friend of his named Billy to the Chambliss home to meet Robert. Billy wanted to join the Klan. He had been in on sessions at a downtown sign shop making Confederate flags and protest signs for NSRP and wanted to do more.

I didn't know who those two visitors were, but I knew that it was Klan business. They talked in the living room away from family members. The next day (September 22) the Cahaba Boys had another of their Sunday meetings near the Cahaba River bridge on Highway 280. A young Klansman named Tommy Blanton, Jr., met Billy and took him to this meeting.

Later statements by Billy indicate that some sort of pledge or oath was signed that day by the dozen or so men present. By the time the group had gotten back to Troy Ingram's house, Billy was frightened and intimidated. During the next few years, Billy's story changed several times about what happened that Sunday, how long he was in the Klan, and how active he was in Klan activities.

Two nights later, Tuesday, September 24, the Center Street home of attorney Arthur Shores was bombed again, this time with two bombs. One exploded very near the house, and a crowd started to gather by the time the police arrived. The second bomb, rigged for delayed detonation, had been placed nearer the curb; it exploded and threw potentially deadly shrapnel through the neighborhood, endangering the people who were gathering and police officers responding to the initial incident.

On Thursday, September 26, Charles Cagle took FBI agents to a field near Gardendale (north of Birmingham) to show them where he and John Wesley Hall had hidden the dynamite they had taken from Robert Chambliss's car the night of September 4. The field was empty.

During the last few days of September, several meetings took place at the St. Francis Motel in Homewood, a bedroom community just south of Birmingham. Alabama Highway Patrol Colonel Al Lingo used the motel as his Birmingham headquarters in the sixties. It was a convenient meeting place for clandestine notables; Colonel Lingo was the state's top law enforcement officer and answered directly to Governor George Wallace. The St. Francis was a midscale place with just enough glitz to avoid being suspect of renting hourly rooms.

One meeting of particular note for my story took place on September 29, 1963, in Colonel Al Lingo's room. I know this because much later, in January 1978, I was doing research in the Birmingham Public Library preparing a paper for a class at Birmingham-Southern College during the winter mini-term. As I entered the archives department, a classmate who was working there as an intern called me aside and, whispering, led me to a small room where there were a number of boxes filled with papers. She explained that the papers, files from Mayor Albert Boutwell's office, were discovered in the attic of old Fire Station No. 1, which had been closed by the city and cleaned out. The papers had not been sorted or archived by library personnel, and she left me with them without informing her supervisors.

I made many notes as I went through copies of police reports, surveillance reports, and notations from 1963 to 1965. I photocopied one that read:

Persons in attendance at meeting in Colonel Al Lingo's room at St. Francis Motel September 29, 1963:
Colonel Al Lingo
Major William R. Jones
Bill Morgan (United Americans for Conservative Government)
Herbert Eugene Reeves, a Klansman
Robert Thomas, a Klansman
Wade Wallace, distant relative of Governor Wallace
Art Hanes, former mayor

SUNDAY MORNING COMING DOWN

Robert Shelton, Imperial Wizard, KKK
Hubert Page, a Klansman
Don Luna, a Klansman

Same persons listed in above group, including Robert Shelton and Art Hanes, were also present at the Alabama Highway Patrol Office later in the evening.

Persons picked up for questioning on evening of September 29, 1963:
Ross Keith
Levi "Quick Draw" Yarbrough
Robert "Dynamite" Chambliss
John Wesley Hall ("Nigger" Hall)
Charles Cagle

On September 30, 1963, Captain Bob Godwin took Hubert Page, a Klansman, to Huntsville, Alabama, where he was given a polygraph examination by a deputy sheriff.
Don Luna accompanied state investigator Posey, and these two men knocked on Robert Chambliss's front door on the evening of September 29, 1963, in a joint operation.

"In a joint operation." Evidently an agreement was struck that night, a plan was made. Robert Shelton had told Robert Chambliss "not to worry, the Klan would take care of him." But during the evening Robert had worried and was so agitated he had an acute attack of a chronic stomach problem. The doctor was summoned to make a house call. Robert was medicated and sedated into rest, until the doorbell rang late that night.

Alabama Highway Patrol investigator Posey and Don Luna, a fellow Klansman, were on the porch. Don assured Robert that they would "get him out of it" as the trooper placed Robert under arrest and took him into custody. No search of the house was made; the arrest was quiet and expected.

Along with Robert, John Wesley "Nigger" Hall, and Charles Cagle were later charged with the innocuous crime of "illegal transportation and possession of dynamite," a misdemeanor. The maximum sentence was six months in jail and a fine.

Robert often stated afterward that he "passed" a polygraph, but he was so heavily sedated that he almost went to sleep in the chair and was virtually unable to coherently answer questions. Robert Shelton was at the highway patrol headquarters that night when the men were questioned. He told Robert to "keep the Klan out of it."

Chambliss, Hall, and Cagle stood trial and were convicted. They appealed the conviction and were cleared of the charges. It was clear then and is now that the deal struck between the State of Alabama and the Klan leadership was to foil the possibility of the FBI investigations progressing. Whatever evidence the city or state had was effectively tied up by these charges, and it would be possible to delay whatever action the FBI might attempt. The charges by the State of Alabama had simply muddied the waters. Charges brought against Chambliss, Hall, and Cagle had no connection to the Sixteenth Street Baptist Church bombing case at all; the charges stemmed from their September 4 movement of dynamite.

When the kudzu field on Mockingbird Lane near Gardendale was checked on September 26 by FBI agents guided by Charles Cagle, no dynamite was found. On October 1, however, Alabama Highway Patrol Colonel Al Lingo, Major Bill Jones, Investigator Ben Allen, and Birmingham Police Captain Joseph McDowell took Cagle back and "discovered" a box containing 130 sticks of dynamite—at the same location.

Captain W. E. Berry of the Birmingham fire department was called to handle the explosives. In his report he stated that the ground under the box was not discolored, indicating that it had only been there a short time, and that the box was "bone dry," indicating that it had not been there on September 28, the last time it had rained in the area.

On October 4, Birmingham Police Captain McDowell took FBI agents to the spot where the state officers had discovered their box of dynamite, confirming it to be the same location the FBI agents had checked with Cagle on September 26.

The state had made their arrests and had produced their evidence, while the "joint operation" ensured that the arrested would eventually be cleared.

Elizabeth, age 4, with her mother, Libby, who was one of Tee Chambliss's three sisters.
Author's archives

The author's grandparents, "Mama Katie" and Roger Whitaker, in 1944, beside the family home on Twenty-fourth Street North.
Author's archives

The author's aunt and uncle, "Tee" and Robert Chambliss, stand in front of their new home at 2505 Thirty-second Avenue North, Easter 1947. *Author's archives*

Elizabeth with her Aunt Flora "Tee" Chambliss in front of the Chambliss home, 1948.
Author's archives

Left to right: Elizabeth's father, John, Elizabeth, Robert Chambliss, Elizabeth's mother, Libby, 1948.
Author's archives

Robert Chambliss by his back porch, 1948. *Author's archives*

Hillhouse family photo (1952): Viola holds infant Kathy (far left); Jim is seated (center) on the sofa with their son at his knee. Jim was the only family member who joined the KKK with Robert in the late 1940s, but he quit a short while after Klansmen killed a black man. After that incident, Hillhouse and Chambliss became enemies for life. *Author's archives*

Mrs. Johnston's 4th-grade class at F.D. McArthur Elementary School. Elizabeth is standing at far left. The same year Elizabeth was taken to a massive Ku Klux Klan rally near Bessemer, Alabama. *Author's archives*

2004 Twenty-fourth Street North, where Elizabeth's family moved in 1944; Elizabeth lived in the house until 1955. Petric Smith stands on the porch talking to the current owner. *V. Jōn Nivens*

Elizabeth (left) holding her 6-week-old son, Robin, with her brother John, Jr. (center) and grandmother "Mama" Katie Whitaker, January 1957. *Author's archives*

Elizabeth, age 19, in 1959, serving at an Eastern Star installation. *Author's archives*

A Southern Ku Klux Klan gathering (early part of this century). *Birmingham Public Library Archives Department*

The Klan's Imperial Wizard kisses the flag during a ceremonial rite. *Birmingham Public Library Archives Department*

Klan members in full dress (first half of this century). *Eirmingham Public Library Archives Department*

The old Cahaba River Bridge on Highway 280, east of Birmingham. The Cahaba Boys met on Sunday afternoons in 1963 in the wooded area beside the bridge. A modern six-lane highway and two new bridges span the river beside this bridge. *V. Jon Nivens*

Top to bottom: Commissioner of Public Safety, Eugene "Bull" Connor; Mayor and President of Birmingham's City Commission, Art Hanes, Sr.; and Public Works Commissioner, "Jabo" Waggoner, were put out of office in 1963 after city voters elected to change to a mayor-council form of government. *Birmingham Public Library Archives Department*

The parsonage of Bethel Baptist Church in North Birmingham, home of the city's civil rights leader, the Reverend Fred L. Shuttlesworth, was bombed on Christmas Day 1956. No arrests were ever made in the incident. Miraculously, Shuttlesworth escaped unhurt. *The Birmingham News*

May 3, 1963. A Negro demonstrator is held by one Birmingham policeman, while a police dog manned by a second officer tugs at the man's sweater. *Associated Press*

Left to right: Dr. Martin Luther King, Jr.; the Reverend Fred L. Shuttlesworth; the Reverend Ralph Abernathy; Birmingham press conference (1963). *The Birmingham News*

Sixteenth Street Baptist Church. The 1963 bomb was placed under the steps at the far right. *Birmingham Public Library Archives Department*

Investigators survey damage to the Sixteenth Street Baptist Church and gather evidence shortly after a bomb planted by segregationists exploded, killing four children on September 15, 1963. Alabama Power Company linesman secures safety of the electrical supply. *Birmingham Public Library Archives Department*

Stained-glass window in the front of the Sixteenth Street Baptist
Church immediately after the bombing. The head of Jesus was blown
out by the explosion. *Birmingham Public Library Archives Department*

Police stand guard, while firemen and church members search the rubble for victims immediately after the blast that killed four young girls on September 15, 1963. *Birmingham Public Library Archives Department*

The altar and pulpit in the sanctuary of the Sixteenth Street Baptist Church was littered with dust and rubble from the explosion. Stained-glass windows and walls were destroyed by the dynamite blast on September 15, 1963. In the ladies' lounge directly below this area, four young girls lost their lives. *Birmingham Public Library Archives Department*

Police and ambulance attendants wait on the street, while rescuers dig through the rubble for victims. The crater (center) from a dynamite blast was 2½ feet deep and more than 5 feet across, crashing a 30-inch stone and brick wall into the ladies' lounge, killing the four young girls inside. *Birmingham Public Library Archives Department*

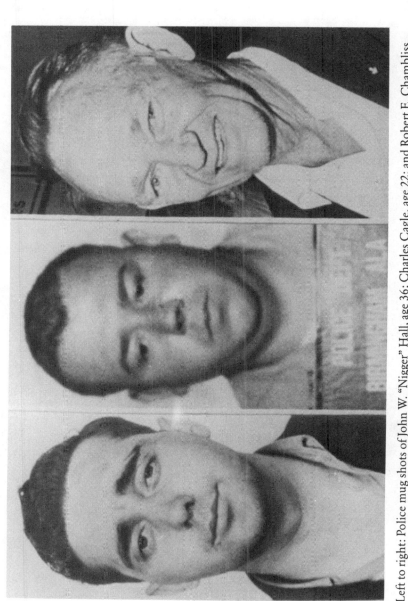

Left to right: Police mug shots of John W. "Nigger" Hall, age 36; Charles Cagle, age 22; and Robert E. Chambliss, age 59. The three men were arrested shortly after the Sixteenth Street Baptist Church bombing and booked on a misdemeanor charge of dynamite possession. The men were Klan "buddies" in the fanatical Cahaba Boys splinter group. *Associated Press*

The Chambliss home at 2505 Thirty-second Avenue North in Birmingham. Robert built the house 1946-1947. *V. Jōn Nivens*

Bob Gafford's place of business, on the corner of Twenty-sixth street and Thirty-second Avenue North, a half block from the Chambliss home. *V. Jōn Nivens*

Elizabeth and son, Robin,
about the time the two went
with Robert Chambliss to a
Klan "plantation."
Author's archives

Elizabeth and son, Robin, at
the Birmingham Zoo (1963).
Author's archives

Elizabeth and her son, Robin (late 1960s). *Author's archives*

1977 bulletin cover of Denman Memorial United Methodist Church, on the city's near west side. *Author's archives*

Elizabeth in the fellowship hall of Denman Memorial United Methodist Church during her pastorate there. *Author's archives*

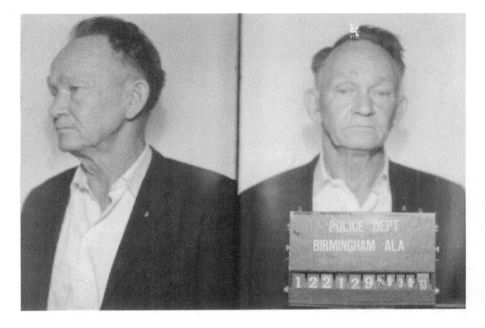

Birmingham police mug shot
of Robert Chambliss, who was
quietly arrested again in 1977
in connection with the
Sixteenth Street Baptist
Church bombing.

Jefferson County Courthouse,
where Robert Chambliss was
tried for murder in the death of
Denise McNair, with Elizabeth
appearing as a state's witness.
V. Jōn Nivens

Alabama State Investigator
Bob Eddy (1994). *Kathy Kemp*

Bill Baxley, Alabama Attorney
General, as he appeared about
the time of Chambliss's trial.
*Birmingham Public Library
Archives Department*

Birmingham Post-Herald front-page story the morning following Elizabeth's testimony.
Birmingham Post-Herald

Elizabeth leaves the courtroom guided by investigator Bob Eddy.
Birmingham Post-Herald

Birmingham Post-Herald

Vol. 116—No. 172
30 Pages Two Sections

Alabama's largest morning circulation

Saturday
November 19, 1977

Final
Edition

15 Cents

Conviction of Chambliss ends his 'one-man war'

"Judge, your honor, all I can say is that God knows I never killed anybody, never bombed anything in my life, and I was not down there at that Sixteenth Street Church... What a shame to put that whole thing on an old 73-year-old man..."

Front-page story following Robert Chambliss's conviction in November 1977. He received a life sentence in the murder of Denise McNair. *Birmingham Post-Herald*

Robert Chambliss (center) with his attorney, Art Hanes, Sr. (right) and court officer during the 1977 murder trial. *Birmingham Post-Herald*

Robert Chambliss, convicted in 1977 of the murder of Denise McNair in the dynamite bombing of the Sixteenth Street Baptist Church 1963, died in prison after serving almost eight years of a life sentence. The Chambliss monument bears the Masonic and Eastern Star symbols. *V. Jōn Nivens*

The Sixteenth Street Baptist Church today, as seen from the entrance of the Birmingham Civil Rights Institute (statue of the Reverend Fred Shuttlesworth in foreground). *V. Jōn Nivens*

The Birmingham Civil Rights Institute opened in 1992 on the southwest corner of Sixth Avenue at Sixteenth Street. Civil rights leader Reverend Fred Shuttlesworth's statue greets visitors from the city and the world. *V. Jon Nivens*

Sculptures in Kelly Ingram Park, where rallies for desegregation took place in the sixties, depict the attacking K-9 dogs used by Birmingham police against demonstrators. *V. Jōn Nivens*

Statue of Dr. Martin Luther King, Jr., which now stands at the entrance to Kelly Ingram Park across from the Sixteenth Street Baptist Church in Birmingham. *V. Jōn Nivens*

Memorial plaque shows the four girls who were killed in the 1963 bombing. The plaque is part of a collection of civil rights artifacts housed in a memorial nook at the Sixteenth Street Baptist Church. *Keith Boyer*

Sculpture by Arizona artist John Henry Waddell, titled "That Which Might Have Been, Birmingham, 1963," symbolizes the unfulfilled maturity of the four girls killed in the Sixteenth Street Baptist Church on September 15, 1963. *Robert Morris*

Petric J. Smith in 1994. *V. Jōn Nivens*

14

FALLING THROUGH THE CRACKS

J. Edgar Hoover and the FBI were called in to investigate the Sixteenth Street Baptist Church bombing for two reasons: the crime's felony status as a civil rights violation and the strong indication of police involvement.

In addition to the regular patrol cars assigned to the area the night the bomb was planted, there had been two special cars assigned to watch the A.G. Gaston Motel and the Sixteenth Street Baptist Church.

At 1:30 a.m. Sunday morning, September 15, a bomb threat was reportedly called to the downtown Holiday Inn on Third Avenue North at Thirteenth Street—six blocks from the church. However, police radio logs from that night document that this call was not broadcast on the police radio; instead there was a broadcast directing the special cars to rendezvous with the shift supervisor. For two hours these special cars were diverted away from watching Sixteenth Street Baptist Church and the A.G. Gaston Motel.

Along with officers on duty between 11 p.m. September 14 and 7 a.m. September 15, several other police officers and sheriff's deputies came under suspicion in the case. These included Robert Chambliss's nephew, Police Officer Floyd Garrett.

Within a couple of days of the bombing, I became aware that FBI agents were talking to various members of our family and that they were being routinely told no one knew anything helpful. I also heard tales of the FBI's harsh attitudes and intention to involve anyone they could; it was easy to feel intimidated by the thought of a Broderick Crawford-type investigation in a small room with a bright light in one's face.

With this set of impressions, it is little wonder that I was upset and unnerved when I received a call from Dale Tarrant at work early in October telling me that the FBI wanted to talk to me. She told me that she had spoken with agents and that I should just cooperate with them. She assured me that everything would be kept secret. No one would know if I told them anything that might help solve the case. She also indicated that they would talk to me whether I cooperated or not.

I reluctantly agreed to meet with the agents after work in the parking lot of the American Liberty Insurance Company, which was shielded from public view. I had a mixture of feelings as I left work that evening. First, I did not believe I could furnish any helpful information because I had not actually seen any crime committed and could not prove any of my suspicions—I just had opinions. Second, for years any mention of the FBI had been charged with distrust, fear, and ridicule, so I was not sure how I should respond to these men. I was trembling from nerves and cold as I sat in the backseat of that car with the two men in the front seat turned to face me.

The driver partially turned and entered the exchange occasionally, while the man in the passenger seat did most of the talking. He was polite and respectful, yet firm and authoritative. This was to be the first of many, many meetings in parking lots, restaurants, and motel and hotel rooms as well as telephone conversations at home and work.

I was shown a large stack of photographs to see if I recognized any of the men as being visitors at the Chambliss home. I was asked if I had any direct knowledge of the bombing itself. I was shown a piece of cloth and asked if I recognized it as belonging to Tee or from any clothing I had seen her wear; it allegedly had been used to tie together sticks of dynamite in one of the bombing attempts.

I did recognize some of the faces in the photographs and told the agents accordingly. Few of the men in the photographs had names to me then, and they gained identities as I was told more about the ones I pointed out.

I was shown a photograph of a "fishing bob" and told it had been found in the street amidst the rubble from the wall and stairs of the Sixteenth Street Baptist Church. I did not see the fishing bob itself. This was when I learned how a bomb can be timed using a decreasing volume of water or other liquid and a fishing bob. As the liquid leaks out of its container, the bob lowers and finally exerts the tiny amount of pressure needed to break either a chemical capsule or a hair-fine trip wire. The blast itself wipes out evidence, usually even destroying the lightweight plastic bob.

The FBI agents assured me that they knew who had done the bombing, but they needed more physical evidence or incriminating testimony to build a case that would hold up in court. I was asked (or told) to visit often in Tee and Robert's house, to watch the house whenever possible, and to report what I might see or hear. And I was to keep to myself any of the conversations I had with FBI agents. I was also told that our conversations should not be shared with the police department; if police investigators contacted me, I should let the FBI know.

The FBI agents were planning to interview my parents and told me that it might look better if I were asked to be present so that they could get the entire nuclear family at one time. I was instructed to behave as though I had not previously cooperated with them. Therefore I was at my parents' home the evening those interviews took place, and I spoke briefly with the agents at that time. They took each of us into a room apart from the others so that the content of each interview was private. Family members were unaware of the conversations I had with FBI agents; Dale Tarrant, who had called me at work to arrange my first meeting with the FBI, was the only person who knew. She and I spent many hours together and separately with FBI agents trying to help gather information and shreds of conversation and observations to assist the succession of agents assigned to the Sixteenth Street Baptist Church case.

During my almost five-year involvement in the original FBI investigation, the only agents I remember vividly are Robert Womack, Timothy Casey, an older gentleman named Cashdollar, and Mel Alexander. There were others, but those I've named are the ones I had most contact with and felt that I got to know. During that period I learned to check my telephone connection box for a tap and take the extra wires loose; I learned to carry a gun at all times and sleep with it hanging on my bedpost; I learned to recognize when I was being tailed in the car and to lead a merry chase; and to recognize by headlights several of the autos used regularly by FBI agents.

From early on, the Klan knew there were informants and routinely threatened to eliminate any who were discovered. The FBI pledged to protect Dale's anonymity and mine, but I did not learn for many years that the agents created more than one file on me: one under my real name, which held only information on those early routine interviews, and a second code-named file, which contained reports of my many other meetings with the FBI as well as agent surveillance of my own activities. (Years later I tried, under the Freedom of Information Act, to obtain my FBI files. I was told that the "photocopying" cost would be $1,000. This, of course, was a prohibitive amount; it effectively denied my access to the information.)

I knew that after the bombing of the Sixteenth Street Baptist Church, FBI agents conducted visual and sound surveillance of Robert's home and there were tapes of several conversations in which he had made self-incriminating statements. However, the FBI did not always know who was present in the house during those conversations, and no one came forward to cooperate.

I was told there was a tape of the conversations of Saturday, September 14, including Robert's conversation with me. I assumed that this was from the bug that deputy sheriff James Hancock had managed to have placed via Dale Tarrant. All of the "bugged" evidence gathered was rejected by FBI director J. Edgar Hoover as insufficient for indictment.

The months of investigation became years, and as one year followed another, the sixties became what seemed like a series of random events against a backdrop of frustration and waiting. Waiting for the other shoe to drop. Waiting for the FBI agents to call and say they finally had Justice Department approval to make arrests or that there would be evidence presented to a federal grand jury. Waiting for Robert to figure out that we were talking to the FBI, that we were watching him as much as possible, and that we would tell what we saw and heard.

Apparently the FBI agents working on the case in Birmingham were also frustrated by the waiting and the dead ends. Mel Alexander was the primary FBI contact with Dale and me from 1964 through the closing years of that early investigation. I don't recall that I ever met with him alone, although I had been alone when I had met with agents previously. There were several meetings in motel rooms and a couple of dinner meetings, but always Dale and I would be together when a meeting with Alexander took place. On those occasions I did more listening than talking.

He and the other agents kept insisting that they needed more evidence or direct testimony to tie together all the things they knew and make a prosecutable case. We were also told that there had been more than one eyewitness to place Robert and the other men at the church in the early hours of that Sunday morning. I wondered why that was not sufficient to indict. It finally dawned on me that either they did not know who that eyewitness actually was, or the witness was not credible. Or … Mel was simply baiting us, thinking that one or both of us had been involved and eventually would admit it.

Dale Tarrant and I discussed all of this, among many other things, and she speculated that the FBI might reveal to us whether there really was enough of a case to prosecute if they, in turn, were baited with a "what if … ." She said to me, "Remember, we were out that night. We went bowling late, and … just decided to drive through that part of town to see if we could see anything going on? Remember?"

I didn't, actually. "If we tell them that, maybe they will decide that there's enough to prosecute. They wouldn't put us on the stand. They promised." She urged me. "I want to see what they say. You just back me up. You may not remember, but you were with me that night. I'm just going to ask, 'What if I told you that we drove down there that night?' "

The truth is that the FBI agents had given us so much information that we probably could not have been credible witnesses during those years if the case had been prosecuted. We had been told in great detail the events of that night, what could be proven and what was speculation. Tee had also provided information that would never see a witness stand. In order to "prod memory" and "make connections" we were told of activities and conversations that we might have never been able to ferret out otherwise. This, of course, added to the conspiratorial atmosphere of the exchanges.

Dale and I were out together so many weekend nights—and on occasion, we had seen Robert and some of his buddies out carousing in cars or on the street—but we had not discussed any such events immediately after the weekend the church was bombed. So which weekend was which was up for grabs. Now a year later, I wasn't at all sure whether I had actual memories of driving on Sixteenth Street or Seventh Avenue North in the early hours of September 15, 1963.

After we discussed the possible "what if ... ," Dale contacted Mel Alexander and set up a meeting. We went together to the motel. She spoke to him and another agent alone while I waited in the small sitting room of the two-room suite. Then I was taken into the back room alone, while Dale waited. We had not detailed a story between us or anything of that nature, but Mel asked me about details surrounding the planting of the bomb that Saturday night/Sunday morning. I remember being a bit alarmed at some of what he was saying. I recall telling him that I felt he could rely on what she had told him, but I could not say specifically that I had seen anything significant. I did ask whether it would make a difference to the strength of the case. He said that it might.

For a while after that meeting with Mel, not much happened. Just more waiting and watching and listening. More being careful. Spring 1965 brought new terrorist activity to Birmingham, and attention was diverted from the 1963 church bombing somewhat. In April and May a series of boxes started showing up on selected people's doorsteps. Painted an industrial shade of green, the boxes each contained several sticks of dynamite and an alarm clock. Only the first one exploded, at the home of a black family. Others were placed on the doorsteps of prominent people like Mayor Albert Boutwell and City Councilwoman Nina Miglionico.

During these weeks, FBI activity increased again, checking on all of the usual suspects and trying to find connections between the material used in the bombs and equipment in Klansmen's garages, homes, or cars.

One morning when Dale was at our house we talked about those green-box bombs, convinced that the same bunch of hooligans were responsible and equally convinced by now that they would never be caught. "If I knew how to make a bomb, myself, I think I would put one on Robert's porch—just to see his face!" I voiced my irritation and frustration in the absurd.

"I would, too." Dale agreed. "God, just think how he would react if he opened his door and saw a green box sitting there. It wouldn't even have to have anything in it. He would be so scared!"

"If only to say, 'We know you are the bombers, and you're vulnerable, too,' it would almost be worth it." By this time we were almost in hysterics, laughing at the morbid humor of Robert being targeted so pointedly.

"We ought to make a dummy bomb. Then take it up there. Knock on the door, and when he answers the door say, 'Look Robert, what is that?' " Dale continued the joke.

I went to the back porch and brought in a cardboard box and a can of green spray paint. Dale retrieved a cylindrical tube from a roll of paper towels in the kitchen garbage can. My grandmother watched us like we were ready for the loony bin as we collected things to go into the box. Green plastic "straw" from a recent Easter basket. Another cardboard cylinder from the bathroom paper towel roll. Old electric wire that had been on the back porch for years—and the alarm clock from my bedroom. All nested in the box, they looked absolutely lethal—at least to us. We sat around the kitchen joking about the effect such a prank would have ... until the doorbell rang! Then we flew into action taking the thing apart and hiding the pieces while my grandmother went to answer the door. Fortunately it was not Robert. We giggled like kids about our version of a "green box" bomb for weeks.

Also in spring 1965, Dr. Martin Luther King's Southern Christian Leadership Conference was gearing up drives to register black voters again. Selma, where Sam Englehardt had formed the first White Citizens' Council in Alabama, was the starting point for a demonstration march to the state capital in Montgomery. In their March 7 attempt to cross the Edmund Pettus Bridge out of Selma marchers were thwarted by Alabama state troopers and Dallas County sheriff's deputies using clubs and tear gas. From March 21 to 25, led by Dr. King, the marchers were joined by civil rights workers, both black and white, and federal officers for their second attempt. Among the whites in the effort, people labeled "outside agitators" by segregationists, was Viola Liuzzo, a Detroit mother of five children.

Liuzzo was shuttling marchers back to Selma from Montgomery after the march when her car was overtaken by another car—bullets fired from that car by the four Klansmen in it killed her almost instantly. Three of the four men in the car were charged with murder; the fourth, Gary Thomas Rowe, broke his cover as an FBI informant and testified against the other three Klansmen.

The FBI had a large number of paid informants, more than 2,000 according to some sources. J. Edgar Hoover's reports to the Justice Department boasted large numbers of new informant recruits. By the time Tommy Rowe's cover was blown, there were several others already on the payroll, including John Wesley Hall, who had been arrested with Robert Chambliss and Charles Cagle on September 29, 1963. Hall's polygraph tests had indicated that he was concealing information about the bombings and had possibly helped build the Sixteenth Street Baptist Church bomb. His polygraph also indicated that although he probably had not been present when the bomb was placed at the church, he had direct knowledge of the bombers' identities.

It seems that the greatest sources of information available to law enforcement, however, were the women who were married to Klansmen or girlfriends of Klansmen, as well as the Klansmen's sisters, mothers, nieces, and in-laws. Female informants were used by city and county officers and by the FBI agents, but few, if any, were paid informants. Most simply cooperated with authorities at great risk, just as Dale Tarrant had been working with a county deputy sheriff for many months prior to the bombing of the Sixteenth Street Baptist Church. She had given information that could have prevented some of the violent acts and information that could have been used to charge and try many of the responsible Klansmen.

As I have mentioned, it has become obvious to me that a systematic attempt was made to identify and engage family members and associates of Klansmen—people who might be helpful in investigations leading to convictions. The detective, officer, or agent could then isolate the informant, effectively neutralizing, if necessary, any danger they might present to the Klan.

There were times when the female informants became too dangerous for various reasons. Perhaps they lost trust in the deputy or detective with whom they were cooperating. Perhaps their knowledge became too vital and too close to the mark. The law enforcement officer, of course, would be close enough to know when a possible information leak was becoming dangerous and would be able to eliminate the threat.

At least two female informants were murdered in the two years following the church bombing. The mangled body of one was found on Highway 31 North; her death was listed as a "hit-and-run" accident, although according to a description given to me by an FBI source, she had "apparently" been repeatedly run over and possibly beaten to death before being placed on the highway. The second was Marguerite "Brown," whose father-in-law was a Klansman; she had been working with a Birmingham city detective, meeting him regularly to pass information in a small motel also on Highway 31 north of the city. On the last night of her life, in spring 1965, she went to meet the detective, but she was reportedly dead of a gunshot to the head when the detective "found her." Although it was physically impossible for a person to accomplish the contortions necessary to self-inflict the fatal shot, Marguerite's death was officially listed as a suicide.

In June 1965, I moved from my grandmother's house into a duplex in Tarrant City near my parents, and when I took my son to register for the first day of school that fall, I met Marguerite's widower, who had a son in the same grade. We began a friendship and dated for several weeks before I learned the circumstances of his wife's death. She had been dead five months when I met him, and he was struggling to parent their four children, who were still at home—and he was, I'm sure, anxious to have a second parent for his large brood.

When he suggested marriage, I felt sorry for the children and was reasonably fond of him; I was also tired of the pressures of my own life raising a child alone, so I entertained the idea, though with more than a little trepidation. Within a few days, I received a telephone call … warning me. I was told the circumstances of Marguerite's death and that it had not been suicide. The FBI contact who called me said that one of Marguerite's family members, an old-line Klansman, was being watched and it was uncertain what her husband's possible involvement might be. My son was used as a point of coercion to break off the relationship. I was told that if I persisted in forming this alliance, I might lose custody of Robin because of the "conditions" I would be putting him into.

I wasn't sure what that meant exactly, but I took the threat seriously. I also understood the additional danger of being in another family that was under watch, added to the one I was already in. I simply told my suitor that I needed to put off marrying because I was unsure. I certainly was not sure enough of him to tell him the truth!

I avoided seeing him for several weeks, and finally he called and asked if I had made a decision. I told him no, and he explained, not unkindly, that his children needed a mother and he needed a wife's help, so that if I were not going to consider marrying him he was going to ask another woman to marry him. I told him to go ahead.

I felt used, manipulated, and held captive. But I also was relieved. I had had time to think what that arrangement might have cost me in time, strength, and possibly my life. I grew very despondent over the situation I was in. Not the broken relationship itself, but the power the situation of being associated with a Klansman had over my life. I had not been allowed to make my own decisions.

Also during this time, my mother's inability to cope with the stress and embarrassment caused her to isolate herself and her health became frail. She became more and more demanding, mistrusting, and accusative. It was not possible to confide in family or friends—so my only outlet for tension concerning the KKK or the FBI was Dale Tarrant.

The months of secrecy after the church bombing had stretched to more than two years, with no end in sight. Yet the FBI presence was always there ... and so was the Klan's.

This despondency led me the closest to suicide that I have ever come. I sat in the living room of the shotgun duplex I rented for myself and my son—he was asleep in the next room. I picked up the .25 automatic that had become my constant companion. I slid a shell into the chamber and took off the safety. I looked at that gun for a long, long time, crying. After a while, my sorrow gave way to anger. I decided that my aggravation value to those people who inspired my feelings was greater than my need for escape. I wanted to stick around as long as possible and, I hoped, cause enough aggravation to make a difference.

Carefully I disarmed the gun and returned it to its holster. Quietly I kissed my sleeping eight-year-old son and lay down on the other twin bed in the room we shared, reflecting that there was only hope as long as there was life. Too many people were already dead—I still had a choice.

After the call from the FBI warning me about associating with Marguerite's widower, there were just the routine check-in contacts with the FBI. I still went by to visit Tee and Robert frequently, but not as regularly.

Robert's political activity was the primary topic of conversation in 1965 and 1966. Heavy campaigning for George Wallace in the presidential race in 1964 fed the machinery of the United Americans for Conservative Government and launched several successful endorsements, including the election of Robert's crony Bob Gafford to the state legislature in 1966.

Then came the day when I learned that the Justice Department was shelving the Sixteenth Street Baptist Church bombing case. Evidence that had been sent from Birmingham to Washington, D.C., had disappeared. There was no record of federal authorities ever having received the infamous fishing bob or other bits of forensic material evidence. The five-year statute of limitation for a federal indictment would expire in 1968, so effort ceased when it was obvious there would not be time to bring the case to trial—nor was more evidence forthcoming.

J. Edgar Hoover declared that convictions in the Sixteenth Street Baptist Church bombing case could not be obtained at this time in the South. End of story.

Mel Alexander was frustrated. Dale was frustrated. I was frustrated, a feeling that soon turned into anger. I felt as used and abused as it is possible for a person to feel. All the intrigue, all the real and perceived danger, all the risk of discovery … for nothing. Absolutely nothing.

And now we had the rest of our lives to watch every word, lest we betray our involvement in this aborted attempt to do the right thing.

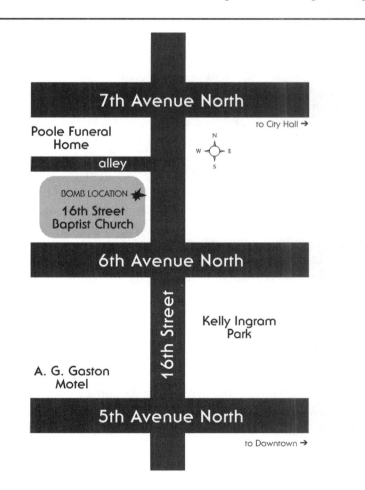

15
RECKONING

It seemed that the decade between 1962 and 1972 was punctuated by gunshots. Life was full of violence and change, and the periods were bullets: Medgar Evers and John F. Kennedy in 1963; civil rights workers Michael Schwerner, Andrew Goodman, and James Chaney in Mississippi in 1964; Viola Liuzzo in 1965; James Merideth in 1966; Martin Luther King, Jr., and Bobby Kennedy in 1968; George Wallace on the campaign trail in Maryland in 1972.

These and many less well-publicized hate-attacks added to the horror story of history that was the sixties and early seventies and to the horror story that our family was plunged into. Added to the gunshots were the bombs, the fires, the "accidents," the "suicides," and the "apparents": apparent heart attack—no autopsy, apparent stroke—no autopsy, apparent cirrhosis, stomach cancer, etc., etc.— no autopsy. Even the "apparent" heart attack that ended the life of J. Edgar Hoover in 1972 was never investigated, and no autopsy was performed.

Convinced that there would never be a satisfactory outcome and that the bombing cases were closed issues, I had to try to put myself back together. Yes, there were other things happening: there were old people dying, younger people getting married and having babies, the highs and lows of life went on. What I had to do was try to figure out what "normal" meant for me.

Deeply disappointed in religious people, I had withdrawn from church in 1963, denounced religion, and swore that I would never darken the door of a church again. I stayed broke a lot back then; the women's movement hadn't started up yet, and I found myself training men making twice my salary how to do my work. In spring 1966, I had the assertiveness to point this out during my annual evaluation and consequently was put on probation for three months.

In an attempt to save my credit, I advertised my car for sale. The ad was answered by a dapper and learned man who turned out to be the pastor of Woodlawn United Methodist Church. On his second trip to look at the car, he worked the conversation around to me. He told me he saw pain in my eyes—and I was instantly in tears. He didn't buy the car, but I found a faith again and a new church home in the summer of 1966.

After that I began to change. I first went back to work in retail display, but a severe injury to my knee brought that to a quick end. I again got a job in insurance, this time with a general agency, underwriting automobile insurance.

I also went through a number of romances, drank myself calm enough to go to sleep almost every night, and lay awake the others. Between 1966 and 1968 I had two major surgeries, one to try to repair my injured right knee. Ironically, Tee was sitting nights with the other patient in my semiprivate hospital room. That first night after surgery, she bathed my feverish head and said she was paying me back for bathing hers with a sock so many years before.

When I left the hospital to recuperate at home between a wheelchair and bed, there was no one to care for me except 11-year-old Robin and a friend from work who stopped by each evening to cook our supper, give me pain medication, and move the cigarettes too far for me to reach. She was afraid I would burn up the bed when the medication kicked in.

That's when I started to wake up ... to come out of it. Flat on my back with nowhere to look but up, I realized there is more to life than wallowing in victimization. That's when the world changed from black-and-white to living color for me. I knew there would be no quick fixes. No instant sainthood here. No walking on water—in fact, after the surgery I had to learn to walk again on an altered and atrophied leg.

In the next couple of years, I made a lot of mistakes. Stupid stuff. By 1970, I was tired, bankrupt, and desperately determined to close that dark era. Besides, the world had Vietnam and Watergate. It had forgotten Birmingham, it had forgotten the Sixteenth Street Baptist Church, it had forgotten the Freedom Rides, unless someone happened to pick up one of the few books turned out.

The forgetting world hardly knew who Robert Chambliss and his "buddies" were, and it knew nothing of me.

In the fall of 1970 I met a young Vietnam vet and married him. Since no one seemed to think our marriage was a good idea, we enjoyed each other with a you-and-me-against-the-world attitude. For a year or so after I remarried I tried pretending to be a normal, stay-at-homebody, but soon I found that I was too restless, and besides, we needed additional income. I began to sell real estate, studying for and passing the state licensing examination.

This was an excellent diversion for awhile. Previously I had worked as an insurance underwriter, and I had studied contract, agency, and tort law in preparation for the Chartered Property and Casualty Underwriter designation. So the challenges of putting together real estate deals in the inflation-ridden boom of the seventies occupied my mind pleasantly for a time. Soon, however, the unrest again took hold, and I started yet another new phase in life.

God and I had gotten on pretty good terms by this time. I had stopped drinking and usually slept nights, I knew the returns of tithing and praying, and I was strongly spiritual (if not theological) in my thinking. I gave in after all the years of fighting off God, and in spring 1975, I announced my intention to study for the ministry in the United Methodist Church.

This was a singularly pivotal time in life for me. The years of stress and duress, fear and frustration, disappointment and disillusionment had given me a strength of resolve that I might not have had, and perhaps could not have had, otherwise. Daily knowing that a slip can end one's life gives a very clear perspective of the brevity of life and the high cost of wasted years.

I would not acknowledge closed doors. With a G.E.D. from 1961 and credit for four courses from the University Extension Center, I applied for admission to Birmingham-Southern College, declaring myself a ministerial student.

I stood the examination of the Charge Conference of my local church and was touched and amazed to hear people one after another stand to speak in witness of my calling to ministry. The district superintendent at that time was openly opposed to my ministerial candidacy, yet I quietly and consistently kept taking the prescribed steps toward that end.

I said above that this was a pivotal time in life for me. Not only did it reflect strength gained from prior years, but, although I could not know it at the time, it also established me as a person whose credibility was so unimpeachable that my testimony could make a profound difference on the witness stand a few years into the future.

I started classes with "Intro to Theology" under Dr. Earl Gossett in summer 1975. In June 1976 I was appointed to my first pastorate, Acmar United Methodist Church, a rural church, about 25 miles northeast of Birmingham, that met every other Sunday and alternate fifth Sundays. It was my privilege to baptize my goddaughter, Maria, in that little church, and while there I increased the frequency of services to weekly and brought about some repairs to the building. Not a particularly spectacular first year, but it was good, very good.

My husband and I had moved into married student housing on the Birmingham-Southern College campus after I was appointed to Acmar.

For about a year prior, we had lived in a house owned by Woodlawn United Methodist Church while I studied, taught in the church, and served as director of the church's child-development center. Robin had quit school and married at age 17, and early in 1977, at age 20, with the advent of a divorce, he moved in with us in the small two-bedroom apartment on campus, and worked in a record store in the nearby town of Hoover. That, too, proved fateful as 1977 rolled around.

In January I did my chaplaincy internship at Carraway Medical Center under the Reverend Wayne Vickery, and in the spring my attention was drawn inexplicably to Denman Memorial United Methodist Church. Not knowing why and not being familiar with the church, I simply put it on my prayer list and started praying about it.

In April, I received a call from Denman's pastor, telling me that he was going to Nashville for further schooling and had been asked to help select his replacement by the superintendent and the bishop. Faculty members at Birmingham-Southern College had given him a list of possible names, and mine was among them. We met, and he later suggested to the hierarchy that I be appointed to the church. This is just the way things were happening in my life. It didn't matter where I lived—for the first time I knew the meaning of "home." The only vow I ever made God was to do what I found under my hand to do—the rest was up to Him.

My life was so busy during that spring and summer that I hardly paid any attention to any world outside my own. It was demanding, it was challenging in a way I enjoyed, and I was content. Not satisfied, but content.

Life was basically good, and there was very little contact with my family. A cousin married, and I conducted the ceremony. That was a joyous occasion.

My Uncle Jim Hillhouse died in July 1977, and I performed the graveside service. This event marked one of the few times during those years that I saw Robert Chambliss; I was deeply disturbed and sickened by his presence and by his flicking of cigarette ashes into Jim's grave. Still, conducting the service was a favor I gladly did for Jim's wife, my Aunt Viola.

Pulpit appointments were made during the North Alabama Conference of the United Methodist Church in June 1977, and I started to pastor Denman Memorial's small congregation. Many of those people at Denman were champions of love and support, and they would be sorely tried before the year was out.

Robin took his G.E.D. exam late in summer 1977 and was set to begin college classes in the fall semester; his freshman year would be my senior. We were both excited. It had taken me a long time to get back to school, and I was anxious for him to be able to go to college while he was young.

Before moving into the parsonage at Denman toward the end of August, we took a short and much-needed vacation to the Great Smoky Mountains. On the Friday we were to leave, I finished my work early in the day, had the car serviced, and went home to our apartment on the Birmingham-Southern campus. There I found a telephone message from Sergeant Cantrell of the Birmingham Police Department; I tried to return his call, but he had left the office for the weekend. My Aunt Mary called a few moments later to tell me that Birmingham Police Department Captain Jack LeGrand had called her—he also was trying to locate me. Unable to return LeGrand's call either, we left on vacation, going first to Mobile to visit friends, then to Atlanta and into the mountains.

When we returned the following Thursday, August 12, 1977, I turned on the evening news to hear that the grand jury was hearing testimony in the Sixteenth Street Baptist Church bombing case. FBI agent Mel Alexander had told us that the bombing case had "fallen through the cracks" at the U.S. Department of Justice a decade before, but now in 1977, Alabama Attorney General Bill Baxley was calling for a "day of reckoning."

The first image I saw on the television screen was Robert Chambliss in the hallway outside the sixth-floor grand jury room; he was attacking a news cameraman. The look on Robert's face and his balled-up fists were so familiar and so disquieting, the relaxed effects of my vacation were instantly negated.

About the same time my telephone rang. It was my Aunt Mary. She told me that "they" were looking for me and had a subpoena to call me to testify before the grand jury. Jack LeGrand had called her again, trying to locate me. She said she had been pestered all week with calls. I started to tremble a bit inside as I verified with her who in particular would be the person to contact. I called police headquarters and learned that LeGrand had left for the day this time, also. Rather than speak to anyone else, I looked up his number and called him at home. I realized it was better to speak to him at his home, for there was almost no chance that the call would be traced. I'm not sure why I felt so strongly, but the atmosphere in Birmingham and the South as I grew up was not one to give honest people faith in law enforcement—crooks and conspirators consorted openly with neighborhood cops.

I still was distrusting of all law enforcement personnel. I did not know Jack LeGrand, but I recognized Ernie Cantrell's name. Cantrell had been one of the officers on duty from 11 p.m. until 7 a.m. the night of September 14-15, 1963, assigned to patrol the church and A.G. Gaston Motel. That night, a special car had been posted a half block away with a clear view of the Sixteenth Street Baptist church's street-side steps under which the bomb had been placed. A "decoy" bomb threat was said to have been called in to the Holiday Inn Motel on Third Avenue North, and the special car then "rendezvoused" with other cars and watched the motel rather than the church property that night. However, the "decoy" bomb threat was not broadcast on the police radio band, and transcripts of police radio transmissions for that night do not show a call received for the motel about 1:30 a.m. It does show, at 1:34 a.m., a call ordering a rendezvous between two cars, but there were no instructions to abandon watch on the church.

Old feelings of mistrust stirred up in me. When I reached LeGrand by telephone and told him who I was, he started to say something excitedly, but I cut him off by saying, "I understand you are looking for me."

He regained his composure somewhat, and I'm sure saw my call as a real stroke of luck that he would be able to take some kind of credit for. "You have to report to the grand jury at 10 a.m. tomorrow," he gruffly demanded.

"No, I won't do that," I replied as calmly and politely as I could manage.

"You have to! I've got a subpoena for you, and I'll serve it on you tonight. You'll be arrested if you don't cooperate!" he was shouting, blustering.

"I'll be glad to try to cooperate, but I will not come to the courthouse and be filmed in that hallway with speculation as to what I may be saying. I have a family and a church congregation, and I won't subject either of them to that." I was still outwardly calm, but my insides were trembling; yet I was entirely deliberate in my refusal.

"You can be charged with ... ."

"If you will listen just a minute, captain. I will make an appointment to speak to someone from the attorney general's office and try to help in any way that I can, but I absolutely will not testify before a grand jury."

He was quiet for several seconds and then said, "Give me your number, and I'll call you back."

Taking a deep breath, I gave him the number and listened as he told me to stay there until he called back. Of course I was afraid that the next sound I heard would be sirens, but I had figured it right. He was taking no action without direction from the attorney general's staff. They were letting him front for them ... do their legwork.

I received a call back in less than a half hour, with instructions to contact a state investigator—a telephone number, a room number, and a name. I called, and a man answered the telephone. "Is this Bob Eddy."

"Yes."

"Jack LeGrand said you would be expecting my call," I told him, amazed that I actually sounded calm.

Eddy asked me to come to the Roadway Inn near the University of Alabama at Birmingham. My husband went with me, which for him was a brave thing to do; after that trip, however, he was kept out of and away from my contacts with these investigators. That night he sat at the far end of the suite while I talked to them.

There was a small table covered with papers and file folders. The state investigator Bob Eddy sat down at the table after he let us into the room. There were two other men present, but introductions went right past me, if there were any; I was not impressed that one of them might be the attorney general.

Bob Eddy was a big man. Tall and solidly built. Thin brown hair, a round face, big hands. He greeted me politely and asked me to sit with him at the table. He seemed just a bit disoriented when we began, as though he did not know what to ask me and was not sure why I was there.

After a few general questions that I answered honestly, if vaguely, I decided that we might as well see where this was going. I told him, in effect, that I was sure he had a file from the FBI containing everything I knew as fact, and I couldn't really add anything that I had not told to the FBI years before; so just what was it I was expected to tell a grand jury? I as much as told him that I was not willing to publicly make any statements and then be left hanging out to dry as the investigation came to nothing … again.

Bob's attention level visibly changed, and he asked me a few pointed questions. Then he said, "Just tell me what you do know."

"What I know or what I believe I know?"

"Everything."

I told him I believed that Robert had, in fact, been involved in placing the bomb that exploded that Sunday morning and that there had been four men, possibly five, in a two-toned Chevrolet belonging to the younger Blanton. I had been told about the car and shown a picture of it by FBI agents during the 1960s investigation. I told him that most of what I knew or believed I knew was from knowing Robert, his history of violence, and statements he had made to me.

"Do you know who the other men in the car were?" he asked.

"I'm not positive."

"Who do you think they were?"

"I believe that Tommy Blanton was driving the car and that Troy Ingram may have been one of the other men, and probably Jack Cash." I told him that I didn't know about the other man, perhaps Charles Cagle or Hall or someone else.

"Why couldn't Bobby Cherry be the other man?"

"Why not?" I returned.

A short time later, he ended the interview, and I agreed to meet again in a few days. "Does this negate the subpoena to appear before the grand jury?" I asked him as I started to leave.

"Don't worry about that. I'll take care of them. You don't need to talk to anyone except me or to someone I introduce you to—with me present. OK?"

"All right," I agreed. "But what about the city police?"

"Don't talk to the city. Don't talk to the county. If they try to talk to you, make them call me."

I assured him that I would. It occurred to me that this could be a reenactment of the isolation of informants that had been such a hallmark of Klan-related investigations in the past. There was something about this big yet gentle man, though, that made me feel he at least cared whether I were safe. I made a conscious decision that night to trust Bob Eddy to a degree I had not trusted anyone before or since. I also made a decision that I really could not totally trust anyone except him and myself. When we returned home, I sat my husband and Robin down and told them that the next weeks or months would be out of my control. Remembering the years dealing with FBI agents, I told them that there might be times I could not and would not tell them where I was going or when I would return.

I explained that this was not to worry them and I would not involve them where it was not necessary, nor would I tolerate any interference; there would be things I could not tell them, so they were not to ask.

I did not know then that Bob Eddy had been working out of an office in the FBI headquarters and that he had been given (bit by bit) information that agency had deemed "all right" for him to have.

I did not know how much time and money the state had expended in interviewing Gary Thomas Rowe. I did not know that when the investigation got close to him, Robert's buddy Troy Ingram had been found dead in his vehicle.

I did not know that Klansman and former FBI informant John Wesley Hall had agreed to talk to Bob Eddy when he came back from a few days in Florida, but that he did not return—he was found dead in his bed in Florida.

Nor did I know that Klansman and former police informant Ross Keith had also died shortly after being located for Bob Eddy by Birmingham police.

There was a great deal that I did not know because I had not been watching these people. My current life was in a world removed from Robert Chambliss and his cronies, and that had been the way I wanted it.

16
OPENING FILES

When I first met him, I did not know how much Bob Eddy did not know. He did not seem to know who I was other than a niece of Mrs. Chambliss. He was apparently wondering why I had refused to appear before the grand jury and seemingly expected, from the information he had, that this might be just another "I don't know anything, I didn't see anything" interview—the sort of thing he had gotten from other family members, friends, neighbors, Klansmen, and politicians who had been interviewed.

Attorney General Bill Baxley, I learned later, had (during much of his time as attorney general) attempted to obtain FBI files on the case. The FBI in Washington had refused to turn over files, evidence, and information for years. When finally some of those files had been made available, Bob Eddy had been given office space, and the FBI had doled out information to him as it saw fit.

The information Bob had available on me was a rather slim file with nothing of substance in it other than a summary report written by special agent Robert Womack on October 12, 1963, after they had interviewed me a couple of times. It contained the Saturday morning conversation between Robert Chambliss and me and my own impressions of Robert as a violent man capable of almost anything. There was, however, another file. A file that had been code-named and that had had most of its telling details (which might have revealed the person's identity) expunged.

Bob Eddy and his fellow investigators and prosecutors had spent hours upon hours going over files, and as I spoke to him, bits and pieces of information had jumped into his mind. I saw it in his face when he realized that I was one of the missing links.

Frankly, I left the hotel room that first night feeling that I might be stepping into a hopeless situation, again. It might be just another political show to appear to be doing something for votes, I thought. I feared that Bob might be just another street agent with no authority and no initiative. He, too, might be subject to the boss pulling the plug, as the FBI agents had been a decade earlier. Yet how could I not stick with it at least long enough to see?

My next meetings with Bob Eddy were much more intense. He was armed with more detailed questions and asked about events and conversations that were more pertinent. Soon he introduced me to assistant attorneys general Jon Yung and George Beck.

Jon Yung was a small man, dapper and tough. Yet he, too, was gentle and respectful during our meetings. He was present at many of the ensuing meetings I had with Bob, and on a couple of occasions, I met with him alone. Jon was to conduct the questioning in court, and I started to realize that he was building a rapport toward that end: helping me to trust him and feel at ease with his questions.

During those many interviews, I repeatedly told both of them that I would not testify unless the case (with my testimony) had an absolute certainty of conviction; nor would I testify if there were a possibility of convicting without my doing so. I wanted to help, I wanted the horror put to rest, I wanted Robert, whom I knew to be a human monster, to face a penalty for his crimes. Here was a man who had talked about, even bragged about, a long career of assaults, batteries, maimings, and murders and yet had never been convicted of a crime more serious than "flogging while masked."

No, I did not want to testify in open court. I did not want to subject my family or my church congregation to that. I did not want to risk acquittal, which would have meant a very sure death sentence for me and perhaps for others I could not protect. I did not want to, but I knew—and they knew—I would.

I was assured that the other men in the car with Robert Chambliss that night would also be charged. I was assured that J. B. Stoner, Robert Shelton, and others who were believed to have furnished support, financing, and approval (if not orders) would also be prosecuted. I was assured that the relationships of police officers to the crimes would probably result in charges of conspiracy.

Yet there was no pretense about the risk involved. It was obvious from the beginning that no one could be allowed to know that I was continuing to meet with investigators, telling them everything I could think of that might lead to other testimony or tie together facts they already knew. Nor could anyone be told if the decision were to be made for me to testify—not even family members could know in advance of the actual court appearance.

All of this evolved over a period of weeks, and although I was trying to be cooperative and they were being polite and kind, there were some cat-and-mouse tactics going on.

One factor, which should be obvious, is that I had had many years to shove all of this far back into the recesses of memory so that it would not haunt me to such an extent that I could not live and function. During that process of purposeful forgetting, some details had blurred. I could not always be sure that I actually remembered certain things of my own knowledge or whether I was recalling information given to me by the FBI.

On the other hand, when my current offerings were not as complete as these investigators expected, there seemed to be doubt about my willingness to cooperate.

Only weeks away from a trial date that had been awaited for more than fourteen years, they were still putting pieces of the puzzle together! During September and October 1977, several rather drastic or unorthodox steps were taken to establish the truth and usability of any testimony I might give. One problem was that Bob was aware of but had not been given the code-named files on me; the FBI was still holding files coded for witness protection. So it was still problematic to tie together details, and they had still not talked to the "other" witness who had been with me during so much of the FBI's investigation. Bob asked me if I would go over the FBI file on me with him. It seems that the local office still would not release some information without my expressed permission and that perhaps there was confusion. I agreed.

Bob picked me up, and we went to the Federal Building, usually known as the "2121 Building," on Eighth Avenue North in downtown Birmingham. This structure housed the FBI offices as well as local offices of other federal agencies. He parked the car in the underground parking garage accessed from the alley behind the building.

We were joined by Jon Yung and another man who seemed to be escorting us. We rode the elevator to the fourteenth floor and exited into a hallway.

We then entered a large meeting room with a huge rectangular table ringed by upholstered chairs, like one would expect to find in the boardroom of a successful corporation. This was not, however, our destination; we went through this room to a doorway in the far corner of the left-hand wall. This opened onto a stairway leading down one flight to the "nonexistent" thirteenth floor. Leaving the stairwell through a door with a coded lock, we went into another room and then another hallway. There we waited at a locked door until we were identified and a code was keyed into the lock.

Aside from the intimidation factor of this routine, it seemed unnecessarily obtuse. It also struck me that a person could disappear into this labyrinth and never be heard from again. Paranoia? Perhaps.

Once admitted into the inner sanctum of the FBI's offices, we went through windowless halls and finally into a very small windowless room that held a desk with a chair behind it and a chair in front of it. Half a dozen or so men ranged tightly packed around the walls. A large man sat facing me across the desk, upon which he placed a ledger-bound volume of pages four or more inches thick. Obviously Bob and I were not to "go over" the file, as his request had suggested to me.

The man at the desk first carefully verified my identity and then opened the file before him and started to scan the entries, reading excerpts and asking, "Was that you?" or "Did you say that?" to each. For quite some time this continued, with me answering either in the affirmative, or not recalling specifically.

Then, almost lulled into the routine of the process, he read an excerpt that jolted me to attention as I denied the truthfulness of the entry. "Mel Alexander wrote this report on ..." he recited the date in December 1964 and read on from the report which had been sent to FBI headquarters in Washington, D.C. In the report Alexander said that he had uncovered, at last, the evidence that would ensure a conviction: Then he had recorded the "what if ..." scenario that Dale Tarrant had presented and that I had not denied. But it was different.

I had not denied it in 1964 because I didn't think it was presented as knowledge on my part. Whether it was presented to Mel Alexander as a fact that we had driven by the church, curious to find out what might be going on that night, or whether he had decided to use it to push his superior into action on an indictment, I do not know. Dale had said the scenario was not presented as fact but as a question: "What if ..." such witnesses would testify, would it be enough to prosecute?

Mel's report claimed that an account of the sighting was given to him as fact and that an offer to testify had been made. Weighing Mel Alexander's reputation against Dale's life, it's difficult for me to believe that she would falsify anything she gave him after so many years of trying to help gather information. Her efforts to gather evidence had predated Mel Alexander; her efforts to bring an end to the bombings and violence in Birmingham by passing information to deputy sheriff James Hancock predated the bombing of the Sixteenth Street Baptist Church and any involvement with the FBI. Hancock had betrayed her trust in him, and yet she had risked passing information to the FBI.

Were there actually two witnesses to the bomb being placed that early Sunday morning about 2 a.m.? Did we ride downtown and drive down Seventh Avenue North and see the two-toned Chevrolet that belonged to Tommy Blanton near the alley that ran behind the church? Did she see a man carrying something by a handle going toward the building? Then after going around several blocks, did we again see the car parked on Seventh Avenue apparently waiting for the man on foot to return to it? Were Chambliss and at least two other men recognizable? Were there four or five persons in the car? Mel Alexander's report allegedly answered these questions, and even in the face of such compelling "evidence," J. Edgar Hoover had refused—twice—to turn the information over to the Justice Department to seek an indictment.

What did I know or not know about the Klan and its terrorist activities? During 1963, all of 1964, and partway through 1965, I was not certain that Tommy Rowe was a paid FBI informant, though Robert often said that he was.

I was never specifically told that the FBI had put John Wesley "Nigger" Hall on its payroll as an informant. I was not told that Henry Alexander, one of the night-riding Klansmen from Montgomery and one of the traveling men between Birmingham, Montgomery, Tuscaloosa, and Anniston, had also been put on the FBI payroll.

I did know, in general, that hundreds of Klansmen were recruited onto the informants' dole by FBI agents in the South. These men routinely engaged in violent behavior, committing crimes against black citizens and destroying property, and were rewarded for calling in occasionally—or for following (as it was later revealed in Senate investigations of FBI agents) "suggestions" for Klan activity. Testimony before the Senate task force indicated that Klansmen on the take were routinely encouraged to sleep with other Klansmen's wives and were given instructions to instigate violence on occasion.

In answer to questions about the night of the bombing, however ... I've wrestled with the events that took place so many times, I've visualized the streets and the faces, had my dreams invaded with nightmares. Was I there that night?

I think I was in the car with Dale, but I was not aware of where we were. My own attention was not drawn to the specific events, and that night blended in with many others when she and I were together going bowling, eating out, or just riding around talking.

Do I think she saw what she reported in the "what if ... " scenario? No. Was the "what if ... " a description to cover up the presence of yet another person who was witness to the events of the evening of September 14-15, 1963, whose safety could not ever be guaranteed? Yes, I believe that it was.

I believe that Robert's wife, my Aunt Tee, had either firsthand knowledge of exactly what happened or knew who was in the car and had details of the plan to place the homemade bomb under the side steps of the building. I believe that Dale tried to let Mel Alexander know this for Tee, and he misinterpreted the scenario.

I was not satisfied, however, to settle with this speculation. By this time, I had spoken with Dale Tarrant and convinced her to meet with Bob Eddy. She had done so, but she adamantly refused to testify and denied having been personally near the church that night.

So much was at stake, and underlying everything was my personal ethic that demanded my memory be completely accurate. I had to verify my recall and sort all of this out for my own peace of mind.

During this period of time, I was blessed in having a varied circle of supportive friends of unique talents whom I could trust implicitly. I called upon two of them: Dr. Barbara Lester, sociology professor at Birmingham-Southern College, in whom I had confided during the earlier weeks of the renewed investigation, and a woman I knew less well, who was a clinical psychologist and also an acquaintance of Barbara's. I knew this woman was trained in hypnotherapy, so I asked Barbara to approach her about exploring the accuracy of my memory through hypnosis. I also asked Barbara to act as monitor to any sessions should her friend agree.

A few days later, the three of us gathered in a Highland Avenue apartment. I lay on the living room floor, my head on a pillow, relaxing as the psychologist led me into trance, with Barbara and a tape recorder witnessing the session.

It says a great deal about trust to recall that, although I was nervous about being hypnotized and what I might recall, I went into an altered state of awareness quite easily; while I had not been able to trust local, state, or federal law enforcement officers and had found it necessary to make a conscious decision to trust Bob Eddy. And I was only beginning to trust Jon Yung.

When I was guided back to full and current awareness of my surroundings by the psychologist, I did not instantly remember the content of the session. I was a little puzzled and embarrassed that both the psychologist and Barbara were rather wide-eyed and excited. Barbara played the tape back, and I, too, became wide-eyed. My statements under hypnosis established—to my satisfaction—that I did not have a memory of witnessing any events at or near the church during the evening of September 14 or the early morning of September 15, and I had not personally seen the car on that particular night. The images in my mind were due to information I had received—they were not visual memories.

I had also, in response to questions about the morning of September 14, repeated Robert's remarks—in a tone and modulation of voice that could almost have been him on the tape rather than a mimicry. I wept from the emotional impact.

I never told Bob Eddy nor any others connected with the investigation that I had done this; nor did it change even one detail of what I had told him already. I had recited earlier my account of Saturday morning, September 14, to Bob and Jon during one of the first of our evening meetings. Jon had taken notes. Several days later, when I met with Jon alone, he handed me a tear sheet of the front page of the September 14, 1963, Birmingham newspaper. He had circled, in red near the bottom of the page, the article about the girl being stabbed. I had told them that it had been on the front page below the fold.

I remembered Robert laying the newspaper on the table still folded with the headlines on bottom and the fold toward me as I sat across the table. He had pointed and gestured that morning, and at one point he had put his open hand palm down on the page in emphasis. This was when he was telling me to "Just wait until after Sunday morning ... ."

When he had first said that to me, and the first several times that I repeated it, I had thought that it sounded rather clumsy. The construction of the sentence sounded strange—contrived. Why had he, on Saturday, said "Just wait until after Sunday morning ... ."

Why not "Tomorrow morning" or something like "After tonight ... ." There seems only one reason why Robert would phrase it the way he did; that morning was not the first time he had made the statement. He had used the same words before, probably several times ... to several people. And he had been saying it for less than a week, for he simply said "Sunday morning"—meaning the next one. It was not a threat in his mind—it was a promise, it was a plan.

17
SAVANNAH

Even though, as a result of the hypnosis session, I had satisfied my own mind and assured myself I'd given accurate information to Bob Eddy and Jon Yung, the questions raised by the FBI files and Mel Alexander's reports were of some trouble to the investigative team. It had not been established that I would, in fact, be called upon to testify; or rather, I had not been told as a certainty. And if I were to take the stand against Robert, would the testimony include only the information Robert himself had given me or was there an "eyewitness" account to be had? More to the point—was I being totally honest?

Bob Eddy asked if I would take a polygraph test. My first thought was that any polygrapher accepted as an expert in Birmingham would also be a part of the local law enforcement establishment or would be an FBI employee. This apparently was on Bob's mind, also. I don't recall who brought it up, but I do recall that we discussed it. He said that he would do some checking and find someone who could be trusted and would ensure that the tests would be confidential. With this assurance, I agreed. He also told me that he was going to ask Dale Tarrant to submit to a test.

Now life goes on and circumstances change for people—and circumstances change people. There had been 14 long years for things to get in the way. People who might have been willing to cooperate in 1963 or 1964 were less than enthusiastic in 1977. There were children who were grown and had lives and families of their own that would be disrupted. There was also the embarrassment of being put on exhibition and the shame of association for so many years with the defendant.

Aside from these issues, there were others even more disturbing. There were personal safety and the safety of loved ones. There was also Tee: how would all of this affect her after so many years? She was 65 years old in 1977, had never been alone, and was in poor health. Yet she would at least be free of the tyranny of Robert, wouldn't she? I reasoned. It was important, however, to protect her from any indication that she may have provided information that passed through informants to the FBI or the state investigative team.

All of these reasons for not testifying were multiplied during the investigative phase because it makes a lot more sense to silence a potential witness than it does to punish one who has already spoken. Besides, I was not convinced, nor was Dale Tarrant, that the matter would, in fact, ever come to trial. It had not come to trial during the sixties; why was 1977 any different?

When Dale and I spoke on the telephone, I could not let even her know that I had agreed to testify, if needed, though she undoubtedly guessed that I would. She may not have understood at the time, but this was also a way of protecting her and her family.

If I were able to speak effectively, it might not be necessary for her to take the risk, especially since she had been one of the informants who had been isolated by a sheriff's deputy into ineffectiveness and had been in danger all of those years. If she had come forward publicly, she would have been disgraced by lies about her reasons for the many meetings with the deputy—had she been allowed to live. Paranoia? No. Several years later when both her name and that of the deputy became public, he did, in fact, discount the value of her efforts because he did nothing with the information she gave him. He led her on. He made her believe he was building a case while he compromised her credibility.

After a couple of days, Bob Eddy called me to say that the polygraph examination would be conducted in Savannah, Georgia. At first I protested. That arrangement would take so much time and effort, it seemed impossible. I was pastor of a church participating in a four-church parish program of community service. I was running a household with a spouse and my son, and I was a full-time student in my senior year at Birmingham-Southern College. I was busy, too busy to take a trip to Georgia.

There were also moments when I questioned my decision to trust Bob Eddy. Since he had learned of the Mel Alexander report, he had seemed a bit tense and guarded with me. I had never taken a polygraph examination before, and I had no reason to believe the tests were particularly credible.

"One day," he promised me. "We'll fly over, take the test, and fly back in the same day."

"I want Robin to go with me."

"You can take him if you'll be more comfortable," he agreed. He then set the date and time.

It turned out that Robin couldn't take the day off from his job, so he just took me to the airport with plans to drop me off. When we arrived in the hangar area where the state-owned airplane was housed, we went into the small waiting area. Bob Eddy, Jon Yung, and a pilot were there.

Someone asked who Robin was and seemed upset by his presence. Bob explained that he was my son and was to go with us. We told them that he would not, after all, be able to go—and were informed that since he was there and knew about the trip, he had to go. One of the men, I think that it was Jon, escorted Robin to a pay telephone to call his employer and claim to be sick. The man Robin worked for was demanding and unreasonable and tried to insist that Robin come to work, "sick" or no. Finally Robin told him that he simply wasn't coming and hung up.

Dale Tarrant joined us at the airport, and we gathered on the tarmac near the hangar where the small six-passenger plane sat waiting. As we smoked cigarettes and made small talk while the pilot did some last-minute things, the subject of security came up. Dale questioned our safety. Bob assured her that every detail was attended to and there were no weapons or bombs on board.

We were at the doorway to the small plane by this time, and she turned to me and joked, "I guess I'd better take this one out of my purse then." I was horrified that she would so innocently say exactly the wrong thing. Bob stopped her with a hand on her arm. He took her purse and had the pilot stand by while he went through the purse's contents on the wing of the plane. She repeatedly told him that she was joking and was both angry and embarrassed that he reacted so strongly. He did not know her, and I can understand that he could not behave otherwise under the circumstances.

The flight was long and boring, but napping was impossible due to tension and crowded conditions. After a while conversation lulled except for quiet exchanges between Bob and the pilot. Bob sat beside the pilot, Dale and I occupied the center seats, while Robin and Jon sat in the rear. I felt vulnerable and isolated, but I did not feel alone. There was also a sense of trepidation in facing a polygraph, yet this had to be faced with resolve the same way every other step had had to be.

I learned that the polygrapher was a man past middle age whose services were often used by the FBI; he was the same one who would later be seen on television when he administered a test to Gary Thomas Rowe. His offices were in an upscale building fronting one of the many downtown parks or squares in Savannah; we could hear the river sounds, but there was no opportunity for sightseeing.

He wired me up to his machine in a small inner office and explained the procedure to me. His voice was kindly but efficient; nothing wasted. He asked a few questions to set criteria for the test, including, "Are you nervous, now?" Then without preamble he began the actual examination.

There were ten or so target questions, but only two or three upon which a great deal hinged. Had I been at or near the Sixteenth Street Baptist Church the evening of Saturday, September 14, 1963, or the morning of Sunday, September 15, 1963; and had I told the FBI that I had been? These questions were asked in several different ways, but the effect was the same. Who was correct; was Mel Alexander or was I? After the test was complete, the polygrapher unhooked all the wires and buckles, handed me a tissue and walked me to the door of the room. Bob was standing there waiting just outside, a look of question on his face.

"You are either the most honest person I have ever tested or the calmest," the examiner said to me as the three of us stood in the doorway.

"I'm certainly not calm," I replied.

It was Dale's turn then, and it seemed to take forever. At some point we had lunch and later coffee. I don't recall eating much or even what I ate.

Robin and Jon had walked around out in the parks while the tests were being done. During this time, Robin started to feel more at ease with the slight, boyish-looking attorney, and some of the tension of the day lifted for him. Having planned on going to work that morning, Robin was too warmly dressed for the muggy Savannah afternoon, so at some point during their walking, Jon bought Robin a shirt; my own distraction during that day was such that I lost sight of this for some years.

After Dale's test was finished, Bob and Jon took me aside. They told me that she had not done very well on the test, and that they had to decide what to do. The two men suggested that it might be necessary to take her in custody; the attorney general might want to lodge charges against her as an accessory.

Every red light and panic button in me went on alert. "No!" I told them bluntly. If they did either, I would not testify and would have nothing further to say. I told them that if, and I emphasized "if," she had not "done well" on the test, it was due to being highly excitable and intimidated. Her performance had nothing whatsoever to do with any "guilt" on her part. They looked at each other and led me back to where she and Robin were waiting. Nothing more was said about the results of her test to me.

When we were all together, they said only that the tests would be evaluated after we got back. Bob Eddy told me later that Dale would not be asked to testify, though he accepted the truthfulness of her statements.

So far as I know, when Dale reads this, it will be her first knowledge of the exchange between Bob, Jon, and me. As I reflect on that conversation and later conversations, I think I did exactly what they wanted me to do. I believe they were baiting me into a commitment. At that particular point in time, I don't think Bob Eddy or Jon Yung realized that my only hesitation was that I didn't want to become a target. I did not want to be publicized and then left hanging. Nor did I want to testify in open court in a weak case so that Robert and his cronies would come after me, after they had been acquitted. I knew what they could (and would) do to someone they felt had betrayed them. I knew that violence was not only a practice for them, but a form of recreation. These men did their night riding the same way other men played sandlot baseball.

I had also been made aware through the years that there were more subtle methods for eliminating enemies. Had no one noticed that "weak links" kept turning up dead just ahead of Bob's investigation? Had he missed the implications that at least two Klansmen had died once he had made it known that he wanted to talk to them? Two men who had been FBI or police informants: John Wesley Hall and Ross Keith. And earlier, Troy Ingram had suddenly died, once the reactivated investigation had started to look serious.

We were in Savannah in order to be safe taking a polygraph, for heaven's sake!

18
NO TURNING BACK

Bill Baxley called the grand jury back into session in September 1977, and on September 24 indictments were returned against Robert Chambliss for four counts of murder resulting from the dynamite explosion at the Sixteenth Street Baptist Church on September 15, 1963. He was arrested at his home that same afternoon by a deputy sheriff. Bob Eddy went with the deputy and waited while Chambliss changed his clothes and sat for Tee to comb his hair. Subsequently bond was set at $200,000.

I had hoped that Robert would remain in jail until the trial, but friends and family members managed to raise the money to post bond after about ten days. Once the wheels were in motion and Robert knew that he would be tried, the danger was great.

I do not know how Robert learned that I might speak against him. That question has never been answered. The only possibility I have been able to discover is that either Ernie Cantrell or Jack LeGrand let it be known that I had spoken to Bob Eddy rather than the grand jury. Perhaps Robert's attorneys noted my name on the grand jury witness list. However he found out, I learned that he threatened to make a phone call and have me killed and my church bombed.

I took his threats seriously—against me and my church. Yet I continued to conceal my cooperation and my intention to testify, if needed.

Late in October, I was told that a trial date had been set—November 14. From that point on, there was a sense of urgency about every meeting with the men who worked for the attorney general of the State of Alabama. Each meeting was gravely serious, and I would be asked the same questions a dozen different ways, as well as new ones. I was also given occasional tidbits of information about the other evidence to be presented and other witnesses. There was also mention of other investigations that were expected to become of primary focus when the trial of Robert Chambliss was over.

It had become pretty well established that my personal knowledge and observations—to which I could give direct testimony—would be useful in this case but probably not in the other cases. Yet it was crucial that those others be pursued because those were the men who would feel threatened and vengeful enough to cause me and other innocent people harm after the Chambliss trial was completed and the information was public.

I started to feel like a fish on a hook. They wanted to hang on and play me until all was safely in the boat, but then what? Would I be thrown out wounded to fend for myself? Would I wind up fried and served up on a platter?

I had one last meeting with Jon Yung just days before the trial was scheduled to begin; all contact after that would be by telephone. I went to the motel near the civic center where we had met several times before; he was in a first-floor room visible from the parking lot. I parked some fifty feet or so from the door and walked to the room—I had learned not to park by the room I was going to. That way, if someone recognized my car, they might not figure out which room I was in; and then I had to be careful and not be noticed going in or out.

Jon was in his shirt sleeves, but he did have on his tie; his suit jacket was on a chair near the dresser. The rooms were always neat where we met. Except for papers and files, tape recorders occasionally, cameras, and other equipment, there was little sign that the men occupied the space. There was usually a coffeepot or some sort of soda available.

I knew that Bob Eddy had been away from home for months, except for an occasional day or two. I assumed the same was true for Jon Yung. Both of them were looking tired and often seemed harassed and worried.

I sat in a chair near the door facing into the room with my back toward the window. The drapes were closed. Jon sat down occasionally on the corner of the bed or on the dresser, but mostly he paced about.

I recall that I was chilled. I recall my muscles being very tight and painful trying to avoid trembling. I do not remember that it was particularly cold, though, just the usual early November nip in the air.

It was definite now; the only things that would make it unnecessary for me to testify would be either a confession—which was not likely—or the death of one of us: Robert or me. As the trial date approached, it became more and more real. For all those years it had been a hope, a dread, a fear. Now it was a scheduled event. It felt somewhat like preparing for surgery. You have to be there, but you have absolutely no control over the outcome.

Of course I was nervous. Of course I was afraid. It seemed that we had covered everything there was to cover and the afternoon meeting had turned into early evening. As I started to get up, preparing to leave, Jon stepped in front of me. He had a large envelope in his hand. "Are you ready for these?" he asked as he handed me the contents of the envelope.

I took the eight-by-ten sheets of heavy paper, and although I do not know what I did expect, I looked at something that was totally unexpected. At first it was hard to focus and become aware of what was in the black-and-white overexposed glossy photograph at the top of the stack. As my eyes adjusted, the details started to emerge; walls, cabinets, instruments, a gurney with a wadded sheet and ... these were the morgue shots of the victims of the bombing. Perhaps there were a dozen prints. Different angles. A few of them included more than one of the victims.

I forced myself to look at the photos, one by one. Each one became more blurred by my tears. These horridly cold, brutally clinical photos of once beautiful, once alive and whole children, were burning into me trying to erase the picture of the four children I had carried in my mind for 14 years.

I had been able to close my eyes and see the smiling faces from photographs that became so well-known after their deaths. The photos used in a plaque mounted in the sanctuary on a wall near the church altar. Those smiling faces had protected me from the other picture I had in my mind all those years of the scenes we had watched on television of the shrouded bodies being brought—one by one—from the rubble that had been their church.

I had wept the morning they had died. I had wanted Robert to bear the public shame of his acts all those years and had tried in every way I had known to help bring that about, but this ... this was ... oh, God, the facts. I looked at the pictures, tears welling into my eyes and running down my cheeks. I handed them back to Jon. He didn't speak, but he watched me and waited.

"I'm ready," I told him, and I left the room. I managed to get into my car and start the engine before my control broke. I could no longer contain the flood of emotion. This was not simple grief, this was not just shock, this was not limited to anger—this was years of pent-up rage and pain.

I can remember to this day, as I write 17 years later, how the streets looked as I drove home in the darkness. Lights blindingly bright as they were refracted through my tears. I can hear in my ears that voice that was my own ... screaming, keening, and crying out to God in sorrow, in rage; railing at the injustice, the cruelty, and at the guilt of impotence: to have not known what to do when it might have made a difference.

Memory can be a blessed tool or it can be a crippling burden. In work and in school my ability to recall detail and even verbatim conversations had been valuable to me. And though I had spent several years pushing the memories of the sixties into a contained place so that I could live and be productive, they flooded back. Vivid, detailed, and absolute.

When I arrived home, I was drained. Perhaps I felt purged. I think that I thought the release of those emotions would strengthen me and that the coming days would provide healing of the wounds, for myself and for others.

I still could not discuss the case with other people, and all I wanted to do was to shout in accusation at a city, a system, a people who could allow ... not just allow ... but also accept, such atrocities.

I wanted to tear it up and put it back together right. I used the weekend to pull myself together. I conducted the regular worship service in my church on Sunday, quietly prepared my son for the inevitable, and slept little.

The trial began on Monday morning; Robert Chambliss would stand trial for one count of murder. They would try him on only one count, explaining that, "If something goes wrong on this, we'll immediately arrest him on another count." The victim named in the charge was 11-year-old Denise McNair.

19
DAY IN COURT

All that was left was to determine when—the day and hour—I was to appear in court to testify. It was not a matter of going to the courthouse to sit around waiting to be called forth from the spectators or a witness room as it's done on television. Nothing that simple.

I waited and tried to behave normally on Monday. I knew that a string of technical witnesses would be called first. This was the nuts-and-bolts of establishing that a crime had, in fact, been committed. The cause of the death of Denise McNair would be established by coroner's reports, by those who had investigated the scene, and by people who were there when the blast occurred. Police and fire department witnesses would establish that an explosion had taken place and that it had been caused by dynamite. Attorney Art Hanes had won the point on barring the use of the word "bomb" in describing the explosion.

No one could say how long all of this would take, so I was simply on standby until I was needed. Yet I couldn't be there in the courthouse. There could be no questions or speculation; better that no attention was drawn to me. And I think my showing up at the last minute ensured that my story would already have been told before I could be intimidated by the cross-examination skills of defense attorney Art Hanes, Jr., or the process of the trial itself.

Monday evening I read the evening newspaper and watched stories about the first day of trial on the television news. During the early evening, I received a telephone call telling me that they should be getting to me on Tuesday, so I should stay home and be prepared to come downtown when I was notified.

Tuesday morning, November 15, 1977, I read the morning newspaper, the *Birmingham Post-Herald*, which carried several stories about the trial. The first witness called had been the Reverend John H. Cross who had been pastor of Sixteenth Street Baptist Church in September 1963. He told about that morning. The Sunday School lesson was on "the love that forgives," he said. He had been teaching the women's Bible class in the sanctuary of the church when "all of a sudden an explosion went off. It sounded like the whole world was shaking, and the building, I thought, was going to collapse."

Then Sarah Collins Riley, the younger sister of Addie Mae Collins, testified. Sarah had been the fifth child in the ladies' lounge that morning, and she described the scene and told the court that she lost an eye in the explosion.

Captain William Berry, Assistant Fire Marshal, testified about the explosion itself from the evidence on the scene. After Captain Berry, came Dr. Joe Donald, who was the chief resident in surgery at the University Hospital, which in 1963 was the old Hillman Clinic.

Early Tuesday morning, November 15, Bob Eddy called making sure I was available.

"Should I come down there? Will you pick me up, or what?" I asked.

"Stay there. Don't go anywhere. I'll call you back and allow time to get you here. Just sit tight."

"OK."

"Are you all right?"

"I don't know."

"You'll be fine. I know you will. It'll all be over soon. Just hang on."

We hung up. I remember puttering about the house putting things in order.

I remember sitting and just looking at the telephone. I remember that it rang a couple of times with other calls. I would hurry each time to get off the line as quickly as possible. When Jon Yung and George Beck had passed the word to me that it was definite I would be called to testify, I told them that I would on one condition.

There was visible tensing against what I might demand. This was one of the few times I saw George Beck prior to the trial. He was in town, and he, Jon Yung, and Bob Eddy met with me that day.

"The only way I can walk in there is if Bob is with me every step of the way," I told them.

"I'll be there," Bob Eddy had responded quietly.

"I mean actually with me. And stay with me, in and out," I was emphatic.

"You got it! I won't let go," Bob grinned as he made that promise. He knew that I meant for him to act as bodyguard. He knew I meant for him to physically take the risk with me. And he agreed. I almost felt vindicated in my initial decision to trust him—had it truly been only three months?

The call to come to the courthouse that Tuesday morning came much earlier than I had expected, although I had been dressed and waiting for several hours. I left the parsonage immediately and drove east into downtown. I passed the courthouse on Twenty-first Street and proceeded another block on Eighth Avenue to Twenty-second Street, turned right onto one-way Twenty-second beside the 2121 Building, as I had been instructed to do. As I eased the car slowly along the line of cars parked at meters, I saw Bob. He was waiting on the sidewalk by an empty parking space. I parked my car at the curb, and Bob put coins in the meter. He then led me to another car, and I got into the back seat.

The drive to the courthouse was short, but it seemed to take forever. The driver went around an extra block or two and Bob sat sideways in the front passenger seat scanning behind the car and to the sides. The precautions seemed elaborate, yet there was a long list of murders and unexplained deaths leading up to this day. As we rode, it seemed to sink in to me for the first time that these men were doing a job. A duty. Whatever deeper motivations there might have been, no matter how honorable, they were there because it was how they earned their paycheck—that was not a comforting thought. I forced those thoughts down and consciously reinforced my decision to trust and my resolve to do this thing. It had been so long, and now the hour had come.

Soon the driver swung the car onto Twenty-first Street heading toward the Jefferson County Courthouse. He turned left off the one-way street into a driveway that led us under the tall old impressive front steps of the courthouse to a basement entrance near the loading docks. Bob and I got out and entered the building, taking an elevator upstairs. Getting off the elevator into a deserted hallway, he led me to an empty room and showed me where I might sit to wait. Then he left me alone, with instructions to stay there until he came for me. I waited for more than a half hour, sitting, standing, pacing, and wanting a cigarette. I wandered around in an empty courtroom alone. At one point someone opened the door and then went away when I said I was waiting for someone.

At last Bob came back. "They are waiting for you," he said as he took my hand and led me back into the corridor and then onto the elevator again.

When the elevator doors opened, the quiet of the building gave way to a din coming from the hallway. The elevator lobby of each floor in the building forms a T with a long hallway that runs the length of the building north and south, so I could not see the source of the noise until we rounded the corner.

The trial was taking place in Courtroom 306, at the end of the hallway. There were a crowd of reporters, camera personnel, lights and wires and microphones. There was a cordon of uniformed officers down each side of the hallway leading to a standing metal detector at the doorway into the courtroom itself.

Bob led me down this guarded path wordlessly until we reached the officer manning the metal detector.

"You can't go in. The court has been sealed," the officer ordered.

"They are waiting for us," Bob told him.

"The courtroom has been sealed. I can't let anybody in. It's for security."

"This is the witness it was sealed for, you idiot! Now let us pass through," Bob growled inches from the man's face so he would not be overheard by the crowd behind us. He still had hold of my hand, and I think I was trying to hide behind him.

The deputy flushed and stepped inside, to reappear in seconds. He verified my name and muttered an apology. Meanwhile, the news reporters who were being held back several feet behind us were demanding to know, "Who is that? What's happening?"

As the door opened, every eye in the room seemed to be glued to it—apparently it had not been announced who was being called as the next witness. I was told that the media and the spectators as well as the defense team expected Tommy Rowe, and defense attorney Art Hanes, Jr., was prepared for him.

There was an almost absolute quiet that was unnerving after the din in the hallway. The quiet gave way to a murmur and then a buzz of whispers. I focused on Bob's back and the witness chair ahead as he led me toward it.

As we approached the table where the prosecution attorneys were seated, Attorney General Bill Baxley stood up and formally called me to the stand. I saw Art Hanes, Jr., and his father, the city's former mayor, lean in toward Robert. And I saw Robert's face set in anger as he shook his head from side to side.

When I had been sworn in and seated, I looked out over the crowd assembled in the room and instantly recognized several faces. Courtroom 306 is a very large room with a main floor and a balcony, and it was packed. The jury was to my right; the judge, the Honorable Wallace C. Gibson, to my left. The prosecution attorneys were directly in front of me, and the defense was in front of the judge's bench.

Each time I would glance toward my left, I saw Robert staring at me as though his stern anger would enable him to intimidate me into silence as it had so many times for so many years. I found that if I leaned just a little to the left and did not sit up perfectly straight, the corner of the judge's bench blocked my view of his face. I believe that was what enabled me to maintain control enough to accomplish what I had come to do.

Jon Yung conducted the questioning, and it went smoothly enough. Even with an occasional objection from Art Hanes, Jr., I was able to remain composed and deliberate.

I responded to Jon Yung's questions as to my name, residence, occupation, and whether I was related to the defendant. He then moved on to ask whether I remembered the September 15, 1963, bombing of the Sixteenth Street Baptist Church. Art Hanes, Jr., objected to Yung's using the word "bombing." The wording of the question was changed to "explosion," and the questions continued.

When asked about my visit to the Chambliss house on Saturday morning before the Sunday bombing, I told the court that there had been an incident the evening before that I brought to Robert's attention. The newspaper article concerning a white girl being stabbed through a bus window and the hundred dollar reward that Bob Gafford had offered. Art Hanes, Jr., again objected. The judge and the attorneys talked back and forth, and finally the judge sent the jury out of the courtroom. For the next 15 or 20 minutes, I testified about the angry and harsh statements Robert had made. This is called "voir dire evidence," when the judge determines whether the jury should hear the testimony.

Judge Gibson interrupted to tell me that I should repeat the language Robert had used. He said, "I am not trying to embarrass the witness, but I think the language—I mean, sometimes we can't deal in niceties, and I think this is one of those times."

I told the court that he had said that if his "buddies" had backed him up, he would have "had the 'niggers' in their place by now" and that he had been "fighting a one-man war since 1942." When I was answering questions about Robert's demeanor, Hanes objected again and the judge instructed me that I could say he "appeared to be angry" but I couldn't say that he "was angry." Then Hanes argued that none of this should be heard by the jury—and Yung argued that it should. They cited cases and precedents until at last the jury was brought back in, and I had to repeat that portion of that testimony for them.

Also I told the court that Robert had told me he had "enough 'stuff' put away to flatten half of Birmingham" and that "the FBI or police could pick him up and search all they wanted to but they wouldn't find it unless he pointed it out to them."

I told the court that he had warned, "Just wait until after Sunday morning, and they'll beg us to let them segregate!"

I told the court that the Saturday evening after the explosion at the church, I had sat in the room while Robert watched a news broadcast during which Robert had said, "It wasn't meant to hurt anybody; it didn't go off when it was supposed to" when the announcer said that murder charges might be lodged against the bombers.

At length Jon Yung finished direct questioning and handed me off to the defense for cross-examination. Robert had written something on a legal pad while I testified, and Art Hanes, Jr., referred to it as he got to his feet. I noticed that Robert continued to write on that yellow pad.

After a few easy questions reminding everyone in the courtroom that George Wallace, too, had said he was fighting to save segregation, Hanes started with the hard questions. He picked at my testimony, trying to discredit and confuse me—which is, after all, what cross-examination is all about.

He questioned such things as the use of the word "stuff," asking had I seen any "stuff." He seemed to think something was refuted by my not defining what was meant when Chambliss had used the words "stuff" that would "flatten half of Birmingham." He argued that the words I had repeated from Chambliss were angry words used by many white men in the sixties. He referred to the use of "nigger" in Robert's remarks which I had testified to, saying that was common in those days.

Then he asked whether these things happened before or after I divorced my first husband. The way the question was worded was, however, as a slur on my character. It was the tone of voice and the grin on his face that indicated his meaning. I swallowed a little flare of anger as I answered; simultaneously Baxley objected to the question and his objection was sustained.

Then Hanes attacked my memory of those conversations. After 14 years, he ridiculed, the court was expected to believe that I remembered so perfectly what had been said. He pulled a couple of dates at random and asked me what I had been doing on those dates. Now this was where it almost got funny; nerves can easily spill over into hysteria, so I struggled a bit to maintain composure. It happened that he named dates that were on or near significant events or routines so that I actually did recall something of what I was doing and answered him accordingly.

After several of these, he named a date that meant nothing to me, and as I started to get angry at this treatment, the prosecution again objected. Again, the objection was sustained. Art Hanes, Jr., soon ended his cross-examination, reserving the right to recall me to the stand.

Before I was allowed to step down, I was questioned again about my memory of those statements of Robert's, and I said that it was "a weekend that I shall never forget."

"No further questions, your Honor," I finally heard them say after I'd been handed back and forth for questioning nine times … five by the prosecution and four by the defense.

"The witness may step down," Judge Gibson dismissed me, instructing the prosecution to keep me available. As I stood up, my legs were weak and my hands were cold, but Bob Eddy was right there. He had stayed nearby throughout the time I had been on the witness stand. It was nearing 2:30 p.m.

Bob took my arm and led me back along that aisle and out through that cordon of uniforms in the hallway. I kept my eyes down watching the floor until we were out and clear of the crowd. I think I was worried I might stumble and fall I was so shaky. I saw my Uncle Howard trying to get to me in the hallway, but we did not stop.

Bob took me toward the elevators and then changed his mind, and we went down the stairs. Not to the basement to be taken away by car, as I expected; instead we left the stairwell on the first floor and calmly walked out through the front doors of the courthouse. Breathing deeply the crisp November air, I walked with him across the wide plaza between the heavy sets of brass doors to the steps and down to the sidewalk.

We crossed Twenty-first Street just as though we had been in the building to buy an automobile tag or business license, and walked down the alley behind the 2121 Building to Twenty-second Street where my car was parked. Bob took me first to the coffee shop at a nearby motel. When I had regained my calm and we had established which route I was to take, he put me into my car and followed me to the refuge that I had prearranged for my seclusion until the trial was over and the verdict was in.

Robert Chambliss was free on bond. He was going home every night after the court recessed. In court, he scowled, he glowered, and (I learned later) he scribbled on his yellow legal pad: "Art Hanes, Tommy Rowe, Libby Cobbs …" over and over.

20
HOME BUT NOT HOME FREE

The next few days were to be some of the most difficult I've ever spent. A week or so before the trial began, I had spoken to Millie, one of the handful of friends I felt that I could trust, preparing her for a favor I might ask. Millie was a tall and portly woman-of-color from Boston studying for ministry in the Episcopal Church and a fellow student at Birmingham-Southern College. We had grown close through the past couple of years of classes, studying, discussions, and shared burgers.

"Millie, I may need a favor in a week or so," I had told her.

"What is it. I'll do you any favor I can." she assured me.

"I'm possibly going to need a place to stay for a few days, and no one can know where I am—absolutely no one. Can I stay with you, if it is necessary?"

"Are you having marriage trouble?" she asked, her face registering concern.

"No, that's not it, Millie. I can't explain, so please don't ask me for details. But if I need you, I'll really need you, and you will understand then."

She agreed, more readily than I would have expected, and the next day she gave me a key to her dorm room.

After my testimony Bob Eddy and I had coffee and then I drove directly to the college campus. Bob followed in another car. On the way the music on the car radio was interrupted by a recording of part of my testimony, and the announcer said, "This voice made history today," plugging the upcoming news broadcast.

Millie was asleep when I arrived. I told her who Bob was, and he checked the room and left me there. Caught off guard, Millie fretted as I explained what had happened, and we started a vigil of watching every news broadcast on a small black-and-white television and reading both morning and evening newspapers. She brought food back to me from the cafeteria and picked up newspapers, checking in between classes.

I had been given the option of staying in a motel, but I was glad not to be alone. I was also glad not to be at home with the telephone and doorbell.

The house monitors did not know that I was in Millie's room. The room had two twin beds, but she did not have a roommate. The bath, however, was shared with the adjacent room, so we kept the connecting door closed and locked.

Only two people figured out on their own where I was: Jesse and Andrea, a mixed-race couple who were friends of Millie's and mine. They had heard the news broadcast of my voice—then noticed Millie buying cheeseburgers. Millie had perpetual money problems, going to college on far fewer resources than requirements. She was often quite inventive in meeting her food needs, usually filling up on the peanut butter-and-jelly sandwiches the cafeteria kept available. When Jesse and Andrea saw Millie buying food and leaving the cafeteria with it, they put two and two together.

They knocked on the door and called softly, "It's Jesse and Andrea. It's OK, nobody saw us come up." Millie looked at me and I nodded. We let them in and the four of us sat around for hours talking and getting nerves settled.

From television and newspapers we learned much of what had happened in the courtroom. The first witness Tuesday was J. O. Butler, Sr., who was coroner in Jefferson County in 1963. He testified to the nature of the injuries sustained by the four victims of the bombing. After Butler, W. L. Allen, a deputy in the coroner's office, was called. Art Hanes, Jr., objected strenuously against admitting reports from the coroner's office into evidence. On the death certificates of each of the four girls, the cause of the injuries was shown as "dynamite blast," and two of them added the word "bomb."

Judge Gibson took out his pocket knife and cut each document—he apologized to the jury that the holes were asymmetrical—taking out the words "dynamite blast" and "dynamite blast-bomb." The death certificates were admitted into evidence and passed to the jury with holes where the "conclusionary statements" of the coroners had been.

Denise McNair's father, Christopher McNair, took the stand next and described that last day of his daughter's life.

Having established the crime and the nature of the crime, the prosecution changed to a different type of testimony.

Tom Cook, retired by 1977, had been a Birmingham policeman for more than 30 years. Cook's name came up several times in investigation reports (including statements by Tommy Rowe), raising suspicion that he furnished police intelligence to the Ku Klux Klan, aiding the Klan's cause. On the stand, he testified about a conversation he had with Robert Chambliss about the Sixteenth Street Baptist Church in December 1975, wherein Chambliss said, "Well, you know I got arrested for having that dynamite" and that he had given "that dynamite to Rowe and them."

After the lunch break, Birmingham Police Sergeant Ernie Cantrell took the stand and described a time in November 1976 when Robert Chambliss came to police headquarters and talked to Cantrell, Captain Jack LeGrand, and Captain Bill Myers. That time Chambliss had come to cast blame on Don Luna. Former Klan investigator Luna had just been arrested for securities irregularities. Luna had given both the state and FBI agents information, and he was with the state officer when Robert Chambliss was arrested on September 29, 1963. Attorney General Bill Baxley said they were showing that Robert was accusing his enemies to police whenever it looked as though someone were talking too much.

Cantrell also testified that during the conversation in November 1976, Robert had told him and the other officers that "a fellow" had told him how to make a "drip-method bomb" using "a fishing bobber, and a bucket full of water with a hole in it." Then Cantrell told the court that Robert said, "If I had bombed the church, I would have put enough stuff there to flatten the damn thing."

When I was called, I had no idea what had gone before I came in, but it was little wonder that Mr. Hanes tore into my testimony on the word "stuff."

Bob Eddy had led me out of the courtroom, and we were well out of the building when Bill Baxley called William "Billy" Jackson, a former Klansman, to the stand. He told of being with Robert and Tommy Blanton, Jr., at the Modern Sign Company downtown the night before the bombing. The group was using the sign shop's equipment to make Confederate flags and protest signs. He also told of going to Robert's home to join the Ku Klux Klan and attending a meeting on the Cahaba River. His testimony differed from earlier statements to police and FBI, however, in that he said these meetings were before the bombing rather than after.

The last witness called on Tuesday was Gertrude Glenn from Detroit, Michigan. Mrs. Glenn had been visiting friends who lived at 1521 Seventh Avenue North behind the church on the weekend the church was bombed. She and her friend's son were returning to that house about 2 a.m. that Sunday and saw a two-toned 1957 Chevrolet parked at the curb near there with the inside light on. Shortly after the bombing she had identified Robert Chambliss from photos as being one of the men in that car, and she selected a photo of Tommy Blanton, Jr.'s, car.

Art Hanes's objections to her testimony brought about legal arguments causing court to adjourn midway through and resume the next day. When I heard this, I felt so sorry for her having to go back the next morning. I had known about her since 1963, of course, having been told of her eyewitness account by FBI agents.

Wednesday morning court resumed a little after 8 a.m., and evidence was taken on voir dire for over two hours. The jury was finally brought in after 10:30 that morning, and Gertrude Glenn was questioned on both direct and cross at great length about the car she had seen and the men in it.

When she was excused, FBI special agent Tim Casey, who was one of the first agents on the case back in 1963, was called. He verified the photos of Tommy Blanton's car that Gertrude Glenn had identified.

Next to take the stand was Yvonne Young, a woman who told about going to Tee and Robert's house with Ross Keith (one of Robert's buddies in both Eastview Klavern 13 and the Cahaba Boys and an FBI informant who died before Bob Eddy could question him), two weeks before the bombing. Trying to find the bathroom, Young had opened a wrong door and saw several bundles of "oversized firecrackers" the color of masking tape lying on the floor. She described how Robert started "cussing" and "scolding" her for going into the wrong room.

After lunch, former fire marshal Aaron Rosenfeld was called for more expert testimony on the use of dynamite in the blast at the church, and Sergeant Cantrell was recalled. Cantrell was questioned more about the drip-method bomb Robert had talked about in 1976 and about his patrol duty and other police cars around the church through the night of September 14 and morning of the 15th.

Following Cantrell was FBI agent John McCormick, who had been in Birmingham for about a week before the Sunday morning bombing. He said that he reacted to the odor of dynamite with a headache—and got one investigating the scene. He further told about being present when another agent found the much-talked-about, little-seen fishing bobber in the street.

When I heard the television announcer say that the prosecution had rested its case and the defense portion of the trial would begin that same day, I was stunned. Was that all they had? I had expected it to take the rest of the week. The defense would drag on forever, right?

Art Hanes, Jr., had reserved the right to recall me, and I feared he might do just that. Surely Art Hanes, Sr., former mayor of Birmingham, former FBI agent, allegedly a former Klansman, would leave no stone unturned.

The defense led off with three Birmingham policemen. Billy Webb and Paul Hurst had been in the special patrol car on the 11 p.m. to 7 a.m. shift, and both testified that nothing unusual had happened. No white men in the area. The third police officer was Robert Chambliss's nephew Floyd C. Garrett, whose testimony was quite different from statements made to the FBI in 1963, except that he said he had gone to borrow a shotgun from his uncle on his way to work.

On cross-examination, Jon Yung quizzed him about telling his supervisor, Maurice House, that he had gone because he was suspicious that Robert was involved and wanted to see if he were at home. Garrett denied that.

Then the defense brought out nine character witnesses before court was adjourned for the day. All of them were asked on cross-examination if they had heard of the various times Robert had been arrested for violence and about his Ku Klux Klan activities. None of them admitted to knowledge of these things in forming their good opinion of Robert's character.

Wednesday evening, Millie and I huddled in her little dorm room. I was disturbed that the trial was going so fast. To me, the prosecution's case against Robert seemed weak and disjointed.

Thursday morning Robert's sister, Bennie Mae Brown, took the stand to say she had gone to Robert's house soon after the explosion looking for his neighbor, Clarence Dill, and found the two of them playing dominoes.

Next came a man named Edward Walker, an automobile salesman who testified that DeSoto automobiles were not made after 1961. Gertrude Glenn had said she was driving a 1962 model; supposedly Walker's testimony was to refute her identification of the Blanton car.

Then the defense rested. Robert Chambliss had surprised his attorneys by refusing to take the stand in his own defense.

There was one rebuttal witness for the state. Birmingham Police Captain Maurice House testified that Floyd Garrett had told him and Detective V. T. Hart that the reason for going to Chambliss's house that morning was because he (Garrett) was suspicious that Robert had done the bombing.

After final arguments, the jury received the case at 4:09 p.m., Thursday, November 17, 1977.

Bob Eddy and Jon Yung had called me several times since my testimony in court to make sure I was all right and to see if I needed anything. When Bob called Thursday evening, there was no enthusiasm in his voice. He sounded tired and we questioned how long the jury would deliberate.

"Nothing to do now ... but wait," he said.

But the telephone in the hallway rang Friday morning a little after 11. Jon Yung's voice said, "It's over. We won."

He told me to wait an hour before going home so that he could have the city police meet me and check the house and the church before I went in.

Millie and I hugged as I left. We were both in tears. A police car was waiting at the parsonage. I gave them my keys, waiting outside until they had checked the house and found it secure. Jesse and Andrea stayed with me during the afternoon, fielding calls and stopping people at the door.

A woman in my church congregation came with food and visited for a short while. I learned later that she thought Jesse and Andrea were police officers there to protect me, but the only police courtesy I received was when they had checked the house and church for bombs at Jon Yung's direction.

The district superintendent of the Birmingham east district of the United Methodist Church, Dr. Montgomery, called to determine if I was all right and to commend me for courage. The Bishop, Carl Sanders, called also, and after a few comments, he asked whether I would have testified if the death penalty had been a possibility. I had to tell him that I had struggled with the same question but had no answer. I do not believe in a death penalty, and in 1963 when the church was bombed, the death penalty had previously been ruled unconstitutional. That ruling was subsequently overturned, however, so that by 1977 it had been reinstated and Alabama had again hooked up "Yellow Mama," as the electric chair is euphemistically known.

I received letters from church people and citizens. I received a call from Mary, the church secretary of the Sixteenth Street Baptist Church. And I received threats.

As it turned out, there would be no further indictments in the Sixteenth Street Baptist Church bombing case. Extradition of J. B. Stoner from Georgia for bombing the Bethel Baptist Church in 1958 was in process, but no charges were lodged against him in the 1963 bombing. Only one man was convicted for the crimes of many in the Sixteenth Street Baptist Church bombing case.

Bill Baxley was running for governor in 1978. He lost despite, or perhaps because of, his efforts to solve civil rights era crimes. Governor

George Wallace sent Bob Eddy to Huntsville to serve the remainder of the term of Madison County's deposed sheriff.

Charlie Graddick was elected attorney general in 1978 and refused to pursue prosecution of the other men in the car that Saturday night in 1963: the one who got out and placed the bomb and set the crude timer, the young man who drove the car, and others who knew and helped. Graddick said the case was "too political," so he put it aside.

It had been hoped that once convicted, Robert would implicate the others. He said there was a "kiss of death" on Tee if he ever talked, and he must have firmly believed in this because he died in 1985, never having admitted to the bombing nor naming any accomplices. However, he did write letters accusing other Klansmen, his nephew Floyd Garrett, and Tommy Rowe.

In his letters and interviews with Ernie Cantrell and Jack LeGrand and district attorney David Barbour while in prison, Robert contended that there had been a CIA plot to frame him. He also accused his attorneys, Arthur Hanes, Jr., and Sr., of framing him—"just like they did James Earl Ray." I've been told that he often threatened me from his cell.

Robert had very few visitors, and after a time his threats and attempts to intimidate caused even the few to stop going to see him, especially after Tee died in 1980.

During the weeks just after Robert's trial I tried to resume a normal life, so I agreed to only one interview. Bill Baxley and I were taped in the living room of the parsonage for ABC's "Good Morning America." I agreed because the show did not air in Birmingham at that time.

About that same time a *Reader's Digest* writer came to see me. I did not give him material that he could use in his article, so he wrote his story using other sources.

I stayed in Birmingham just over a year after the trial. My second marriage had never had a secure foundation, and after the stress and publicity of the Chambliss case, it crumbled. The spring after the trial my husband divorced me. In June, I left the Methodist Church; feeling that my congregation (and I) had endured enough. I asked for a leave of absence. I moved several times and had my unlisted telephone number changed several times, but the harassment never stopped. Someone stood outside my bedroom window and lined up bullets on the windowsill. Someone broke into my car and left a hunting knife in the driver's seat. My telephone rang at odd hours of the night ... every night. Some callers were heavy breathers, most were threats, and some only said, "We know where you are."

I could not get a job in Birmingham; I was told repeatedly that people were afraid to hire me. I pastored a small independent church for a few months for $50 a week and housing and then worked as a security guard for several months.

I left Birmingham the first week of January 1979 under an assumed name, with one friend and all my possessions packed in a subcompact car, having sold or given away virtually everything I owned. I had no destination in mind except somewhere out of Alabama.

During the years I was gone, I was located several times even though I had changed my name and my appearance. I wasn't always sure just who had found me, but when it was a threat, I assumed it to be the Klan. Yet when three men wearing business suits in a nondescript car take your picture through the car window, you assume it to be the FBI and wave.

In 1980, during one of my many moves, I lost contact with my son. It would be four years before we reestablished communication. For that purpose I had quietly slipped back into Birmingham a couple of times. Then in winter 1985, a month after Robert died, I moved back to Birmingham. Only a few people knew who I once was.

Having been censured by my immediate family after the trial and further as my life changed, I did not feel free to reestablish contact with other relatives. I also feared that such associations would make me easier to locate for those who might still want to silence me. I had been warned (in writing in 1980) that should I try to make contact with any family members, I would be killed. So instead of taking up my old identity initially, I formed new friends and new activities. For several years I earned my living in an antiques restoration business.

During that time, I granted the only newspaper interview I have given in all these years. Kathy Kemp of the *Birmingham Post-Herald* reached me through a mutual acquaintance, and after meeting her, I agreed. She was kind enough and professional enough to guard my location and appearance at that time. That interview was published in October 1988.

I was not paid for either of the interviews I gave. I was never on the FBI payroll and received no money from them, nor have I ever received any reward money for my testimony or for cooperation with the State of Alabama's investigation. The State of Alabama has no witness protection program, so changing my name and appearance and all relocations were at my own expense and by my own efforts.

I readily admit that a year after I moved back to Birmingham in poor health and with poor prospects, I contacted a secretary in Bill Baxley's law office. There were no longer funds available, which I felt sure would be the case before I called. I did not speak with Bill Baxley himself.

Birmingham changed too—a great deal between 1963 and 1977. J. Edgar Hoover had said that it was impossible to get a conviction during the sixties. He might have been right. When I came back to Birmingham in November 1985, I found a city that had changed even more. But I still found an atmosphere of prejudice and fear.

Birmingham has now outgrown its nickname "Bombingham." Its current city government reflects its racial makeup with some very talented and dedicated individuals.

Yet it is still a city prone to violent division. It is still a city that does not take a stand for tolerance and mutual respect among its citizens. And, unfortunately, its understanding of "human rights" seems to still be locked in the dichotomy of black/white and has not opened to embrace all people.

Those who were children in 1963 are adults now and have raised another generation, still divided by race, religion, class, age, lifestyle, and neighborhood.

Had they lived, Denise, Carole, Addie, and Cynthia might have told us that hate and fear are sides of the same coin. Freedom begins by breaking free—free from fear, without hate, able to embrace all who are different because they are human, and therefore precious.

I toured the new Birmingham Civil Rights Institute shortly after it opened in 1992, and on the street outside I embraced a friend—a black businesswoman—and we agreed that Birmingham has come a long way. But we all still have a long way to go.

21
LOTS OF QUESTIONS AND VERY FEW ANSWERS

Former Governor George Wallace is an invalid now. He has suffered for more than two decades since he was crippled by an attempt on his life while campaigning in Maryland for the U.S. presidency in 1972. He is an honored guest at meetings of black mayors and has been "forgiven" his role as enabler of the violent and the vicious.

I, too, forgive him; yet I do not understand how we, as a people, can forgive ourselves for not asking the questions—and insisting on answers—as to how much his terms in office contributed directly to the grief of the state: by political posturing, by allowing crimes to go unpunished, by financing and encouraging violence for votes.

Why did George Wallace send Bob Eddy to Huntsville to serve out the term of that county's deposed sheriff, effectively getting Eddy "out of the way" during 1978?

So far as I know, no one has ever asked Ku Klux Klan Imperial Wizard Robert Shelton about being with Robert Chambliss that Saturday night, September 14, 1963. He was. Chambliss picked him up at the airport. When did he go back to Tuscaloosa? How much did he participate in or coordinate that night's activities?

No one has answered why the head of the state police (Alabama Highway Patrol) Colonel Al Lingo met with Robert Shelton and other Klansmen at the St. Francis Motel just before Chambliss, John Hall, and Charles Cagle were arrested on September 29, 1963 two weeks after the Sixteenth Street Baptist Church bombing.

No one has asked why the chairman of the United Americans for Conservative Government was at that meeting.

No one has asked why Bob Gafford (who was later elected to the Alabama House of Representatives) was offering to help Edward Fields (National States Rights Party) get use of the National Guard Armory for a rally after Fields was released from jail in 1963; or why bombing suspect Bobby Cherry, after being questioned by Bob Eddy near Fort Worth, Texas, in 1977, made a call to Birmingham—to Bob Gafford.

No one has asked why, as attorney general, Charlie Graddick fired Bob Eddy, who had rejoined the attorney general's staff after completing his time as sheriff of Madison County, spurring Jon Yung to quit, thus breaking up the investigative team, which was urging Graddick to prosecute other bombing suspects after J. B. Stoner was convicted.

No one has questioned J. B. Stoner's bomb-making classes or dared to call the Birmingham bombings "conspiracy" and charged others known to have participated.

No one has questioned why a Birmingham police officer (out of uniform) was warning people on the morning of September 15, 1963, to keep their mouths shut (about the bombing). Or why his alibi given to the FBI in 1963 was significantly different from his testimony in court—testimony that was rebutted—and he was not charged with either conspiracy or perjury.

Nor has there been an investigation into the deaths of at least two female informants, linking their demise to the roles they were playing.

No one has officially questioned how Troy Ingram died in his vehicle that day in 1976. Was he about to discuss the things that went on in his garage or at his house after the Cahaba River meetings of Klansmen in 1963?

Apparently no one suggested extensive forensic examination on Ross Keith or John Wesley Hall, two Klansmen who became FBI and police informants after the bombing, both of whom died when Bob Eddy tried to get to them for questioning in 1977.

No one has questioned publicly a report from a man who was eating chili in Jack Cash's restaurant, a Klan hangout, on Friday, September 13, 1963, and overheard Jack make a phone call and ask someone if they had the "case." The informant reported that Jack told the someone on the phone to take it to the "church" in Powderly. (Klansmen called their meeting halls "church.") The number Jack is said to have called was FA2-9481, a service station on First Avenue South at Thirty-first Street, where Baggett Transfer trucks hauling dynamite were parked.

There are police reports that indicate that two and perhaps three carloads of white men were in the area of the Sixteenth Street Baptist Church in the wee hours of Sunday, September 15, 1963: the car that Robert was in, one with six members of the National States Rights Party in it, and another with at least two men who were said to be wearing police uniforms.

Which car actually had the bomb that was planted and timed to go off? Who were the two men in police uniforms, and whose uniforms were they?

Several witnesses saw two white men running between houses on Seventh Avenue North moments after the blast—one was limping—but these men have never been identified. Had they been sent to retrieve or check on the bomb? Why did police officers testify at Robert's trial that there were no white men in the area at the time of the bombing, and that nothing ususual took place?

The dynamite purchased from Leon Negron's General Store in Daisy City by Robert Chambliss on September 4, 1963, was different from the case "found" by state investigators in the kudzu field near Gardendale, the case used as evidence when Chambliss, Hall, and Cagle were charged with illegal possession and transportation. The "found" case was placed in the field after September 28, when it had rained ... yet the original case has not been traced. Why has there been no grand jury investigation of those events? No charges of "obstruction of justice?" "Tampering with evidence or creating evidence?" "Conspiracy?"

Perhaps there will never be answers to these and the many other questions remaining in the Birmingham bombing cases, especially in the bombing of the Sixteenth Street Baptist Church.

Perhaps it is sufficient to ask them, lest we forget that we all have an obligation to demand truth and candor from those we appoint to serve and protect us as law enforcement officers and government officials. From those to whom we have given authority, we must exact responsibility. For this is the essence of freedom, the very definition of democracy, and our only hope against oppression.

EPILOGUE

In the early months of 1979, when I found myself totally removed from everything and everybody I had known and it seemed that the only asset left to me was a determination to survive, I went to the local United Methodist Church in the Texas Gulf Coast city I was in. The church offered professional counseling at low cost. One of the things I had learned through the years was the value of absolute honesty—especially with myself—and I was having trouble with the things that honesty was telling me.

After a couple of months, the retired navy officer/psychologist who was my counselor suggested that I should go to another city where the state university medical complex included a gender clinic. I moved to that city, and after several more months of counseling, evaluation, and physical tests, I entered the Gender Dysphoria Clinic for gender reassignment.

After two years of treatment, surgery, and a court evaluation, I was documented as "being of the male gender" legally, in December 1981. After another four years I returned to Birmingham.

I became very active in the city, coming out for various issues including gay and lesbian rights, jobs with justice, antiracism, women's rights, and other human rights related issues. I joined the volunteer staff of the *Alabama Forum* and over the years have done most of the jobs involved in producing a monthly newspaper with senior editor June Holloway. I still do book reviews and a monthly column for that publication.

Between 1986 and 1989, I tried to revert to my former identity for my parents, for my friends—but it no longer fit.

I debated whether any of this information should be included in this book because I did not want any hint of sensationalism to detract from the message of the work itself.

The decade of the seventies was a time when I could testify without there being any spectacle made to deflect from the value of my testimony. Today that may not hold true.

In a society that lives in a tabloid world, the messenger is often defamed at the expense of the message, and that is always a risk when a person speaks out. All too often today truth-of-content is lost while style-of-context is debated; still, I hope that will not be the case with this work.

I realize that by coming forward as I have with this full revelation of my current identity, I will frustrate readers who now wish to know more.

Yet that is another story best saved for another telling. I will say that simply needing a good place to hide played into some of the decisions I have made. I feel that my years of hiding, silence, and identity changes since the 1977 trial might be seen as testimony to the lengths one individual may be driven by fear and the need to escape it. Who I am today, I believe, is a direct reflection of the urgent desire to be free.

I would also like to say here that I could never have sustained myself without the support, understanding, and compassion of my dear friend, companion, and spouse Joni. She has made the last five years pleasant and productive as I struggled, in the development of this book, with what could have been a nightmarish resurrection of the past. I have not undertaken this work to glorify myself or to attract attention to myself but to help clarify a time in human history that was painful and harmful and that wrongfully damaged so many persons.

When J. Edgar Hoover died, tens of thousands of documents were destroyed. Hundreds of thousands more remain sealed by the FBI, classified for "national security" or "witness protection" purposes.

There are still too many secrets. There are still too many lies. There are still too many people suffering while the powerful manipulate and the political posture. If I am to call for truth, I must offer truth. We all should settle for nothing less. For it is only in an atmosphere of truth that freedom can ever prosper. It is only in an atmosphere of truth that those men and women who dare to do violence to others can be halted and brought to justice.

And it is only in an atmosphere of truth that we can learn to relate to each other by our compassion and our honesty rather than to judge each other on the points of difference between us.

None of us will be free until we all are free.

DOCUMENTATION

FBI interview with Elizabeth Cobbs, 1963

This FBI report, dated 10/12/63, documents the initial interview of Elizabeth Cobbs (then Elizabeth Hood) with federal agents. Note that the underlined and highlighted material reflects the Chambliss statements that Cobbs ultimately repeated in court in 1977—and that played a key role in Chambliss's conviction. *Birmingham Public Library Archives Department*

FBI interviews with Cobbs / Garrett, 1963

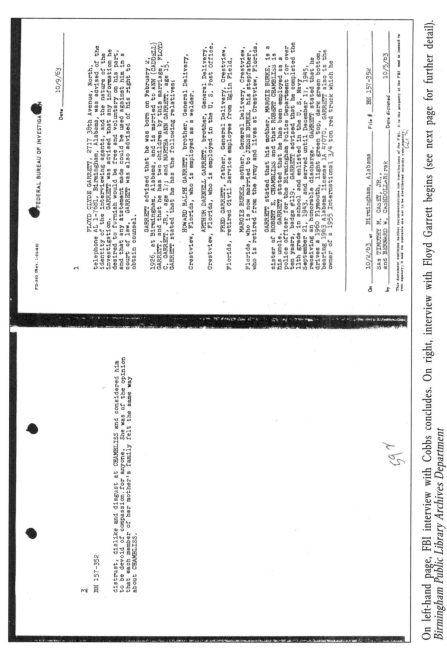

FEDERAL BUREAU OF INVESTIGATION

Date 10/9/63

1

FLOYD CLYDE GARRETT, 2717 38th Avenue, North, telephone AL 1-7681, Birmingham, Alabama, was advised of the identity of the interviewing agents, and the nature of the investigation. GARRETT was advised that any information he desired to furnish would be free and voluntary on his part, and that any statement made could be used against him in a court of law. GARRETT was also advised of his right to obtain counsel.

GARRETT advised that he was born on February 2, 1926, at Birmingham, Alabama, and is married to ANN (CADDELL) GARRETT, and that he has two children by this marriage, FLOYD C. GARRETT, JR., age 1½; and MARTHA ANN GARRETT, age 15. GARRETT stated that he has the following relatives:

HOWARD RALPH GARRETT, brother, General Delivery, Crestview, Florida, who is employed as a welder.

ARTHUR DARNELL GARRETT, brother, General Delivery, Crestview, Florida, who is employed in the U. S. Post Office.

FRED GARRETT, father, General Delivery, Crestview, Florida, retired Civil Service employee from Eglin Field.

MARGIE BURKE, mother, General Delivery, Crestview, Florida, who is now married to JESSE BURKE, his stepfather, who is retired from the Army and lives at Crestview, Florida.

GARRETT stated that his mother, MARGIE BURKE, is a sister of ROBERT E. CHAMBLISS and that ROBERT CHAMBLISS is his uncle. GARRETT stated that he has been employed as a police officer for the Birmingham Police Department for over ten years, badge #119. GARRETT advised that he completed the 11th grade in school and enlisted in the U. S. Navy September 21, 1943, and served until December 1, 1945, receiving an honorable discharge. GARRETT stated that he drives a 1960 Plymouth, light green top, dark green bottom, bearing 1963 Alabama license 1A 4/070. GARRETT also is the owner of a 1955 International 3/4 ton red truck which he

On 10/2/63 at Birmingham, Alabama   File # BH 157-352
by SAs TIMOTHY M. CASEY, JR.,   Date dictated 10/5/63
and BERNARD W. CashDOLLAR:rok

3

BH 157-352

distrust, dislike and disgust at CHAMBLISS and considered him to be devoid of compassion for anyone. She was of the opinion that each member of her mother's family felt the same way about CHAMBLISS.

On left-hand page, FBI interview with Cobbs concludes. On right, interview with Floyd Garrett begins (see next page for further detail). *Birmingham Public Library Archives Department*

BH 157-352
2

recently purchased from a Reverend KING, license number unknown. He stated that his wife has a 1960 Impala Chevrolet, four door sedan, white over green; however, he does not know the license of his wife's car. GARRETT stated that he also works part time on a commission basis as a landscape man for Sears and Roebuck, 1517 First Avenue, Birmingham, Alabama. Mr. GARRETT stated that he is not a member of any fraternal organizations nor has he ever belonged to the Ku Klux Klan or United Americans for Conservative Government (UACG). He stated that he attends the 35th Avenue Baptist Church on occasions.

GARRETT is a white male, 5' 10", 210 pounds, brown hair worn in crew cut, medium complexion, chunky build.

GARRETT advised that on Sunday, September 15, 1963, he was at home and that his children departed for Sunday School about 9:30 a.m., and that his wife left to go to church about 10 a.m. He stated that he did not attend church this day. He stated that shortly after feeding the dogs he heard an ... as he stated upon his arrival ... stated that the pastor of the Birmingham Police Department that it was necessary for him to return to duty. He stated that he got dressed, stopped at the church and told his wife that he had to go to work. He stated that his shotgun was "hung up" and that he desired to obtain a shotgun before going to work. He stated that he went to the home of ROBERT E. CHAMBLISS, his uncle, in an attempt to borrow CHAMBLISS' shotgun. He stated that he opened ... could not recall who was there other than CHAMBLISS and Mrs. CHAMBLISS. He stated that he asked CHAMBLISS if he had a shotgun, and CHAMBLISS told him that he did not have one but that he had a rifle. GARRETT stated to CHAMBLISS that he did not need a rifle, as he had one in his car. GARRETT stated that CHAMBLISS asked him what the trouble was and he told him that he had been called in. CHAMBLISS stated to GARRETT, "What's the matter, more Nigger trouble or bombing?" GARRETT stated that he told him that he did not know but that he had to go. GARRETT stated that he turned and ran out of the house and proceeded to the police station. He stated that it was about 10:45 a.m. when he arrived at the station. He stated that

BH 157-352
3

upon his arrival at the station he got into his uniform and that at this time had talked to Sergeant L.JONES, and that Sergeant JONES had assisted in clearing the shotgun. He stated that he proceeded to the scene of the 16th Street Baptist Church with Sergeant JONES, Sergeant FORD and Officer PEACOCK and arrived on the scene at about 11 a.m. He stated that he worked from about 11 a.m. at the scene until approximately 12 midnight. GARRETT stated that he recalled, there was another woman at CHAMBLISS' home when he entered to seek a shotgun, and that this woman wore curlers and glasses and may have been one of Mrs. CHAMBLISS sisters. GARRETT stated that he did not speak to her.

GARRETT advised that one JAMES H. HILLHOUSE of 2518 36th Avenue operates Reed's Service Station, 34th Avenue and 27th Street, and is a brother-in-law of CHAMBLISS, as his wife and CHAMBLISS' wife are sisters. GARRETT stated that he knows from the past that HILLHOUSE has no use for CHAMBLISS. GARRETT advised that many years ago he had heard that CHAMBLISS was a member of the Ku Klux Klan, but that he had heard that CHAMBLISS had pulled out of the organization. GARRETT stated that he himself has never been a member of the Ku Klux Klan or any other organization promoting segregation. GARRETT stated that Mrs. CHAMBLISS has always taken care of Mr. and Mrs. HOWARD MANNING's children as MANNING and his wife work, and that HOWARD MANNING is a brother of Mrs. CHAMBLISS.

GARRETT stated that his wife on two or three ... CHAMBLISS was sick, and that GARRETT's mother was in town, had come up from Florida, and that his wife took his mother to visit with Mrs. CHAMBLISS. GARRETT stated that he sees CHAMBLISS on occasions, mostly at CHAMBLISS' place of employment or in the vicinity thereof, Rebuilt Auto Parts, 919 3rd Avenue, North, which establishment is located on his beat. He stated that he seldom goes to CHAMBLISS' home, although he lives fairly close to him.

GARRETT stated that on September 14, 1963, the day prior to the bombing of the 16th Street Baptist Church, he was on duty from 3 to 11 p.m. and did not on this occasion recall seeing CHAMBLISS. He stated that at about midnight after getting off work, he and his girl friend, BETTY GRIFFIN, who

The FBI interview with Chambliss's nephew, Birmingham Police Officer Floyd Garrett, in which Garrett tells agents he heard the explosion on September 15, 1963, while his wife and children were at church, and was later called by phone to report in for duty. In sworn testimony during Chambliss's 1977 trial, Garrett said he never heard the explosion and that the call to report came early in the morning, while he was asleep, and that his wife woke him. *Birmingham Public Library Archives Department*

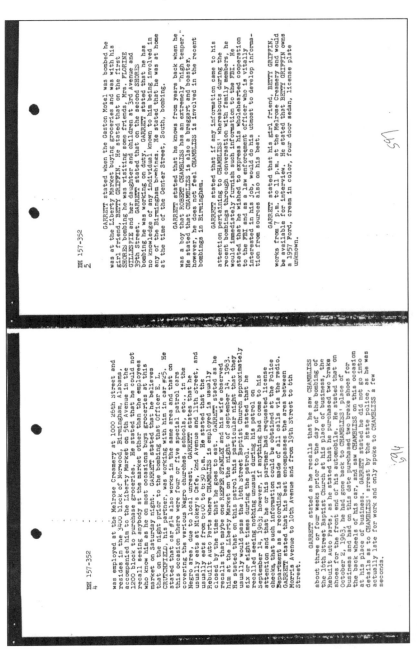

BH 157-352
4

was employed at the Melrose Creamery at 1000 26th Street and resides in the 3400 block of Norwood, Birmingham, Alabama, accompanied him to the Liberty Market on 5th Avenue in the 1200 block to purchase groceries. He stated that he could not recall seeing anybody at the market other than the employees who know him as he on most occasions buys groceries at this market on Saturday night. GARRETT stated that he believes that on the night prior to the bombing 15th him car #25. He stated that car #14 also works in the same area and that on this occasion there were four or five special patrol cars covering the various Negro churches, schools, etc. in the Negro area, due to local unrest. GARRETT states that he usually eats at Nickey's Cafe, 2nd Avenue and 11th Street, and usually eats from 6:00 to 6:30 p.m. He stated that the Rebuilt Auto Parts where CHAMBLISS is employed is usually closed by the time that he goes to eat. GARRETT stated as he recalls that maybe one REEPER STANLEY and his wife observed him at the Liberty Market on the night of September 14, 1963. He stated that on this patrol this particular night that they usually would pass the 16th Street Baptist Church approximately six or eight times during the patrol. He stated that he recalled seeing nothing unusual during his patrol on September 14, 1963; however, if anything had come to his attention and that he or his partner had requested license checks, that such information could be obtained at the Police Department as a recording is made of all calls via the radio. GARRETT stated that his beat encompasses the area between Morris Avenue to 10th Avenue and from 19th Street to 6th Street.

GARRETT stated as he recalls that he saw CHAMBLISS about three or four weeks prior to the day of the bombing of the 16th Street Baptist Church at his place of business, the Rebuilt Auto Parts, as he stated that he purchased two brake shoes for the front end of his automobile. He stated that on October 2, 1963, he had gone back to CHAMBLISS' place of business and had on this date purchased two brake shoes for the back wheels of his car, and saw CHAMBLISS on this occasion at his place of business. GARRETT stated he did not go into details as to CHAMBLISS' arrest by the police, as he was actually late for work and only spoke to CHAMBLISS a few seconds.

BH 157-352
5

GARRETT stated when the Gaston Motel was bombed he was at the Liberty Market buying groceries and was with his girl friend, BETTY GRIFFIN. He stated that on the first SHORES bombing he was visiting some friends, Mrs. FLORINE GILLESPIE and her daughter and children at 3rd Avenue and 39th Street. GARRETT stated that on the second SHORES bombing he was working on duty. GARRETT stated that he has no knowledge of any individual known to him being involved in any of the Birmingham bombings. He stated that he was at home at the time of the Center Street, South, bombing.

GARRETT stated that he knows from years back when he was a boy that ROBERT CHAMBLISS has an extremely "high temper." He stated that CHAMBLISS is also a braggart and boaster, however, he does not feel CHAMBLISS is involved in the recent bombings in Birmingham.

GARRETT stated that if any information came to his attention pertaining to CHAMBLISS' whereabouts during the recent bombings through conversation with family members, he would immediately furnish such information to the FBI. He stated that he wished to express his wholehearted cooperation to the FBI and as a law enforcement officer who is vitally interested in his job, would do his utmost to develop information from sources also on his beat.

GARRETT stated that his girl friend, BETTY GRIFFIN, works from 7 to 11 p.m. at the Melrose Creamery and would be available for interview. He stated that BETTY GRIFFIN owns a 1957 Ford, cream in color, four door sedan, license plate unknown.

SUMMARY OF INVESTIGATION,
BOMBING OF 16TH STREET BAPTIST
CHURCH, BIRMINGHAM, ALABAMA,
SEPTEMBER 15, 1963

I. PHYSICAL EVIDENCE AT SCENE

A complete crime scene was conducted with the aid of laboratory experts and Bureau Agents. The scene was protected by the Birmingham Police Department by roping off the area and placing armed guards.

a. An examination of the material, consisting of wood, metal, and masonry located in the vicinity of the explosion forwarded to the FBI Laboratory failed to identify the type of explosive due to a lack of residue.

b. No fragments of a mechanical timing device, fuse, or blasting caps were found. It should be noted, however, that a small red plastic and wire piece was located at the crime scene and was identified as part of a fishing bobber.

II. CHRONOLOGICAL SUMMARY OF PRELIMINARY INVESTIGATION

A complete neighborhood embracing several blocks in each direction from the church was conducted. Interviews in this area number in the hundreds. The owners of all license numbers recorded by persons on the bomb site 9/15/63, as well as those recorded by Bureau Agents during the pertinent time frame, ████████████ all stores open in the vicinity at the pertinent time, was conducted. Automobile owners were identified and interviewed as to reasons why they were in the vicinity and for investigative leads.

The church has a membership roster of 400 names. Of these, about 150 were in attendance at the time of the bombing. All have been located and interviewed, but nothing pertinent developed.

The neighborhood investigation and interview of church members has resulted in the location of over a dozen individuals who were on the street adjacent to the church when the bomb actually exploded. However, none can remember seeing a person whose actions they questioned. (It is felt highly possible that some sort of a timing device, operated by chemicals or non-metal device, could have been used.)

An immediate program was initiated to account for the whereabouts of individuals known to both the Birmingham Police Department and the FBI as capable of committing bombings. Also, members of the Ku Klux Klan and other so-called hate groups in Birmingham and surrounding offices were located and interviewed as to their whereabouts during the pertinent periods.

All suspects developed by other investigative agencies were checked out. All current information furnished anonymously or through logical sources was checked immediately for authenticity and possible importance.

Numerous tips, anonymous and otherwise, conscientious citizens supplying names of suspects, members of other investigative agencies furnishing names of suspects, all have been checked out.

III. INTERVIEW OF PEOPLE IN VICINITY AT TIME OF BOMBING

JAMES EDWARD LAY, Civil Defense Captain, advised that he noted a 1957 black two door Ford parked under the mimosa tree immediately adjacent to the explosion point at approximately 12:10 a.m., 9/2/63. This vehicle was occupied by two white men. After viewing a series of photographs, ████████████ BLANTON, Jr. strongly resembles the man who left the automobile and walked over to the area near the stairs which were blown away later. He said the photograph of ROBERT EDWARD CHAMBLISS strongly resembles the individual driving this car. He stated the car left the area before he had the opportunity to obtain the license or to check the car out any further.

JOEL A. BOTKIN, 524 12th Terrace North, retired dentist, age 75, advised he was parked in his car about two

-2-

Summary of FBI investigation of the Sixteenth Street Baptist Church bombing case. This report and other FBI documents were slowly released to Alabama attorney general's office investigator Bob Eddy; his

Birmingham Public Library Archives Department

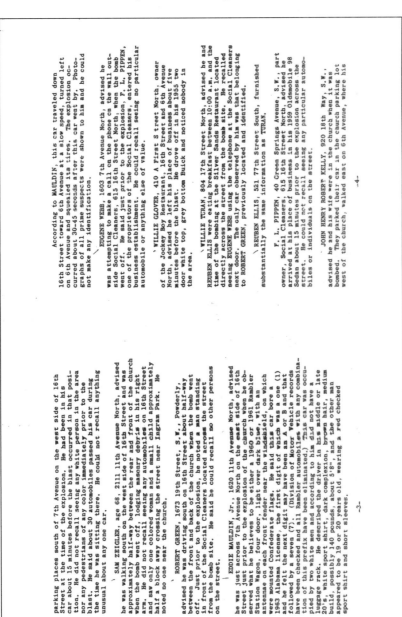

FBI summary of investigation, continued

parking places south of 7th Avenue on the west side of 16th Street at the time of the explosion. He had been in his car about 15 minutes before the blast occurred in that position. He did not recall seeing any white person in the area nor any pedestrians of any color immediately prior to the blast. He said about 30 automobiles passed his car during the time he was sitting there. He could not recall anything unusual about any one car.

SAM ZEIGLER, age 68, 2111 11th Avenue North, advised he was walking south on the west side of 16th Street and was approximately half-way between the rear and front of the church when the bomb went off, lodging masonry debris in his right arm. He did not recall seeing any automobiles on 16th Street and saw only one colored woman and a small child approximately half a block away crossing the street near Ingram Park. He noted no one near the church.

ROBERT GREEN, 1673 19th Street, S.W., Powderly, advised he was driving south on 16th Street about half-way between the front and back of the church when the bomb went off. Just prior to the explosion he noticed a man standing in front of the Social Cleaners located across the street from the bomb site. He said he could recall no other persons on the street.

EDDIE MAULDIN, Jr., 1620 11th Avenue North, advised he was just across 7th Avenue North on the east side of 16th Street just prior to the explosion of the church when he observed what he believes to be either a 1960 or 1961 Rambler Station Wagon, four door, light over dark blue, with an antennae on each front fender near the windshield, on which were mounted Confederate flags. He said this car bore a 1963 Alabama license, the first digit of which was a one (1) and he felt the next digit may have been an A or B and that followed by a seven (7). (Division of Motor Vehicle records have been checked and all Rambler automobiles with any combination of this prefix have been eliminated.) This car was occupied by two white men and according to him did not have a luggage rack. He described the driver in his middle or late 20's, white sport shirt, dark complexion, brown hair, medium build, possibly 140 pounds, about 5'8", and the other man appeared to be 19 or 20 years old, wearing a red checked sport shirt and short sleeves.

-3-

According to MAULDIN, this car traveled down 16th Street toward 6th Avenue at a slow speed, turned left on 6th Avenue and squealed its tires. The explosion occurred about 30-45 seconds after this car went by. Photographs of all prime suspects were shown to him and he could not make any identification.

EUGENE WEBB, 1603 7th Avenue North, advised he was attempting to make a call on the phone on the wall outside Social Cleaners, 615 16th Street North, when the bomb went off. He said just prior to the explosion, F. L. PIPPEN, one of the proprietors of the Social Cleaners, entered his business establishment. He could recall seeing no particular automobile or anything else of value.

WILLIE GLOVER, 410 A First Street North, owner of the Jockey Boy Restaurant, 16th Street and 6th Avenue North, advised he left his place of business about five minutes before the blast. He drove off in his 1955 two door white top, grey bottom Buick and noticed nobody in the area.

WILLIE TURAN, 804 17th Street North, advised he and REUBEN ELLIS were eating breakfast between 10:00 a.m. and the time of the bombing at the Silver Sands Restaurant located directly across the street from the bomb site. He recalled seeing EUGENE WEBB using the telephone at the Social Cleaners next door. The only car observed by him was that belonging to ROBERT GREEN, previously located and identified.

REUBEN ELLIS, 521 77th Street South, furnished substantially the same information as TURAN.

F. L. PIPPEN, 40 Green Springs Avenue, S.W., part owner, Social Cleaners, 615 16th Street North, advised he arrived at his place of business in his 1959 Oldsmobile 98 Sedan about 15 minutes prior to the explosion across the street. He could not recall seeing any particular automobiles or individuals on the street.

JOHN HENRY ROBERT KELLY, 920 18th Way, S.W., advised he and his wife were in the church when it was bombed. They parked their car in the church parking lot west of the church, walked east on 6th Avenue, where his

-4-

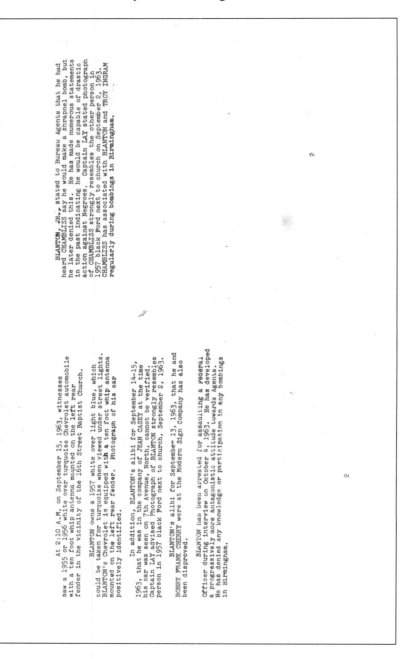

At 2:10 A.M. on September 15, 1963, witnesses saw a 1955 or 1956 white over turquoise Chevrolet automobile with a ten foot whip antenna mounted on the left rear fender in the vicinity of the 16th Street Baptist Church.

BLANTON owns a 1957 white over light blue, which could be taken for turquoise when viewed under street lights. BLANTON's Chevrolet is equipped with a ten foot whip antenna mounted on the left rear fender. Photograph of his car positively identified.

In addition, BLANTON's alibi for September 14-15, 1963, that he was in the company of JEAN CASEY at the time his car was seen on 7th Avenue, North, cannot be verified. Captain LAY advised Photograph of BLANTON strongly resembles person in 1957 black Ford next to church, September 2, 1963.

BLANTON's alibi for September 13, 1963, that he and BOBBY FRANK CHERRY were at the Modern Sign Company has also been disproved.

BLANTON has been arrested for assaulting a Federal Officer during interview on October 4, 1963. He has developed a progressively more antagonistic attitude towards Agents. He has denied any knowledge or participation in any bombings in Birmingham.

BLANTON, JR., stated to Bureau Agents that he had heard CHAMBLISS say he would make a shrapnel bomb, but he later denied this. He has made numerous statements in the past indicating he would be capable of drastic action against Negroes. Captain LAY stated photograph of CHAMBLISS strongly resembles the other person in 1957 black Ford next to church on September 2, 1963. CHAMBLISS has associated with BLANTON and TROY INGRAM regularly during bombings in Birmingham.

2

2

197

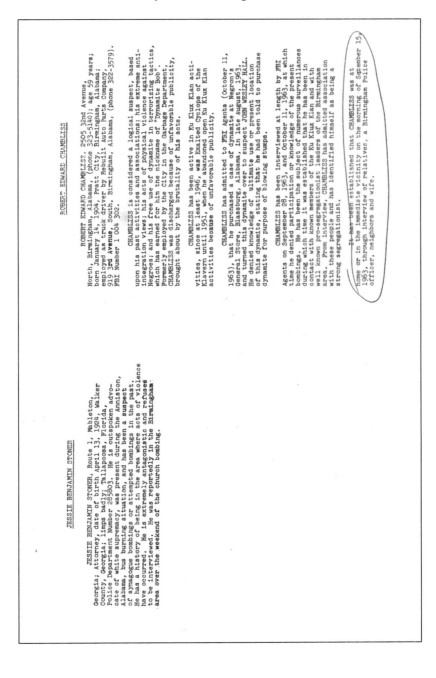

ROBERT EDWARD CHAMBLISS

ROBERT EDWARD CHAMBLISS, 2505 32nd Avenue, North, Birmingham, Alabama, (phone 323-5140); age 59 years; born January 14, 1904, Pratt City, Birmingham, Alabama; employed as truck driver by Rebuilt Auto Parts Company; 919 3rd Avenue, South, Birmingham, Alabama, (phone 322-3579). FBI Number 1 004 302.

CHAMBLISS is considered a logical suspect, based upon his past activities and associations; his extreme anti-integration views; his acts of physical violence against Negroes; and his free use of dynamite in terrorizing tactics, which has earned for him the nickname of "Dynamite Bob". Formerly employed by the City in the Garbage Department, CHAMBLISS was discharged because of unfavorable publicity, brought about by the brutality of his acts.

CHAMBLISS has been active in Ku Klux Klan activities, since at least 1946, was Exalted Cyclops of the Klavern until 1951, when he abandoned open Ku Klux Klan activities because of unfavorable publicity.

CHAMBLISS has admitted to FBI Agents (October 11, 1963), that he purchased a case of dynamite at Negron's General Store, Blassburg, Alabama, in late August, 1963, and turned this dynamite over to suspect JOHN WESLEY HALL. He denied knowledge of ultimate use or present location of this dynamite, stating that he had been told to purchase dynamite for purpose of blowing stumps.

CHAMBLISS has been interviewed at length by FBI Agents on September 28, 1963, and October 11, 1963, at which time he denied participation or knowledge of the present bombings. He has been the subject of numerous surveillances during which time it was established that he has been in contact with known members of the Ku Klux Klan and with well known pro-segregationist leaders of the Birmingham area. From interviews, CHAMBLISS has admitted association with these people and has identified himself as being a strong segregationist.

It has been established that CHAMBLISS was at home or in the immediate vicinity on the morning of September 15, 1963, through interview of relatives, a Birmingham Police officer, neighbors and wife.

JESSIE BENJAMIN STONER

JESSIE BENJAMIN STONER, Route 1, Mableton, Georgia; Attorney; date of birth April 13, 1924, Walker County, Georgia; limps badly; Tallapoosa, Florida, Police Department Number 285803. He is outspoken advo-cate of white supremacy, was present during the Anniston, Alabama, bus burning situation, and has been a suspect of synagogue bombings or attempted bombings in the past. He has a history of being in the area where acts of violence have occurred. He is extremely antagonistic and refuses to be interviewed. He was reportedly in the Birmingham area over the weekend of the church bombing.

JERRY QUILLAN DUTTON

Bessemer Road; NSRP Headquarters, 1865
Gwinnet County, Georgia; Birmingham Police Department
#120100; Youth Director, NSRP.

DUTTON was interviewed at the Jefferson County
Jail, on September 24, 1963, and refused to answer any
questions. He stated his attorney, J. B. STONER, of
Atlanta, Georgia, would furnish any information that
was needed.

Dr. EDWARD REED FIELDS

Dr. EDWARD REED FIELDS, 1509 Mims Street, Southwest;
Information Director, National States Rights Party, 1865
Bessemer Road; white male; date of birth September 30, 1932,
Chicago, Illinois; graduate Palmer School of Chiropractry,
Davenport, Iowa; originally from Atlanta, Georgia; FBI
Number 157 959 E.

On September 23, 1963, he was interviewed, at
which time he denied any knowledge of the bombings in
Birmingham and reiterated his stand on segregation to
Agents, and is currently involved in litigation directed
towards FBI Agents.

FBI summary of investigation, continued

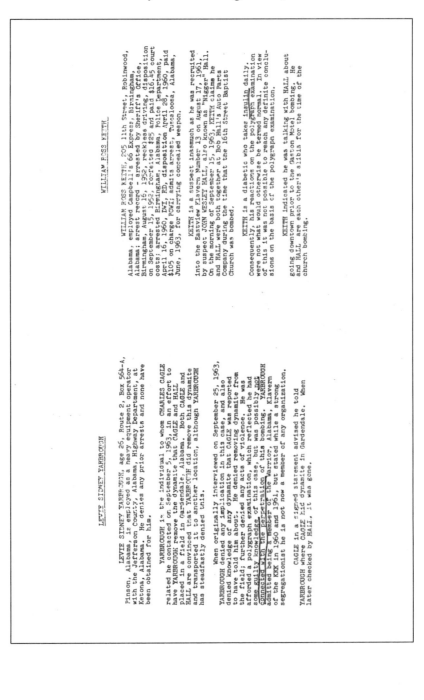

LEVIE SIDNEY YARBROUGH

LEVIE SIDNEY YARBROUGH, age 26, Route 2, Box 564-A, Pinson, Alabama, is employed as a heavy equipment operator with the Jefferson County, Alabama, Highway Department, at Ketona, Alabama. He denies any prior arrests and none have been obtained for him.

YARBROUGH is the individual to whom CHARLES CAGLE related he contacted on September 5, 1963, in an effort to have YARBROUGH remove the dynamite that CAGLE and HALL placed in a field in Gardendale, Alabama. Both CAGLE and HALL are convinced that YARBROUGH did remove this dynamite and transported it to another location, although YARBROUGH has steadfastly denied this.

When originally interviewed on September 25, 1963, YARBROUGH denied any implication in this case, and also denied knowledge of any dynamite that CAGLE was reported to have told him about. He denied removing dynamite from the field; further denied any acts of violence. He was afforded a polygraph examination, which reflected he had some guilty knowledge of this case, but was possibly not connected with the perpetration of this bombing. YARBROUGH admitted being a member of the Warrior, Alabama, Klavern of the KKK in 1960 and 1961, but stated while a strong segregationist he is not now a member of any organization.

CAGLE in a signed statement advised he told YARBROUGH where CAGLE hid dynamite in Gardendale. When later checked by HALL, it was gone.

WILLIAM ROSS KEITH

WILLIAM ROSS KEITH, 205 11th Street, Robinwood, Alabama, employed Campbell's 66 Express, Birmingham, Alabama; arrest record - arrested by Sheriff's Office, Birmingham, August 16, 1952, reckless driving, disposition $16.45 court costs; arrested Birmingham, Alabama, Police Department, April 16, 1960, DWI, PD, disposition April 28, 1960, paid $105 on charge PGWI; admits arrest, Tuscaloosa, Alabama, June, 1963, for carrying concealed weapon.

KEITH is a suspect inasmuch as he was recruited into the Eastview Klavern Number 13 on August 17, 1961, by suspect JOHN WESLEY HALL, also known as "Nigger" Hall. On the morning of September 15, 1963, KEITH claims he and HALL were both together at Bob Hall's Auto Parts Company during the time that the 16th Street Baptist Church was bombed.

KEITH is a diabetic who takes insulin daily. Consequently, his reactions on the polygraph examination were not what would otherwise be termed normal. In view of this it was not possible to reach any definite conclusions on the basis of the polygraph examination.

KEITH indicated he was talking with HALL about going downtown prior to the Gaston Motel bombing. He and HALL are each other's alibi for the time of the church bombing.

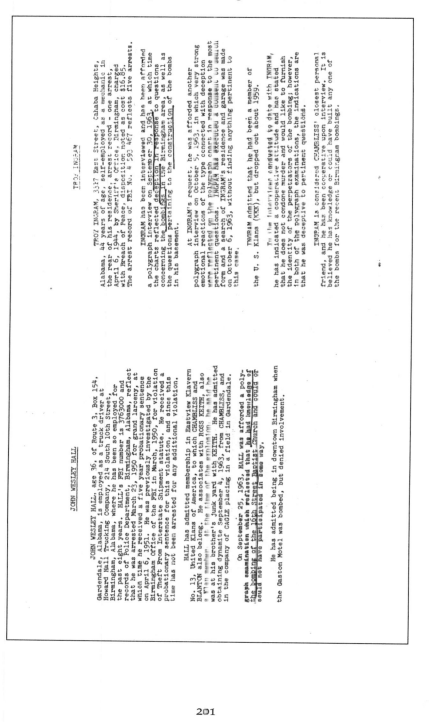

JOHN WESLEY HALL

JOHN WESLEY HALL, age 36, of Route 3, Box 154, Gardendale, Alabama, is employed as a truck driver at Howard Hall Trucking Company, 214 South 10th Street, Birmingham, Alabama, where he has been so employed for the past eight years. HALL's FBI number is 3763000 and records of Police Department, Birmingham, Alabama, reflect that he was arrested March 23, 1950 for grand larceny, at which time he received a five year probationary sentence on April 6, 1951. He was previously investigated by the Birmingham Office of the FBI in March, 1960, for violation of Theft From Interstate Shipment statute. He received a probationary sentence for this violation, and since this time has not been arrested for any additional violation.

HALL has admitted membership in Eastview Klavern No. 13, United Klans of America, to which CHAMBLISS and BLANTON also belong. He associates with ROSS KEITH, also a Klan member. At the time of the explosion, he said he was at his brother's junk yard with KEITH. He has admitted obtaining dynamite September 4, 1963, from CHAMBLISS, and in the company of CAGLE placing in a field in Gardendale.

On September 25, 1963, HALL was afforded a polygraph examination in which reflected that he had knowledge of the bombing of the 16th Street Baptist Church and could or could not have participated in some way.

He has admitted being in downtown Birmingham when the Gaston Motel was bombed, but denied involvement.

TROY INGRAM

TROY INGRAM, 3317 East Street, Cahaba Heights, Alabama, 44 years of age, self-employed as a mechanic in the rear of his residence, arrest record - one arrest, April 6, 1944, by Sheriff's Office, Birmingham, charged with Breach of Peace, disposition noted as cost $16.85. The arrest record of FBI No. 4 593 467 reflects five arrests.

INGRAM has been interviewed and has been afforded a polygraph interview on September 30, 1963, at which time the charts reflected deception in response to questions concerning the bombings in the Birmingham area, as well as the questions pertaining to the construction of the bombs in his basement.

At INGRAM's request, he was afforded another polygraph interview on October 5, 1963, in which very strong emotional reactions of the type connected with deception were reflected on the polygraph chart in response to the most pertinent questions. INGRAM has executed a consent to search form and a search of INGRAM's residence and garage was made on October 6, 1963, without finding anything pertinent to this case.

INGRAM admitted that he had been a member of the U. S. Klans (KKK), but dropped out about 1959.

In the interviews conducted to date with INGRAM, he has indicated a cooperative attitude and has stated that he does not condone murder and would like to furnish the identity of the perpetrators of the bombing; however, in both of the polygraph examinations, the indications are that he was deceptive to pertinent questions.

INGRAM is considered CHAMBLISS' closest personal friend, and he has been cooperative upon interview. It is believed he has knowledge of or could have built any one of the bombs for the recent Birmingham bombings.

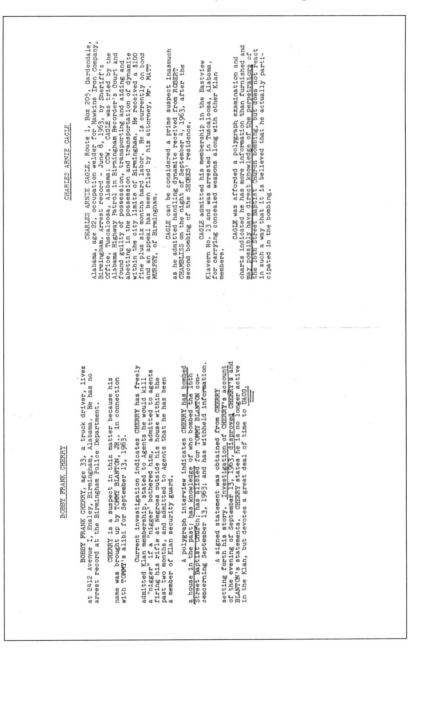

CHARLES ARNIE CAGLE

CHARLES ARNIE CAGLE, Route 1, Box 205, Gardendale, Alabama, age 22, occupation welder for Hawkins Iron Company, Birmingham. Arrest record - June 8, 1963, by Sheriff's Office, Tuscaloosa, Alabama; CCW. CAGLE was tried by the Alabama Highway Patrol in Birmingham Recorder's Court and found guilty of possession, transporting and aiding and abetting in the possession and transportation of dynamite within the city limits of Birmingham. He received a $100 fine plus six months hard labor. He is currently on bond and an appeal has been filed by his attorney, Mr. MATT MURPHY, of Birmingham.

CAGLE can be considered a prime suspect inasmuch as he admitted handling dynamite received from ROBERT CHAMBLISS on the night of September 4, 1963, after the second bombing of the SHORES' residence.

CAGLE admitted his membership in the Eastview Klavern No. 13 and was arrested in Tuscaloosa, Alabama, for carrying concealed weapons along with other Klan members.

CAGLE was afforded a polygraph examination and charts indicated he has more information than furnished and may possibly have direct knowledge of the perpetrators of the 16th Street Baptist Church bombing, but does not react in such a way that it is believed that he actually participated in the bombing.

BOBBY FRANK CHERRY

BOBBY FRANK CHERRY, age 33, a truck driver, lives at 2412 Avenue I, Ensley, Birmingham, Alabama. He has no arrest record at the Birmingham Police Department.

CHERRY is a suspect in this matter because his name was brought up by TOMMY BLANTON, JR., in connection with TOMMY's alibi for September 13, 1963.

Current investigation indicates CHERRY has freely admitted Klan membership, stated to Agents he would kill a "nigger" if a "nigger" bothered him, admitted to agents firing his rifle at Negroes outside his house within the past two months, and admitted to Agents that he has been a member of Klan security guard.

A polygraph interview indicates CHERRY has bombed a house in the past; has knowledge of who bombed the 16th Street Baptist Church; has alibied for TOMMY BLANTON concerning September 13, 1963; and has withheld information.

A signed statement was obtained from CHERRY setting forth his story. Investigation of CHERRY's account of the evening of September 13, 1963, disproved CHERRY's and BLANTON's statements. CHERRY states he is no longer active in the Klan, but devotes a great deal of time to UACO.

Document found in papers of Mayor Albert Boutwell

Persons in attendance at meeting in Colonel
Al Lingo's room at St. Francis Motel September 29, 1963:

    Colonel Al Lingo
    Major William R. Jones
    Bill Morgan (United Americans for Conservative Government)
    Herbert Eugene Reeves, a Klansman
    Robert Thomas, a Klansman
    Wade Wallace, distant relative of Governor Wallace
    Art Hanes, former Mayor
    Robert Shelton, Imperial Wizard, KKKK
    Hubert Page, a Klansman
    Don Luna, a Klansman

    Same persons listed in above group, including
Robert Shelton and Art Hanes, were also present at the
Alabama Highway Patrol Office later in the evening.

    Persons picked up for questioning on evening of
September 29, 1963:

    Ross Keith
    Levi "Quick Draw" Yarbrough
    Robert "Dynamite" Chambliss
    John Wesley Hall ("Nigger" Hall)
    Charles Cagle

    On September 30, 1963, Captain Bob Godwin took
Hubert Page, a Klansman, to Huntsville, Alabama, where
he was given a Polygraph examination by a Deputy Sheriff
who was formerly employed by OSI.

    Don Luna accompanied State Investigator Posey,
and these two men knocked on Robert Chambliss' front door
on the evening of September 29, 1963, in a joint operation.

This unsigned document found in Mayor Albert Boutwell's papers in January 1978 details a meeting in Alabama Highway Patrol Colonel Al Lingo's motel room before Robert Chambliss and four other Klansmen were "picked up for questioning" on September 29, 1963. Three of the men, Chambliss, Cagle, and Hall, were charged with illegal possession of dynamite. They were convicted but later acquitted on appeal. *Birmingham Public Library Archives Department*

Reporter's notes duplicating "St. Francis" report on page 203

15 /   1.23   on newsprint — with Jerry Mitchell (AP) notes

w-t-b-c   steve phillips, tus

shelton: "Well what could you expect. . I think it wa apparent to everyone
that there wasn't going to be any justice in the case."   He also said
he wasn t convicned it was a bombing ithe thought it was a natural gas
explosion. thefbi reported for five days after the incident that it was
a gas explosion. there were no traces of any dynamite.

*Getvory
758-5523*

11-15-77

former mayor Albert Boutwell [*Casey - passport
933 - 1900*
deck.

persons in attendace at meeting in col al lingo s room at st. francis
motel sept 29, 1963; lingo, maj. wm. r. jones, bill morgan, united ams
for conservative government; herbert eugene reeves, a klansman, robt
thomas a k lansman, wade wallace, distant relative of gov. wallace;
art hanes, former mayor; robt shelton, imperial wizard kkk, hubert page
a klansman and don luna , a klansman. same persons listed in above group
including robt shelton and art hanes were also present at the ala. highway
patrol office later in the evening.   persons picked up for questioning
on evening of sept. 29, 1963; ross keith, levi quickdraw yarbrough, robt
dynamite chambliss, john wesley hall (nigger hall), charkes cagle,

on .sept 30 capt bob godwin took hubert page, a klansamn to huntsville
ala where he was given a polygraph examinati n by deputy examination
by dept uty sheriff formerly employed by OSI (intelligence gagent during
wwII)

don luna accompnanied state investigator posby and these two men knocked
en robt chambliss ' front door on the evening of sept. 29, 1963 in a joint
operation .

cagle   *"Bobby could convince the jury
Jesus christ was guilty."
cagle → Page.*

A news reporter's notes during the November 1977 trial of Robert Chambliss include a quote from the St. Francis motel report, indicating this meeting was common knowledge months before Mayor Albert Boutwell's copy surfaced. This document was filed with the archival copy of the trial transcript. *Birmingham Public Library Archives Department*

1125 / 3.13 ③

FD-302 (Rev. 1-25-60)

FEDERAL BUREAU OF INVESTIGATION

Date ___10/6/63___

On October 4, 1963, Special Agents JOSEPH M.
ZIMMERMAN and JOHN F. McCORMACK, accompanied by Captain J. M.
McDOWELL, Birmingham Police Department, went to a field
located off of Highway 31, near Gardendale, Alabama, where
they turned off onto Mockingbird Lane. Captain McDOWELL
drove down Mockingbird Lane to a spot approximately 50 yards
from the intersection of Mockingbird Lane and Laurel Lake Road
where he stopped and stated this was the location where he
had accompanied Colonel LINGO, BEN ALLEN and Major BILL JONES,
as well as CHARLES CAGLE. Captain McDOWELL showed agents the
spot where CAGLE pointed under a kudzu vine and stated a
paper sack containing 2½ sticks of Olin dynamite was found at
this location. It is noted that this is the exact location
where CAGLE originally took agents on September 26, 1963, and
told them that was the spot where HALL and he had placed the
case of dynamite that they had obtained from ROBERT CHAMBLISS'
house.

Captain McDOWELL then walked from the kudzu patch
approximately 100 yards away into a wooded area where he
located a tree, stating this is where Major BILL JONES found
a box of Monobel B dynamite. He stated that CHARLES CAGLE
had walked around the area, looking around trees in the
general direction where BILL JONES found the case of dynamite.

Captain McDOWELL stated CAGLE made the statement to
him that the dynamite had not been here when the FBI brought
him out to this place before.

On ___10/4/63___ at ___Birmingham, Alabama___   File # ___BH 157-352___
     SA JOSEPH M. ZIMMERMAN and
by ___JOHN F. McCORMACK:rak___   Date dictated ___10/4/63___

This FBI report details a trip agents made with Birmingham Police Captain McDowell to the site where McDowell, led by Charles Cagle, found a case of dynamite on October 1, 1963. This document the fact that Cagle told McDowell the dynamite was not at the site when he accompanied FBI agents there at an earlier date shortly after the Sixteenth Street Baptist Church bombing on September 15, 1963. *Birmingham Public Library Archives Department*

FBI interview with Captain W. E. Berry regarding condition of "Gardendale" dynamite

FEDERAL BUREAU OF INVESTIGATION

1

Date _____10/8/63_____

On October 2, 1963, Captain W. E. BERRY, Birmingham, Alabama, Fire Department, advised that the previous day he had been requested by State of Alabama authorities to handle an amount of dynamite which had been recovered by them. Captain BERRY exhibited 130 sticks of Monobel-B dynamite. According to Captain BERRY, this is a permissive dynamite, which means that the duration and size of the fire flash at the time of the explosion is such that it is permissible to use this dynamite in mines or other places where there is danger of the presence of explosive or highly volatile gases.

According to Captain BERRY, this dynamite was contained in a two-piece case, the top portion slipping over the bottom portion, the bottom portion being that part of the carton which actually holds the dynamite. Captain BERRY stated it was his understanding this dynamite had not been moved by the state authorities prior to his, Captain BERRY's, arrival at the scene. Upon removing this case of dynamite, Captain BERRY noted that the grass underneath the case was not discolored, nor were there other indications that this case had been sitting at this particular location for any great length of time. Captain BERRY also noted that the case, as well as the individual sticks of dynamite, were dry, which indicated to Captain BERRY that this dynamite had been placed in the location where it was found some time subsequent to September 28, 1963, which was the last day it rained in the Birmingham area.

This dynamite was weighed by Mr. S. H. FARLEY, Department of Weights and Measures, Birmingham, Alabama, and it was determined that the 130 sticks weighed 50 pounds and 14 ounces.

The bottom portion of the case exhibited by Captain BERRY contained the printed words "Dupont high explosive dangerous" "ICC-23H65". Also on this case were stamped numbers. The bottom half of the first two numbers and first digit did not print and interpretation by means of the remaining portion of numbers and letters indicated that the number may have been 28BH104. Also printed on this bottom half of the dynamite case was "Monobel-B 1¼ x 8".

On __10/2/63__ at __Birmingham, Alabama__ File # __BH 157-352__

by SA HUGH J. SMITH and SA FRANK B. SPENCER:yk _____ Date dictated __10/7/63__

First page of an FBI report of an interview with Birmingham Fire Department Captain W. E. Berry who was responsible for removing the case of dynamite from the field near Gardendale, where police had been led by Charles Cagle on October 1, 1963. Berry essentially tells the FBI the dryness of the case indicated that the dynamite had been placed there recently. The finding of the dynamite conveniently backed up charges of dynamite possession filed against Cagle, John Wesley Hall, and Robert Chambliss in the wake of the church bombing—charges which, at least temporarily, derailed any more serious ones that might at that time have been filed. *Birmingham Public Library Archives Department*

Police investigator's report on the "Gardendale" dynamite

1125. 7.48

li. l.:

BIRMINGHAM POLICE DEPARTMENT

MEMORANDUM

October 16, 1963

Re: Investigation made by J. K. Turner on the dynamite which was found by
State Investigator in the case where Chambliss, Cagle and Hall are the
defendants.

On 10/3/63 at approximately 9:30, I went to the City Powder Storage
Magazine located near Norwood Fire Station with Captain Godwin, State
Investigator and Captain Bill Berry, Birmingham Fire Department.
Upon arriving there we found three (3) men from the City Weights and
Measures Department, Chief Rosenfield, Birmingham Fire Department,
and two F.B.I. Agents. The Magazine was unlocked by Captain Berry
and a carton containing Monobel B-1¼ x 8 dynamite removed. The markings on the box were not clear but appeared to be 28BH104. The net
weight of dynamite was 50 lbs. 14 oz., the count 130.

Captain Berry, Captain Godwin and I then went to DuPont Powder Company
near Watson where we contacted Leo J. Fox, Associate Plant Manager.
After examination of the box which had contained the dynamite and some
checking at the plant, it was determined that the dynamite had been
made at that plant on August 28, 1963. The company had made three
mixings of this particular type on August 27 and 28. The test count
on the mixings was 139, 144 and 145 sticks per case. Mr. Fox says
the name "Permissable Dynamite" which appeared on the carton could be
confusing. This wording means that this dynamite is approved by the

Birmingham Police Investigator J. K. Turner's report on the dynamite retrieved from the Gardendale field.
Turner, along with state investigator Godwin and Birmingham Fire Department Captain Berry, trace the
explosives to the store of Leon Negron. Negron says the dynamite could have been sold to a man in a black
1954 Chevrolet or that it could have been part of a mine shipment that disappeared. *Birmingham Public
Library Archives Department*

Police investigator's report on dynamite, continued

Memorandum   Page 2

Bureau of Mines for use in mines where certain explosive gases may
be present since the flash created by the explosion will not ignite
the gas. This dynamite may be approximately equivalent to 50% Red
Cross dynamite according to Mr. Fox or as much as 60% Grey strength.
We were furnished a list of the places having purchased this type
dynamite since the mixing date. On 9/3/63 Negron Grocery, Daisy
City, 4 cases; 9/10/63 Harrison's Grocery, Dora, Alabama, 60 cases;
9/13/63 Finley Champion Coal Company, Action, Alabama, 3 cases; 9/24/63
Negron Grocery, Daisy City, 4 cases.

Mr. Fox stated that in spite of the fact that we had better than
50 lbs. of dynamite, that we had less than a case of dynamite. According to him the count would not have been below 139 or above 146. Mr.
Fox explained the increase in weight as possibly due to the dynamite
absorbing moisture from the air since the plastic bag which normally
contains dynamite was open.

Leon Negron, Route 3, Box 922, Birmingham, Phone OR·4-7331, was contacted at his place of business, Negron Grocery. His wife was present
at the time of arrival. Most of the questioning was done by Captain
Godwin. Some of the interview was missed by me due to the fact that
I was suffering from a severe attack of hay-fever. Mr. Negron informed us that he had talked to the F.B.I. and State Investigator before and that he had told them that he had sold a case of dynamite
on August 30, but he was of the opinion that it happened before Labor
Day even though he admitted after some questioning that it could have
been later than August 30.

Police investigator's report on dynamite, continued

Negron stated that the sale took place on Saturday at a time when his wife was not at the store. His son-in-law, Larry Murphy, (not sure of name) was in the store at the time of the sale. He states that a man in his 40's, about 6' to 6'2" tall, of medium build, dressed in clean work clothing, and having the appearance of having worked outside drove up in a clean black 1954 Chevrolet pick-up accompanied by a 16 or 17 year old boy who stayed in the truck. The man asked for a case of dynamite paying for it with a $20 bill. Negron and the man then went to a shed in the rear of the store for the dynamite, and the man picked up the case and put it in the back of the pick-up which had been parked on the right side of the front door (facing the building).

Mr. Negron first stated that he thought the man was going to use the dynamite blowing up stumps but later stated that he had a pad in his hand to take down the tag number on the pick-up as it pulled away, but his vision was blocked by an automobile pulling up at the gas pump. When asked why he would jot down the license number of the vehicle if he thought the dynamite was going to be used for blowing stumps, he said then that the first thing he thought of was the trouble that had been happening in Birmingham. Negron states that he had sold only the one case recently.

At one point in his conversation Negron stated that he had sent some dynamite to a mine, which he operates in the rear of his store, on September 6. He says this dynamite was not used in the mine but it

Conclusion, police investigator's report on dynamite

Memorandum   Page 4

disappeared. He was of the opinion that the case may have been taken by an employee (doesn't have the name) who had not been back to work since that date.

Upon checking the shed used by Negron for the storing of dynamite and other merchandise, Captain Godwin and I found a partial case of Monobil B dynamite. This case had the same code markings as that found by the State.

Sergeant Parson, Birmingham Police Department, has known Mr. Negron for years. He called Negron at my request, asking him if he would talk to me at a later date. To this he agreed. Today I have been unable to find time for this interview.

Detective J. K. Turner
Saundra Tate, Stenographer

October 15, 1963

Police radio log, September 14-15, 1963

MEMORANDUM

The following is a list of police radio transmissions which occurred from 10:19 P.M. on September 14, 1963, until 10:22 A.M., September 15, 1963:

RECORD 19:

10:19 P.M., Car 18 requested registration on 1A 44186. (Leroy Hill – 58 Dodge)

All solo motors were directed to go to the downtown area and break up auto parade, autos carrying Confederate flags.

Motor 122 requested that a plain car be sent to 3 Avenue 16th Street North to check on a building across from the old Internal Revenue building. Stated that this building was headquarters for paraders and that placards were being made there.

RECORD 20:

11:00 P.M., September 14, 1963, Car 17 (C. E. Pyle, K. B. Womack, or George Hayes and M. E. Strickland) was directed to go to Golf Center, Highway 78 East, Signal 39 on several. This car reported back in service at 11:08 P.M.

11:20 P.M. Car 137 requested registration on 1A 75237. (Issued to Drummond Motors, '58 Chevrolet, 2-Dr. no report.)

Car 20 requested registration on 1A 75237. Later requested that this request be disregarded.

11:33 P.M. Car 58 was directed to go to 2817 21 Street West. Someone threw something at officer's house. Car 58 later reported everything was alright at this house.

Car 21 asked for a report on 1B 11630. (No arrest order outstanding.)

Car 113 requested registration and report on 1A 10630 issued to A. W. Alexander, Jr. of 352 Marywood Drive, '62 Cadillac. No report.

12:00 midnight, September 15, 1963.

12:01 A.M. stolen report broadcast on '48 Plymouth, two door, 1-72837, dark blue.

RECORD 1:

Car 912 requested to locate a green and white Buick occupied by two Negro males driving at a high rate of speed west on 8 Avenue. Moments later car McBride reported occupants were white. At 12:08 A.M. Car 5 reported that the car was en route to hospital with a male who had a cut arm.

Birmingham Police Department radio log for the night of September 14 and the morning of September 15, 1963. Note: 10:19 p.m. A motorcade of Klansmen was held downtown late Saturday night. With many Klansmen in the area, a plain car was sent to the sign shop on Third Avenue and Sixteenth Street. Here Klansmen were making protest signs and Confederate flags three blocks from the Sixteenth Street Baptist Church. (Police later told federal agents there were no white men seen in the area.) Note: 10:22 a.m. A police car, which is not identified, reported an explosion. Note: 1:34 a.m. The "Gaston" detail was instructed to rendezvous with Car 8. This special detail was diverted from patrolling the Gaston Motel and Sixteenth Street Baptist Church by a "decoy" bomb threat at the Holiday Inn six blocks from the church. This summary transcript of the radio log tapes was prepared by Detective V. T. Hart and showed no indication that the "decoy" bomb threat at the Holiday Inn was actually broadcast on police band radio. The police radio dispatcher on duty 11 p.m. to 7 a.m. was Jack LeGranc. *Birmingham Public Library Archives Department*

Police radio log, September 14-15, 1963, continued

Radio transmissions which occurred
from 10:19 P.M., 9-14-63 until 10:22 A.M.
9-15-63; Page 2

12:15 A.M., Car 22 requested registration on 1B 4444 issued to Benny Still,
of 1120 11 Street, Ensley for a '62 Ford. No report.

Car 35 requested registration on 1A 46679. It was issued to John Montgomery,
of 7???Madrid Avenue, Birmingham, and was a '55 Buick. No arrest order
on subject, John Montgomery.

12:53 A.M., Car 21 requested registration report on 1B 10058 issued to
Robert M. Creel of 1701 13 Avenue, for a '59 Chevrolet. (No report.)

RECORD 2:

1:17 A.M., Car 197, make report on 1-72184. No report.

1:34 A.M. Gaston Detail requested to meet Car 8.

Car 196 reported that an Oldsmobile was turned over on Huntsville Road.
No one in or near the car. License 1-77384.

Car 56 was sent to 3400 Block on Huntsville Road on Signal 21.

At 1:43 A.M. it was broadcast 1-77384 was issued to Milton Abroms of 311
Overbrook Road, '58 Oldsmobile, four-door. (Mr. Abroms no longer owns the
automobile.)

1:48 A.M. temporary report issued for '59 Ford, 31-3154½ white in color,
stolen from 5 Avenue 25 Street North.

3:00 A.M. Car (?) was sent to #29 Greensprings Avenue.

3:30 A.M. it was noted that the electric power was off in the 1000 block
of 19th Street North. Traffic lights out also.

3:34 A.M. Car 35 reported that a line had been laid at the fire.

Car 13, E. Melton and Y. J. Cope requested registration of 1-3344. It
was issued to H. B. Chapplear of 612 26th Street S.W. for a '56 Cadillac,
two door.

3:44 A.M. Car 56 asked if there was a report of a blast anywhere. The
radio man replied an unconfirmed report was that there was one in the
Norwood area.

Car 20 reported there was an explosion at Southern Electric Steel Company,
an industrial explosion in the 2300 Block, Huntsville Road.

Conclusion, police radio log, September 14-15, 1963

Radio transmissions which occurred
from 10:19 P.M., 9-14-63, until 10:22 A.M.
9-15-63; Page 4

RECORD 5:

It was reported at 6:50 A.M. that a '54 Chevrolet, 1A 7014, white over
blue, was under the bridge near the Jewish Cemetery with four tires missing.
This car is issued to Darcus N. Haslip, 1216 4 Pl. North, '53 Chevrolet.

Car 13 requested report on 1ᴴ/1 12773. Issued to Appliance Exchange Company,
2215 2 Avenue North.

7:57 A.M.   Time Check.

8:18 A.M. requested to check 1-94808, 50 or 51 Chevrolet, blue color.

8:52 A.M. Car 56, W. C. Wilhite, asked if there was any hit and run report
on Georgia Tag 9-J 6237. (No report at that time.)

RECORD 6:

9:34 A.M. Car 24 requested report on 1-42820. Car was in in Greensprings
Park. (No record.)

Car 13 subject reported looking in window of Greek Youth Center. Unfounded.

All cars contacted to find driver of black and white '57 stationwagen,
License unknown, driven by Barnard J. Lupo, 1013 11 Place North. Information
is that subject's wife is in University Hospital and he should go there and
contact her.

10:00 A.M. Stolen report for a '61 Rambler, black, 1A 17374, stolen
between 10:30 A.M. and 3:30 P.M. Saturday, September 14, from 130 Finley
Avenue.

10:22 A.M. Car number not clearly heard reported explosion.

V. T. Hart, Detective
Evelyn Trucks, Stenographer
October 24, 1963

FBI interview with Don Luna

FD-302 (Rev. 1-25-60)   FEDERAL BUREAU OF INVESTIGATION

Date **March 23, 1964**

DONALD EUGENE LUNA, Route 1, Millbrook, Alabama, was advised he did not have to make a statement; that he had a right to consult an attorney prior to making any statement; that no threats or promises would be made to induce him to talk; that any information furnished could be used against him in a court of law.

LUNA voluntarily furnished the following information:

He joined the United Klans of America, Inc., Knights of the Ku Klux Klan through the Eastview Klavern Number 13 sometime in 1962 because at that time, he felt integration was being pushed throughout the South. He said he was encouraged to join the Klan by his uncle, WILLIAM H. HOLM, who is an active member of the Eastview Klavern. LUNA added his aunt, MARY LOU HOLM, is an ardent segregationist and a leader in the United Americans for Conservative Government. LUNA claimed he was never a member of the "action groups" and claimed to never have participated in any acts of violence while a member of the "Klan". LUNA stated that he was a "Klan investigator" while a member.

LUNA stated he did not work with the Alabama Highway Patrol during the fall of 1963 when they apprehended CHARLES CAGLE, ROBERT E. CHAMBLISS, and JOHN W. HALL, for possession of dynamite. He said that he had assisted the Highway Patrol prior to those arrests in obtaining information concerning the "Muslim Movement" in Birmingham. LUNA advised he was approached by the State authorities to assist in obtaining CHAMBLISS' cooperation at the time the State planned to arrest and interview CHAMBLISS for possession of dynamite. LUNA said that when he learned that ROBERT SHELTON, the Imperial Wizard, and that he felt the decision as to the amount of cooperation furnished by the "Klan" must be made by SHELTON and the members of the "Imperial Board". LUNA denied furnishing the State authorities any information which led to the arrest of any of the above mentioned individuals. LUNA added the State had already obtained enough information to make their case" against CHAMBLISS, HALL, and CAGLE, for possession of dynamite at the time they sought his assistance.

On 3-17-64 at Birmingham, Alabama   File # BH 157-352

Date dictated 3-19-64

by SA J. BROOKE BLAKE, JR:ras

This document contains neither recommendations nor conclusions of the FBI. It is the property of the FBI and is loaned to your agency; it and its contents are not to be distributed outside your agency.

BH 157-352

2

LUNA claimed he instituted his own investigation shortly after the bombing of the 16th Street Baptist Church and that he felt such inquiry was required of him as a "Klan investigator". LUNA furnished the following, learned through his investigation as to the exchange of the dynamite for which the above listed individuals were arrested:

ROBERT THOMAS, according to ROBERT E. CHAMBLISS, instructed JOHN HALL and CHARLES CAGLE, while they were at a "Klan Rally" on the Bessemer Highway, to go to CHAMBLISS' residence after the rally to pick up a package. HALL and CAGLE, who were drinking heavily, did pick up the package which both HALL and CAGLE told LUNA was a case of dynamite. Both informed LUNA they had obtained the dynamite from CHAMBLISS' residence and the case was opened at the time they obtained it. Both told LUNA they took the dynamite to the same area of the bomb recovered some dynamite later and placed this package beneath some dynamite. LUNA advised CAGLE and HALL told him they planned to return to the location the following night to pick up the case of dynamite.

LUNA stated he learned from JOHN HALL that ROSS KEITH and HALL left the Eastview Klavern Meeting on the following evening and went to the location where CAGLE and HALL had placed the dynamite on the preceding day, but found the dynamite missing. HALL told LUNA that KEITH, and himself then went to CAGLE's residence where CAGLE told them he had given the dynamite to LEVI S. YARBROUGH.

LUNA claimed the State authorities were unable to learn from CAGLE where he gave the dynamite to YARBROUGH in that he, CAGLE, did not want his name connected with YARBROUGH because YARBROUGH, CAGLE, and several other Klansmen had made some hand grenades together several years prior. LUNA said the State authorities believed YARBROUGH when he denied receiving the dynamite.

LUNA stated his investigation ended at the point where YARBROUGH received the dynamite; however, he said he assumed from past history and past associations, that the dynamite went from YARBROUGH to TROY INGRAM, who made the shrapnel bomb for CHAMBLISS.

LUNA stated that he could not prove that the State authorities had planted a case of dynamite which they "recovered".

Klansman Don Luna cooperated with FBI investigators as indicated by this report of a March 17, 1964, interview in which Luna implicated other Klansmen in the bombing and described his own involvement with the Alabama Highway Patrol. Luna was with the state investigator (Posey) who arrested Chambliss on September 29, 1963. *Birmingham Public Library Archives Department*

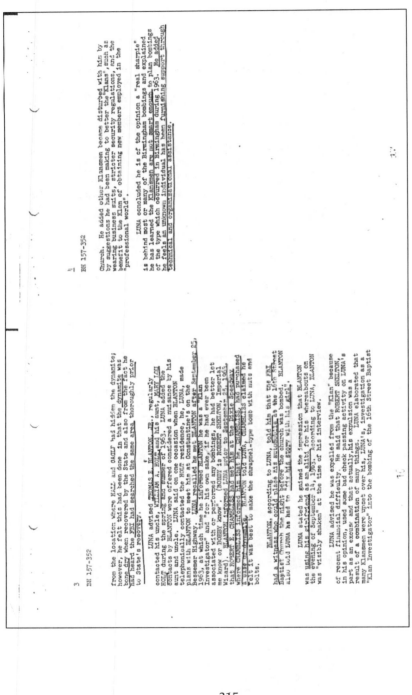

from the location where HALL and CAHI had hidden the dynamite; however, he felt this had been done in that the dynamite was buried when recovered by the State and also from the fact he had heard the FBI had searched the same area thoroughly prior to State's recovery.

LUNA advised THOMAS E. BLANTON, JR. regularly contacted his uncle, WILLIAM A. HOLT, and his aunt, MARY LOU HOLT during the spring and summer of 1963. LUNA added the contacts by BLANTON were offered considered a nuisance by his aunt and uncle. LUNA said on one occasion when BLANTON made plans with BLANTON to meet him at Constantine's on the telephonically contacted the HOLT residence; he, LUNA, made Bessemer Highway. LUNA recalled he met BLANTON after September 25, 1963, at which time he informed BLANTON he was a "Klan Investigator" and "for his own sake, if he had ever been associated with or performed any bombings, he had better let me know or BOBBY know". (BOBBY is ROBERT SHELTON, Imperial Wizard). BLANTON informed LUNA prior to September 25, 1963, that ROBERT E. CHAMBLISS had met him at the Dixie Speedway where CHAMBLISS informed him that they had purchased dynamite, BLANTON told LUNA, CHAMBLISS claimed he felt it was best to make the shrapnel-type bomb with nuts and bolts.

BLANTON, according to LUNA, told him that the FBI had a witness who could place his automobile at the 16th Street Baptist Church the night before the church was bombed, BLANTON also told LUNA he had to "fix his story with his girl".

LUNA stated he gained the impression that BLANTON was using his girlfriend as an alibi for his whereabouts on the evening of September 14, 1963. According to LUNA, BLANTON was "visibly shaken" at the time of his interview.

LUNA advised he was expelled from the "Klan" because of recent financial difficulty. He said that ROBERT SHELTON, in his opinion, used some bad check passing activity on LUNA's part as an excuse and that actually his expulsion was a result of a combination of many things. LUNA elaborated that many Klansmen were upset over his, LUNA's, investigation as a "Klan Investigator" into the bombing of the 16th Street Baptist

Church. He added other Klansmen became disturbed with him by by suggestions he had been making to better the Klans, such as wearing business suits, stricter security regulations, and the benefit to the Klan, of obtaining new members employed in the professional world.

LUNA concluded he is of the opinion a "real sharpie" is behind most or many of the Birmingham bombings and explained he has learned the Klansmen are not smart enough to plan bombings of the type which occurred in Birmingham during 1963. He added he feels an unknown individual has been furnishing support through technical and organizational assistance.

Elizabeth Cobbs's subpoena, 1977

GRAND JURY SUBPOENA – ORIGINAL

Case No. _____ CIRCUIT COURT

Investigation _____   Report to

_____

Room No. 612

THE STATE OF ALABAMA
JEFFERSON COUNTY
CIRCUIT COURT

To any Sheriff of State of Alabama:

You are hereby commanded to summon

Elizabeth H. Hood Cobb

804 12th Street West

Birmingham, Alabama

You are hereby commanded personally to be and appear before the Grand Jury Impaneled for the Criminal Division of the Tenth Judicial Circuit of Alabama, at a Court holden for said County on the ___11___ day of ___August___ 19_77_ at 9 A.M., and from day to day of said term until discharged by due course of law, and to give evidence and the truth to speak in behalf of the State of Alabama in all matters which may be inquired of by said Grand Jury, and this you shall in no wise omit under penalty prescribed by law.

Witness this _____ 19_____
      EARL C. MORGAN . District Attorney

Executed by leaving a copy of this Subpoena with the above witness.

This ___ day of _____ 19___

_____ Sheriff

By _____ Deputy Sheriff

The grand jury subpoena for Elizabeth Cobbs, which was never delivered. Cobbs refused to appear before the grand jury but volunteered to cooperate with state investigators in August 1977. *Birmingham Public Library Archives Department*

Police report on Robert Chambliss, 1968

F-44722   ADD   ART   1-24-68

BOMB THREAT

CARRAWAY METHODIST HOSPITAL
1601 North 25th Street

On January 18, 1968, Captain James McDowell and Sergeant C. L.
Limbaugh went to the Carraway Methodist Hospital, located at
1601 North 25th Street, and interviewed the Director of Nurses,
Mrs. Ann Sorge. Mrs. Sorge stated to us that Mr. Sidney
Hamilton, White Male, 70, of Fultondale, General Delivery, who
was being dismissed from the hospital on January 17, 1968, told
her of an incident that happened on January 16, 1968, in which
he stated to her at that time that Robert Chambless, White Male,
who is well-known to this Department, was in a semi-private
room, 535, Carraway, and when a Negro was assigned to the room
with him, he became very angry and stormed out of the room and
made a scene in the hall. Officer Gordon F. Faulkner was
called to the scene and in his initial report, he stated that
witness said Robert Chambless said he blew up the church where
the little Negro girls were killed. On interviewing Mrs.
                    -CONTINUED-

Sorge, we went to the Room #537, and interviewed the Reverend
Charles King, Methodist Minister, Age 84, house address is
1630 Wharton Avenue, Tarrant City, Alabama, and Mr. Hamilton
stated to Captain McDowell and Sergeant Limbaugh that on
January 16, 1968, Robert Chambless did come into their room
in a very angry mood, and said he was checking out of the
hospital, and he wasn't going to stay any longer that he had
some friends that would take care of them if they gave him any
trouble, but Mr. Hamilton said he did not say he was involved
in the bombing of the church where the Negro girls were killed.
He stated that he was accused of the bombing and held for a
time for it and Mr. Chambless was held by State Troopers, also
investigated by the Birmingham Police Department and the F.B.I.
on that occasion. Mr. Hamilton stated also that Mr. Chambless
had his knife out in his hand made the statement that he
had killed one man with that knife. Mr. Chambless was in the
hospital for a stomach operation for stomach ulcers. Mrs.
Sorge stated that he was at the point of being released anyway
and the doctor released him from the hospital and he left.
It is felt by the investigating officers, Robert Chambless on

                    -CONTINUED-

other occasions, in a fit of anger, would do a lot of talking,
etc. We think that the first report was in error of what was
heard. He did not say he had bombed the church and he did not
say he was going to bomb the hospital. There is a complete
report in file that Mrs. Ann Sorge made by her nurses on this
account.

UNFOUNDED

SERGEANT CARL L. LIMBAUGH

Copy of the police report investigating an incident in 1968 when Robert Chambliss
made threats against Carraway Medical Center and allegedly admitted bombing the
Sixteenth Street Baptist Church. Chambliss had become enraged when a black patient
was placed in the semiprivate hospital room with him. Note the cavalier treatment of
the allegations by the investigators. *Birmingham Public Library Archives Department*

Portion of 1977 trial transcript

```
Q    Was Captain LeGrand with the police department
     then?

A    Yes, sir.

Q    Do you know his rank at that time?

A    Yes, sir.

Q    What was that?

A    Sergeant.

Q    Do you know what shift he was working that day?

A    11:00 to 7:00.

Q    Same shift as yours?

A    Yes, sir.

Q    Were you a sergeant at that time?

A    No, sir.

Q    Was he your immediate supervisor?

A    No, sir.

Q    Do you know where he was assigned?
          Do you know his work area?

A    Yes, sir, I do.  He was assigned as dispatcher
     on the radio.

          MR. HANES, JR.:  Thank you, sir.


          REDIRECT EXAMINATION


BY MR. BAXLEY:

Q    Sergeant Cantrell, did you see any supervisor
```

CIRCUIT- 169

-508-

Excerpt from Robert Chambliss's November 1977 murder trial; testimony of Sergeant Ernie Cantrell states that Jack LeGrand was on radio duty the night of the bombing and that the decoy bomb threat was broadcast. LeGrand and Cantrell were in charge of the Birmingham Police Department investigation through the 1970s and 1980s—although both appear to have been, at the least, less than proficient in the performance of their duties. *Birmingham Public Library Archives Department*

LeGrand's notes from 1976 Chambliss interview

Bob Chambliss —————— 11/10/76
Cagle, Chambliss, Hall   Major Felony Office
Luna, Posey   City Hall

Meeting at St Francis Hotel, Homewood
Lingo, Robt Thomas, B Shelton

Bill Holt

"Water bucket" method
punch hole let the water out.

B' Shelton got $9,000 from Wallace

Luna had a chart of housing
development near Lake Purdy, wanted
Bob to get case of dynamite.
Bob got case from Leon Negron.

Leon Negron shot down by shotgun
at his home a yr. ago.

Tommy Blanton Jr. would not hurt
anyone.

                    Capt. Jack C. LeGrand

Birmingham Police Captain Jack LeGrand made notes during interviews and later wrote formal reports. These notes were taken during an interview with Robert Chambliss on November 10, 1976. Chambliss voluntarily came to police headquarters to talk about fellow Klansman Don Luna. During this interview Chambliss told police he knew how to make a "drip-method bomb." *Birmingham Public Library Archives Department*

Conclusion, LeGrand's notes
from 1976 Chambliss interview

1125 3.20.6

16 St Church Bombing   Date 3-30, 19 78

Memo - Robt C. Chambliss

CHIEF OF POLICE

Interviewed Bob Chambliss at 10ᵗʰ AM this date at Kilby, Mt. Meigs Prison. in the company of his attorney Arthur Hanes Sr. Chambliss insisted that Gary T. Rowe was an agent of the C.I.A., that he Chambliss was never in Blenton's car, that Cochylied, that Rowe at the KKK Hall told of the 16 St Church bombing in front of other witnesses, that he (Chambliss) did not give dynamite to Rowe, denied that in 1963 that he had told a party that the persons in the car were Cherry, Jack Cash, Blenton, and himself,

Chambliss stated after his indictment and before his trial that he had received telephone calls from Stoner and Cherry. Blenton went to Attorneys Williason + Purvis asking why Chambliss had talked to Asst. Att. Gen. John Yung.

It was determined that Chambliss's wife was glad that Bob was convicted and sent to prison, and further that his wife stated Bob was not at home at anytime on the night of Sept 14, 1963.

Concluded interview at 11²⁹ AM

_____

Capt. Jack C. LeGrand

INVESTIGATING OFFICERS

Birmingham Police Department Captain Jack LeGrand interviewed Robert Chambliss four months after Chambliss was imprisoned for murder. These notes from that interview indicate Chambliss attempted to shift blame to others, including FBI informant Tommy Rowe who Chambliss (and Birmingham Police Department Officer Lavaughn Coleman) claims was a CIA operative. Note: No source is cited for statements in the last paragraph of this report. *Birmingham Public Library Archives Department*

Chambliss letter from prison

8/22/78.

Hon. District Attorney.
Selma. Ala. 36701.
Dear Sir.
Why does Bill Baxley. Say Rowe is not a
Suspect in The Bombings When He Was Head
leader in all the Bombings in and around
B'ham Him and 4 other C.I.A. members and 1
Police or more He Paid all that taken the stand
against Me But I Was told He Made them Kick
Back $100.75.000 and I Would Kneel on My
Mothers Grave and Pray to You I've never
Bombed any thing never Killed any Body and
never Ben in Tommy Blanton's Car in My Life
So Help Me God. Can you Help Me or Send a
Reporter.
I Could Help Convict 5 C.I.A. Members and 1
Police or more.

Yours Truly.
R. E. Chambliss.
Kilby Correctional Center.
Montgomery Ala.
Route 5 Box 125
36109.

Robert Chambliss consistently denied his own guilt and accused others. His letters from prison, shown here and on the following page, illustrate his continued efforts to shift blame to others, named and unnamed, especially those he felt had spoken against him. *Birmingham Public Library Archives Department*

Chambliss letter from prison

9/22/78.

Mr Bill Baxley.

Dear Sir.

I heard you Say Rowe Was not a Suspect in the
Bombings When He Was the Head Leader of all the
Bombings in and around Birmingham.
Him and 4 other C.I.A. members and Police or
More I Can name all of them.
I Would Kneel on my Mothers Grave and Pray to
You I have Never Bombed any thing Never Killed
any Body and Never ben in Tommy Blanton's Car
in My Life to Help me God.

Yours Truly.

R. E. Chambliss.
Rt. 5 Box 125.
Montgomery Ala.
36109

Robert Chambliss's letter to Bill Baxley, dated 9/22/78, accuses Gary Thomas Rowe of the Birmingham bombings and states that Rowe and four others were CIA agents. *Birmingham Public Library Archives Department*

FURTHER READING

Bass, Jack. *Taming The Storm: The Life and Times of Frank M. Johnson, Jr. and the South's Fight over Civil Rights.* Doubleday, 1993.

Blumberg, Rhoda Lois. *Civil Rights: The 1960's Freedom Struggle.* Twayne Publishers, 1984.

Chalmers, David Mark. *Hooded Americanism: The History of the Ku Klux Klan.* New Viewpoints: F. Watts, 1981.

Clark, E. Culpepper. *The Schoolhouse Door.* Oxford University Press, 1993.

Cohodas, Nadine. *Strom Thurmond and the Politics of Southern Change.* Simon & Schuster, 1993.

Goldman, Roger and David Gallen. *Thurgood Marshall: Justice for All.* Carroll and Graf Publishers, Inc. 1992.

Hemphill, Paul. *Leaving Birmingham: Notes of a Native Son.* Viking, 1993.

Hentoff, Nat *Free Speech for Me But Not for Thee.* Aaron Asher Books, Harper Collins Publishers, 1992.

Kennedy, Stetson. *The Klan Unmasked.* Florida Atlantic University Press, 1990.

Nelson, Jack *Terror in the Night: The Klan's Campaign Against the Jews.* Simon & Schuster, 1993.

Nunnelley, William A. *Bull Connor.* University of Alabama Press, 1991.

O' Reilly, Kenneth. *Black Americans: The FBI Files*. Carroll & Graf Publishers, Inc., 1994.

Raines, Howell. *My Soul Is Rested: Movement Days in The Deep South Remembered*. G.P. Putnam's Sons, 1977.

Russell, Dick. *The Man Who Knew Too Much*. Carroll & Graf Publishers, Inc., 1992.

Sikora, Frank. *Until Justice Rolls Down: The Birmingham Church Bombing Case*. University of Alabama Press, 1991.

Sims, Patsy. *The Klan*. Stein & Day Publishers, 1978.

Summers, Anthony. *Official and Confidential: The Secret Life of J. Edgar Hoover*. G.P. Putnam's Sons, 1993.

Thompson, Jerry. *My Life in the Klan: A True Story by the First Investigative Reporter to Infiltrate the Ku Klux Klan*. G.P. Putnam's Sons, 1982.

Turner, John. *The Ku Klux Klan: A History of Racism and Violence*. Klanwatch, a project of Southern Poverty Law Center, 1981.

BIOGRAPHICAL INDEX

The following list identifies the key characters in the story of *Long Time Coming*.

Friends and Family of Elizabeth H. Cobbs

Flora "Tee" Chambliss - Elizabeth's aunt, oldest sister of Elizabeth's mother, Libby; married to Klansman Robert Chambliss.

Robert Chambliss - Elizabeth's uncle, Ku Klux Klan member, Klan terrorist. Convicted of murder in 1977 in connection with the Sixteenth Street Baptist Church bombing of 1963.

Mama Katie - Elizabeth's grandmother.

Roger - Elizabeth's step-grandfather, Mama Katie's second husband.

Libby - Elizabeth's mother.

John - Elizabeth's father.

Johnny - Elizabeth's brother.

Robin - Elizabeth's son.

Mary - Another of Elizabeth's aunts, a younger sister of Elizabeth's mother, Libby.

William - Aunt Mary's husband.

Viola - Another aunt, older sister of Elizabeth's mother, Libby.

Jim - Aunt Viola's husband.

Kathy - Viola and Jim's daughter, Elizabeth's cousin.

Howard - Elizabeth's uncle, younger brother of Elizabeth's mother, Libby.

Mary Ida - Howard's wife.

"Dale Tarrant" - Elizabeth's close friend and fellow FBI informant.

Klansmen and "Buddies" of Robert Chambliss

The Cahaba Boys, a violent Klan splinter group associated with Birmingham Klavern 13, included among its members Tommy Blanton, Jr., Charles Cagle, Herman and Jack Cash, Robert Chambliss, Bobby Cherry, John Wesley "Nigger" Hall, Troy Ingram, and William Ross Keith. Robert called these men his "buddies."

Edward Fields - Cofounder with J. B. Stoner of the ultraconservative National States Rights Party, of which many Klansmen—including Robert Chambliss—were members.

Bob Gafford - Referred to by Robert Chambliss as one of his "buddies." Ran an auto parts store down the street from the Chambliss home; later elected to Alabama House of Representatives.

Don Luna - A Birmingham Klansman and FBI informant.

Hubert Page - A Klan leader in Birmingham's Klavern 13.

Gary Thomas Rowe - FBI infiltrator of the Klan; not taken seriously by Robert Chambliss and the rest of the Cahaba Boys.

Robert Shelton - Imperial Wizard of the KKK.

J. B. Stoner - Klan lawyer; founder of ultraconservative National States Rights Party; ultra-right-wing activist; arrested, convicted, and served time for the 1958 bombing of the Bethel Baptist Church.

Robert Thomas - Grand Dragon of Klavern 13 in Birmingham.

Investigators

Mel Alexander - FBI agent with whom Elizabeth had the most contact 1963-68.

Bill Baxley - Alabama attorney general who reactivated and prosecuted the Sixteenth Street Baptist Church bombing case 1976-77.

George Beck - Alabama assistant attorney general under Bill Baxley.

Bob Eddy - Investigator for the State of Alabama, assigned in 1976 to the Sixteenth Street Baptist Church bombing case.

Robert Womack - FBI agent with whom Elizabeth had initial, and then regular, contact 1963-68.

Jon Yung - Alabama assistant attorney general under Bill Baxley.

Local Police and Law Enforcement Officials

Sergeant Ernie Cantrell - Birmingham police officer on duty the night the Sixteenth Street Baptist Church bomb was planted; later assigned to investigate the case.

Officer Floyd C. Garrett - Birmingham police officer whose comings and goings on the morning of the bombing remain largely unexplained; nephew of Robert Chambliss.

Deputy Sheriff James Hancock - Local officer to whom Dale Tarrant reported Klan information, including a warning that Sixteenth Street Baptist Church was about to be bombed.

Captain Jack LeGrand - Birmingham police officer on radio dispatch duty the night the Sixteenth Street Baptist Church bomb was planted; later assigned to investigate the case.

Colonel Al Lingo - Head of the Alabama Highway Patrol at the time of the Sixteenth Street Baptist Church bombing.

Captain J. M. McDowell - Birmingham police captain who accompanied FBI agents and Charles Cagle to the site near Gardendale where dynamite was found.

Police Chief Jamie Moore - Chief of Police in Birmingham during the civil rights struggles.

Detective Don "Stevens" - Birmingham police detective who investigated the Fountain Heights bombings in the 1950s and was later crippled by a hit-and-run driver.

Public Officials

Albert Boutwell - Elected mayor of Birmingham in 1963 under first mayor-council government.

Eugene "Bull" Connor- Birmingham police commissioner put out of office by change to mayor-council government in 1962.

Charles Graddick - Elected Alabama attorney general in 1978. Subsequently, no further arrests were made in the Sixteenth Street Baptist Church bombing case.

Art Hanes, Sr. - With Bull Connor and Jabo Waggoner, served as one of Birmingham's last city commissioners (as president); former FBI agent; Robert Chambliss's attorney in the 1977 murder trial.

Art Hanes, Jr. - With his father, Art Hanes, Sr., represented Robert Chambliss in the 1977 murder trial.

Jabo Waggoner - Birmingham commissioner of public works, put out of office in 1962 by transition to mayor-council government.

George Wallace - Governor of Alabama 1963-1967, 1971-1979, 1983-1987.

Civil Rights Leaders

Reverend John Cross - Pastor of Sixteenth Street Baptist Church at the time of the 1963 bombing.

A. G. Gaston - Prominent Birmingham businessman, owner of the motel where Dr. King made his Birmingham headquarters, and that was bombed in 1963.

Reverend A. D. W. King - Brother of Martin Luther King, Jr. His home was bombed in 1963.

Dr. Martin Luther King, Jr. - Civil rights leader and founder of Southern Christian Leadership Conference. Targeted Birmingham as the nation's "most segregated city" in 1963.

Authur Shores - NAACP attorney whose Birmingham home was the target of numerous bombings.

Reverend Fred L. Shuttlesworth - Pastor of Bethel Baptist Church in Birmingham; local civil rights leader and founder of the Alabama Christian Movement for Civil Rights. Both his home and church were bombed.

INDEX